Be My Baby

How I Survived
Mascara,
Miniskirts,
and Madness,
or
My Life as
a Fabulous
Ronette

Ronnie Spector
with Vince Waldron

HARMONY BOOKS
NEW YORK

Published by Harmony Books, a division of Crown Publishers, Inc., 201 East 50th Street, New York, New York 10022. Member of the Crown Publishing Group.

HARMONY and colophon are trademarks of Crown Publishers, Inc.

Manufactured in the United States of America

Library of Congress Cataloging-in-Publication Data
Spector, Ronnie
   Be my baby : how I survived mascara, miniskirts, and madness, or my life as a fabulous Ronette / Ronnie Spector with Vince Waldron.—1st ed.
      1. Spector, Ronnie.   2. Singers—United States—
Biography.   I. Waldron, Vince.   II. Title.
ML420.S72A3   1990
782.42166′092—dc20   90-32533
[B]

ISBN 0-517-57499-3
10 9 8 7 6 5 4 3 2 1

First Edition

For my mom and
for Austin and Jason

Contents

Foreword
by Cher

I was seventeen when I met Ronnie. I can still remember the day Phillip brought her down to Gold Star Studios for the first time. I'd never seen anybody like her. She had this big hair, these huge eyes, and no hips. I remember thinking that she seemed really, really teeny. And that voice! Well, nobody sounded like her, did they? She really was one of a kind.

I'd just left home and moved in with Sonny, and he still worked for Phil Spector in those days, so everyone just thought of me as Sonny's girlfriend. At first I was a little envious of Ronnie, because even though she was only a year or two older than I was, she'd already been on tour and everything. But I was happy for her, too.

Oh, I was so excited when the Ronettes went to England and brought home all this stuff. Ronnie came back with Beatle boots and leather skirts and poor-boy T-shirts, and I nearly died. It was like she'd gone to Nirvana and brought home souvenirs. She also brought back some pretty incredible stories. I still remember her dragging me into the ladies' room at Gold Star to tell me how the Beatles thought she was cute, and how John Lennon had a big crush on her. "And, Cher," she told me, "you wouldn't believe how much the kids over there loved our music!" I think that was the first time any of us realized that people all over the world were actually listening to these little records we were making at Gold Star, and that just blew our minds.

That was around the time I started my own singing career. In fact, "Be My Baby" was the first record I ever sang on. I'd been dying to sing since the first day I walked into Gold Star, but I never had the nerve to tell anyone except Sonny. Then one day Darlene Love or one of the other background singers didn't show up, and Phillip looked at me and said, "Sonny tells me you can sing." I was so embarrassed that I started making excuses, trying to explain what I thought Sonny meant by that. But Phillip said, "Oh, just get out there. All I need is noise."

So I went out and stood in front of this big speaker and sang "be my, be my baby" with the Ronettes and all these other singers. But I think Phillip got more than he bargained for that day, because my singing voice was so loud that he finally had to ask me to stand behind the other singers so I wouldn't drown them out. He had me take one step back, then two, then three. It got to be like a joke. Every time I opened my mouth, Phillip would say, "Step back a little bit more, Cher." I finally looked at Ronnie and started laughing, because by the time we finished the song, I was standing ten feet behind everyone else.

I sang background on every song Phil made after that, from "Be My Baby" to "You've Lost That Loving Feeling." And I think I made maybe twenty-five dollars the whole time. But when I hear those songs today, I think of the fun we had recording them, and I can still feel the thrill. Of course, it wasn't always so great.

Phillip was very protective of Ronnie even then, and he was always asking me to keep an eye on her. I had this little red MG convertible, so it became my job to take Ronnie shopping or to interviews or wherever she had to go. Phil expected me to act like some kind of babysitter for her, but the funny thing was that Sonny dictated my movements the same way Phil dictated Ronnie's. And yet, for some reason, both of them trusted that nothing would happen to either of us as long as we were together. So for a while there, Ronnie and I were inseparable.

Sometimes we'd just sit around my house talking or watching TV—the usual girl stuff. If we went out to eat, it was always to some place like Tiny Naylor's, which Ronnie really enjoyed because it was a drive-in, and I don't think she'd ever seen a drive-in before she came out to California. We always had a great time together. And the weird thing is, we never even thought of doing the kinds of things that Sonny and Phillip were afraid we might be doing when we went out. We never went wild, and neither of us was ever very interested in other guys. We were just two young and unbelievably innocent girls who were very much in love with our boyfriends.

Sonny and Phillip were both incredibly dominant men, but I think Ronnie had it much worse than I did, because at least with Sonny I was always working, so I stayed in contact with other people. But Ronnie didn't even have that. After Phillip became a recluse, he kept her isolated from the rest of the world, and it's easy to keep someone confused if you keep them isolated. She tried to fit in and make things work, but she ended up making compromises until there was nothing left to compromise. And I know what that's like. I think a lot of women do.

Ronnie went through some tough times, but the important thing is she survived and she's still around to tell the tale. And that's what she does in this book. It's an amazing story. And one of a kind. Just like Ronnie.

Introduction
by Billy Joel

Records are watersheds for the memory. You can name a year to me, or a sporting event, a fashion craze, or a political election—and I'll come up blank. But name me a record and I can usually zero in on exactly when it came out, where I was, and what I was doing when I first heard it. I think that's how a lot of people my age mark time—by the important records in their lives. And for me, "Be My Baby" happens to be one of those very important records.

I grew up in a blue-collar town on Long Island called Hicksville, where most of the kids were from lower- or middle-income working-class families. I was a hitter, or I guess what you'd call a greaser. We had a gang—and music was a big part of our lives. Tough music. We weren't interested in Fabian or Frankie Avalon. We wanted music that was good for dancing, making out, or, ultimately, fucking. So we bought 45's by guys like James Brown, Otis Redding, and Jackie Wilson. And we loved the Ronettes. There were a lot of girl groups back then, but they had the toughest sound of all. Whenever we went to a party, we always tried to bring at least one record by the Ronettes.

Those parties were the center of our teenage social life in Hicksville. The girls would all line up on one side of the room, giggling and talking to themselves; and we guys would stand on the other side, trying to look tough in our iridescent shirts, tight casino pants, and matador boots. Everybody'd kinda be eyeing one another, waiting for the right moment to strike up a conversation or ask somebody to dance. And the music had a lot to do with when that happened. Waiting for the right song to come on before you made your move was crucial, because we knew that if we held out till the Ronettes came on, we'd have it made. If you could make eye contact with a girl while Ronnie sang the opening line to "Be My Baby," then—*bam*—that was it, guy! You were in.

I don't know what it is about "Be My Baby." It just oozes sex, that record. It's got this Latinesque string line that practically throbs. And Ronnie's voice—I mean, it sounds almost lubricated. It's got a smell to it, like sweat and garlic. There's an urgency to that voice, a sexuality that screams *street* to me. Ronnie's sound is like the neon glow that hits the streets under the elevated tracks on a hot summer night. She's got that natural vibrato that sounds like it's coming straight up from her gut— and there's no one else who sings like that. Ronnie can wring more emotion out of one long phrase than most other singers can from a whole song.

About ten years after I first heard the Ronettes, I was sitting in a theater watching *Mean Streets*, the Robert DeNiro film. There's a scene where he's standing in a bar with his gang when all of a sudden "Be My Baby" comes boomin' off the jukebox. When I heard that, I kinda jumped out of my seat remembering how much I liked the song and the way Ronnie sang it. When I got home, I decided to write a song that would make me feel the way "Be My Baby" did.

So I wrote "Say Goodbye to Hollywood," modeled after Ronnie's vocal style; and I recorded it, trying to re-create Phil Spector's wall of sound from the ground up. In interviews, I always said I wrote the song with Ronnie in mind, so when I heard that she wanted to do "Say Goodbye to Hollywood" herself, I flipped. And I loved the version she did with the E Street Band. I thought it was the perfect record for FM radio.

I met Ronnie only once. It was about a year after she did "Say Goodbye to Hollywood." I was doing an interview at the BBC when she just walked into the studio and knocked me for a loop. I'd always been such a fan, and now here she was telling me how much she enjoyed recording *my* song. I just about went over the top. It was like things had come full circle.

Some people might call what I feel about Ronnie's music nostalgia, but I think it's more than that. I'm convinced that "Be My Baby" would be a hit even if it came out tomorrow. Still, I have to admit that if somebody puts on one of her records today, no matter where I am, a part of me does slip back to the Village Green in Hicksville, Long Island, where I'm drinking beer and singing along with my gang. After all these years, I still get that little greaser tremble of excitement whenever I hear Ronnie sing. And that's something I hope I never lose.

1

Ozzie and Harriet in Spanish Harlem

Skinny Yellow Horse. That was the name the black kids had for me when I was growing up, because I had light skin and I was so small that I'd always kick like a little pony whenever I got into a fight. And I was always getting beat up. PS 153 on 145th Street and Amsterdam Avenue was one of the toughest black schools in Harlem, and the kids were always making fun of me. "Hey, half-breed," they'd yell, "get your ass back to the reservation."

I didn't have it as bad as my sister. I was a tomboy and I could run fast, but Estelle was always so poised and proper that the kids at PS 153 thought she was a snob. So they'd pick on her worse than me. Even though Estelle was two years older than I was, there were times when *I* had to defend *her* against some of those kids.

The worst thing about all of it was that I never even understood prejudice until I got to school. I was born in Spanish Harlem on August 10, 1943. My mother, Beatrice Bennett, is black and Cherokee, and my father, Louis, was white, which makes me a half-breed. My sister Estelle and I were raised on 151st Street between Amsterdam and Broadway, in a neighborhood that had Chinese laundries, Spanish restaurants, and black grocery stores. We saw people of every color on the street—black, white, and yellow, with eyes that slanted this way and that. A lot of the kids on our block were half-breeds, so interracial marriage seemed normal to us. But the kids at PS 153 didn't agree.

Estelle and I both had long, straight hair, and that got us into more trouble than anything else. My mother used to put my hair in these long, thick braids that went all down my back, and then she'd tie bright yellow bows on the ends. That was the way I had my hair the day this black girl named Barbara asked if she could touch it. I was sitting at my desk in second grade when she leaned forward from behind me.

"Ooh, Ronnie. Your hair looks so soft," she whispered. "Can I feel it?"

My kind of hair wasn't common on black girls, so kids were always asking if they could touch it. "Sure," I told Barbara, and went back to reading my Dick and Jane.

"Oh, it's nice," she said. "This is some pretty hair."

I could feel her stroking my braid, but I didn't think anything about it until some of the kids sitting around us started to giggle. The teacher hadn't come into the classroom yet, so a lot of the kids turned around and started watching Barbara. I was used to being poked fun at, but I still couldn't understand what was so damn entertaining about what was going on behind my head. Then I found out.

"Oooh, Barbara!" a girl named Cynthia screamed. "Why you do Ronnie like that?"

I turned around to see what she was talking about, and I couldn't believe my eyes. Barbara was dangling a strange piece of brown rope in her hands, and it had a yellow bow tied to the end. I gasped and reached up to touch the back of my head. My braid was gone. Barbara had cut it right off my head.

"This sure is some pretty hair," she said, taunting me by swinging my own long, beautiful brown braid in front of my face. "Let me keep it. Okay, Ronnie? Can I keep it?"

I held my hand over the stubby little patch that was left on my head, and I started crying hysterically, which only made the other kids laugh even harder. "Gimme that," I cried, grabbing the braid out of her hands. Then I ran into the closet in back of the classroom and locked the door behind me, cradling my poor cutoff braid in my hands. I refused to come out, even after the teacher walked into the classroom and ordered me out.

"Come out of there, Veronica," she demanded. "And I mean *now*." I don't know what story the other kids had told her, but she sure wasn't taking my side. So I stayed put. The teacher finally called my mother, who came to carry me home after all the other kids left.

The next week my mother signed us up at PS 92 on 134th, where they had a mixture of Spanish and black kids, along with a few whites. It was a better school, and it was right across the street from my grandmother's house in Spanish Harlem. After school we'd always go straight to Grandma's, where we'd play with all of our other cousins. My mother has seven brothers and six sisters, so you can imagine how crowded it got over there.

Estelle and I used to play with my aunt Hermean's kids, Diane and Elaine, who were about our age. But the cousin who I was closest to was my aunt Susu's daughter, Nedra. Nedra Talley. Her father was a Spanish man, which made her a half-breed like me. Even though she was two years younger, we were inseparable. We even climbed up on the toilet and peed together—that's how close we were. We must have shared a spirit of adventure, because we were always getting in trouble together at Grandma's house.

My grandmother was very strict with us. We weren't even supposed to go outside and play. If we wanted sunshine we had to find it up on the roof, where she could keep an eye on us. We weren't allowed out to the park, because that's where strangers hung out. This was Spanish Harlem, and there were all kinds of weird people out there. I'll never forget the one time Nedra and I did go outside alone. It was the first time I saw a man's penis.

I was about eight years old when I convinced Nedra to sneak across the street to the candy store with me. We got there without anyone catching us, and we were already chewing our licorice whips and candy corn outside the store when we noticed this Spanish guy standing in the middle of the sidewalk with his back toward us. We tried to walk past him, but as we did, he turned around and showed us his penis, which was dangling outside of his pants. We screamed so loud they must have heard us in Queens. Then we ran home and told our grandmother and all of our aunts what had happened. They made us stay inside for a month.

But that wasn't much of a punishment, since we almost never went out anyway. After what happened to us outside the candy store, I was happy to stay inside.

Especially on weekends. Weekends at my grandma's house were the best. That's when all my aunts and uncles would come over, and there would be nothing but food and singing the whole time. Most of my mother's sisters and brothers liked to sing, or act, or tell jokes, so every weekend they'd get together and stage little amateur shows at Grandma's. None of them sang or performed professionally—this was just something they did for fun.

It was all so exciting, especially to a little girl like me. I'd stand in Grandma's living room watching everyone rehearse, and I would be amazed. Four of my uncles would be harmonizing like the Mills Brothers in one corner, while three aunts worked up an Andrews Sisters number in the other. Another aunt would be throwing her leg up in ballet movements in the kitchen while someone else practiced an accordion in the bedroom. On weekends that house turned into a little do-it-yourself Juilliard.

I guess I've got performing in my blood. Besides all the uncles and aunts on my mother's side, my father also loved music. My dad worked in the subway yard all day long, but he had a great big drum kit set up in our living room, which he'd bang all night. His dream was to play drums in a Harlem jazz club. He never did make that dream come true, but he sure passed his love of music on to me.

I've loved singing for as far back as I can remember. Since I was a baby, according to my mother. When I was just sixteen months old, Mom tells me, she was holding me in her arms one cold December morning when I began singing Christmas carols on the Number 1 subway train. The other passengers looked over at this little baby singing "Jingle Bells" in her tiny voice, and they nearly fell off their straps.

"Look at that," one of them said. "That little ole baby's singing!" I was so small that everyone on the train thought I was even younger than I was. "I never saw no baby that could sing before," an old lady said. According to Mom, I just glanced around at all the attention I was getting and smiled. Even as a baby, I loved having an audience.

Everyone in my family knew how much I loved to sing, so it didn't surprise any of them when I climbed up on my grandma's coffee table at the age of four and started singing my little nonsense songs. I liked it up on that coffee table, and once I got up there, I never did climb down. By the time I was eight, I was already working up whole numbers for our family's little weekend shows. And when I stood up to sing, I was always the center of attention in that room. One afternoon my uncles even surprised me with my own spotlight, which was really just an old Maxwell House can with a light bulb stuck in it. But I loved it. That light seemed to focus all the warmth in the room on me as I belted out Hank Williams's "Jambalaya" in my eight-year-old voice.

"Jambay-lie, cold fish pie, diddly gumbo," I sang, with no idea what the words meant or if I even had them right. But when I looked around the room and saw all my aunts and uncles smiling and tapping their feet to keep time, I knew I must have been doing something right. In the middle of the song I stopped singing and improvised a little yodel. I was trying to imitate what all the cowboy singers used to do. And that was the beginning of the "whoa oh-oh-oh-oh-ohs" that would become my trademark as a singer.

When I finished the song I looked out over that seventy-five-watt bulb and saw that everyone in Grandma's living room was clapping and looking at me. When it was over I got down and sat on the rug between my sister and Nedra. That's it, I thought. That's the feeling I want for the rest of my life.

Then Estelle would get up onstage and do a song, or she'd join Nedra or my cousin Elaine and me in a number that we'd worked out in three-part harmony. Our mother loved to see us sing together, and she encouraged our show business leanings in every way she could. She even sent Estelle to Startime, a dancing school that was big in New York in the 1950s. I begged Mom to let me take classes there, too. But she could only afford to send one of us, and Estelle was the oldest. Of course, that made me very jealous.

I'd go down to Startime and hang around outside the dance studio while Estelle took her class. I wasn't enrolled, but I thought I might pick up a few free pointers anyway. I'd stand in the hallway until the class started, then I'd sneak over to the doorway and peek in the window. If I saw my sister's leg go up in the dance studio, I'd mimic her and do the same thing out in the hall, except that I'd lift my leg even higher. I'd stand outside that door until I'd memorized an entire routine. Then I'd practice the routine all week long, until it was good enough to show all the aunts and uncles at Grandma's house.

I wanted to be the best dancer of all. The fact that I wasn't even supposed to be in that dance class only made me all the more determined. And when I was growing up, one thing I had was determination.

The thing I remember most about those early days in Spanish Harlem is how hard my mom worked to make our life at home seem like an Ozzie and Harriet kind of thing. We ate every meal together, and Dad always had a place at the head of the table, just like all those families on TV. We didn't have a lot of money, but our parents always made sure we had toys to play with. And we were creative kids—if we couldn't have a dollhouse, Estelle and I would take our dolls and crawl out on the fire escape and pretend that it was their summer home.

Dolls were a big thing in my life; I loved them so much. All my girl cousins bragged about how they outgrew their dolls, but I never got tired of mine. I slept with dolls all the way up until I was married.

I still remember the most beautiful doll I ever saw—it was in the toy department at Macy's, where I went Christmas shopping with my mother. There, propped up in a little crib, I saw a life-sized baby girl doll with a big, round head, and little wisps of brown hair that made her look almost real. I was only six years old, and I'd never seen anything like it. I pleaded with my mom to buy it for me on the spot, but she took one look at the price tag and winced.

"Go ask Santa for that doll," she said. "Maybe he can bring it to you for Christmas."

I'm sure Mom thought I'd forget all about the doll in five minutes, but I wasn't about to let her off the hook. I dragged her right over to Santa Land and we waited in line. And waited. And waited. When I finally got on that old man's lap, I told him exactly what I wanted—the beautiful baby girl doll with the soft brown hair that looked almost real. Santa told me to be a good little girl, and on Christmas morning I'd find a surprise waiting.

Sure enough, on Christmas I looked under the tree and found a doll. But not the one I wanted. Instead of the life-sized baby doll from Macy's, I got this smiling Kewpie doll whose hair was painted right onto her little plastic head. I took it in my arms and tried to love it, but it just wasn't the same. Looking back, I guess my mother was trying her best to make me happy, but I don't think she realized how badly I wanted that life-sized baby girl doll. I must've had a strong maternal instinct, because I was one little girl who took her dolls seriously.

My father recognized that. He was basically a dreamer, so he understood how important my little fantasies were. If I was enchanted by something, he would always get it for me—no matter what it took. Even if he had to steal it.

Which is exactly what he did one day. We were shopping at the Woolworth's at 145th and Broadway, and Dad had just finished loading our basket with all the household items when I saw a tiny pair of ice skates on a shelf in the toy aisle. They were miniature skates, the perfect size for one of my favorite dolls. They were so beautiful, I reached up to the shelf and pulled them down so I could hold them in my hands. When my father saw me, he walked over and laid his hand on my shoulder.

"I'm sorry, Butchie," he told me. That was his favorite nickname for me. "We don't have any money for doll skates today."

"Oh, Daddy," I begged, "please?" I wasn't about to give in, and finally I made such a fuss that the security guard walked over to see what was going on.

"You folks got a problem?" he asked.

"Oh, no," my father said, smiling. "My little girl just doesn't want to leave without a toy." Defeated, I turned to walk away. But I hadn't gone three steps when I noticed that my father had stopped to start a conversation with the security guy. "You've got some job," Dad said. "It's a shame the way people just come in and steal things from here every day." I stood there for a minute or two while the grown-ups made small talk, until finally my dad turned and said, "Okay, Butch. We'd better get going."

I led the way out to the street, but as soon as we got outside, my father tapped me on the shoulder. "I've got a surprise for you, Butchie," he said. I turned around and looked at the little present he was holding out for me.

"My doll skates!" I shrieked. "Thank you, Daddy. Thank you."

"Now, don't tell your mother how I got those," he cautioned. "That should be our little secret." Of course I knew they were stolen. My father had actually slipped them into his back pocket while he was talking to the security guard. But I didn't care. All I knew was that I wanted those skates in the worst way, and my daddy got them for me.

Estelle and I thought we had the best dad in the world—he always seemed so happy-go-lucky and easygoing. Not like our mom, who was always strict and stern. We never could figure out why she got so short-tempered around Dad. We didn't understand that he had a drinking problem that was getting worse every year. All we knew was that Mom and Dad didn't always get along as well as they should.

Even so, I remember having lots of great times together as a family, especially when my sister and I were younger. On warm summer nights, Dad used to pack us all into the car and take us for long rides on Riverside Drive. We'd crank the windows all the way down, and sometimes he'd even let me ride with my head stuck outside, so I could feel the wind blasting across my face. Estelle liked to sit sideways across the backseat, so I'd climb down and perch on the little hump in the floor. From there, I'd look up and watch my mom and dad laughing and talking with the warm wind blowing through their hair. Those are my favorite memories of childhood, because those were the nights when I knew we really were a family.

There wasn't any one time I can point to and say, "That's the day my family fell apart." My mom and dad finally split up when I was twelve, but even that was a long time coming. My sister and I never saw them argue, but we caught enough cross looks exchanged across the dinner table to know that things weren't all that great. And every so often we'd hear harsh words spoken in whispers after they thought we'd gone to sleep.

Dad's real test came when Mom decided to move to a bigger apartment. She was fed up with our tiny walk-up on 151st, so she went out and found a brand-new two-bedroom place at 405 West 149th Street. The rent was $140 a month, which was a lot to pay in 1956. But with her waitressing money and Dad's income, she figured we could just about make it—so long as Dad kept himself together.

I always felt sorry for Dad. He dreamed of being a jazz drummer, but it just wasn't happening for him. He was white, and in those days most of the jazz bands in Harlem were black. Besides, he couldn't read music, and that limited his chances of going professional more than anything else. But instead of accepting his fate—or working to change it—Dad just drank, hoping that might help him forget his lost dreams. It didn't, of course. His drinking only made him more depressed, and after a while he just started drifting further and further into his depression. By the time I got to junior high school, Dad started coming home later and later every night. And then, when he finally did stumble in, he was usually a mess.

Of course, my mom had no patience for any of that. She put up with it as long as she could, but after they signed the lease on the new place, she knew it was time to lay down the law. "Louis," she told him, "this is our chance for a new life. But we got a lot more expenses now, so we both got to get serious. That means you gonna have to stop drinking and coming home late and running around with all these no-accounts in the neighborhood."

"I will, baby," he promised. But Mom had her doubts.

So did I, especially after the day I went to Macy's with him to pick out furniture for the new apartment. I could smell the alcohol on his breath the minute the elevator doors closed, and all the way up to Home Furnishings all I could do was wonder if Dad was going to be in any shape to buy furniture. He wasn't.

As soon as we got to the showroom, Dad fell back into an easy chair and passed out. I went around with the salesman and picked out a new living room set. When I was done, I walked over and fished the money out of Dad's pocket so I could pay the man. Then I woke Dad up and took him home. I was only twelve years old, but I felt like *I* was the parent and *he* was the kid. I was embarrassed and hurt that my own father would do this to me, and that's when I finally began to understand what my mother had gone through for all those years. It was only a few weeks later that Dad left for good.

It was the night before the second month's rent on our new place was due, and Dad didn't come home with his check. My mother sat up until 2:00 A.M., and when he didn't come home, she locked the door and shut off the light. The next day she called his grandmother in Florida and told her to come and get him. I loved my father, but I can't say that I blamed her. I guess I knew in my heart that we'd lost Dad long before he finally left the house.

By the time I got to junior high I was already very conscious of my looks. Ever since I was ten or eleven I'd gotten a lot of attention from the boy cousins at Grandma's house, who would come sniffing around whenever the girls had a pajama party. I didn't know why, but they always seemed to have their eyes on me. Even then my grandmother had to keep a sharper eye on me than the other girls.

In school I discovered that being a half-breed had its advantages, since light-skinned girls were considered pretty. But even though a lot of the guys at school came after me, I still didn't feel like I really fit in with any one group. The blacks never really accepted me as one of them. The white kids knew I wasn't white. And the Spanish kids didn't talk to me because I didn't speak Spanish. I had a little identity crisis when I hit puberty. I remember I used to sit in front of the mirror, trying to decide just what I was. Let's see now, I'd think. I've got white eyes, but these are black lips. My ears . . . are they white ears or black ears?

I even tried to dye my skin darker one time because I thought that might make me look more like my dark-skinned cousins. I found this stuff at the drug store called Q/T Quick Tanning Lotion. The bottle claimed it was guaranteed to give you a dark, rich tan overnight, so I bought the stuff. And that night, after everyone else went to bed, I snuck into the bathroom and spread it all over my body. The directions said to "use in moderation," but I knew I wanted to be dark all over, so I squeezed out about half the bottle. The next morning when I woke up, Estelle was standing over my bed, staring at me.

"What happened to you?" she said.

"What?" I said, clearing the sleep out of my eyes.

"Those stripes!" she said. "You look like a zebra."

I leaped out of bed and looked at myself in the mirror. She was right. I must've used too much of that stuff, because it had dyed my skin in big wide stripes that made me look like a tiger or something. I tried to scrub it off, but the stripes didn't go away for weeks. I wore turtlenecks and tights to school for about a month.

When I was in junior high my mom waited tables at a place called King's Donuts, so Estelle and I used to hang out there after school. We told Mom we liked to visit her at work, but she knew the real reason we came around was because the diner was right across from the Apollo Theatre.

The Apollo was the most exciting spot in Harlem when I was growing up. All the biggest black stars came to play there, and there always seemed to be bright lights and big crowds lined up around the place. And Estelle and I were both naturally drawn to that kind of excitement. Not that we were ever allowed inside the place; my mother made it clear that the Apollo Theatre was strictly off-limits.

In her mind, the Apollo represented the world of drugs and sex, and all kinds of other grown-up things that she thought we were still too young to see. She didn't even like us hanging around King's. As soon as we walked in the door, she'd stick us downstairs in the employees' lounge, where we would do our homework until she got off work. "Don't talk to anyone on the street," she'd warn us whenever we left King's alone. "A lot of these people are thieves or con men. Or junkies."

Junkies! Somebody was always talking about junkies when I was growing up. I never saw one, but, boy, did I want to! I would cringe getting my polio vaccination, but for some reason I was fascinated by the idea of these people who stuck a needle in their arm every day. I couldn't wait to lay eyes on someone who did that.

One day my cousin Mae spotted a junkie outside my grandmother's house. "Hey, look out the window," she said. "It's a junkie." I jumped up from the couch and ran toward the window, but my grandmother stopped me halfway.

"Don't you go over to that window, Ronnie," she commanded. "You don't need to be looking at no dope addict." That just killed me, because all I wanted was to see what a real junkie looked like. But it was forbidden. I never did get to see a dope addict, unless you count Frankie Lymon. And he wasn't even a dope addict when I first met him.

2

A Whole Lot of 'Ettes

A lot of entertainers can't, or won't, tell you where they got their style from. But I know exactly where I got my voice. Frankie Lymon. If he hadn't made a record called "Why Do Fools Fall in Love," I wouldn't be sitting here writing this today.

I was twelve years old when I first heard Frankie and the Teenagers singing "Why Do Fools Fall in Love" on my grandmother's radio. Frankie had the greatest voice I'd ever heard, and I fell in love the minute that record came on. I couldn't tell if he was black, or white, or what. I just knew that I loved the boy who was singing that song. I would sit by my grandmother's old Philco every night waiting to hear him sing "Why do birds sing so gay?" And when he finally came on—with his innocent little voice and perfect diction—my hands got all sweaty, my toes curled up, and I climbed right under that old box radio, trying to get as close to that sound as I could. I pressed my head into the speaker until I got Frankie going right through my brain.

"Ronnie, you keep on like that, you'll go deaf," my grandmother warned me. But I didn't care. If they'd kept playing that song, I would've stayed under that radio forever.

I was amazed when I found out that Frankie was black. "Where did he learn that perfect diction?" I wondered. Not at home. I went to a black church, and I couldn't understand a word they said. Even more surprising to me was the fact that

Frankie was only thirteen years old—just a year older than I was! When I found that out, I knew I had to meet him, and every night I prayed to God that I would. That's how much this boy meant to me.

When I finally did get to meet Frankie, it happened through such a strange coincidence that I'm sure it was fated to be. My mother was waiting tables at King's Donuts, and one day she was telling another waitress how much I worshiped Frankie Lymon. "That boy is all Ronnie ever talks about," Mom said. "She wants to meet him so bad, but I don't even know where to start looking for him."

"Frankie Lymon?" the other waitress said. "Bebe, he's sitting right there in your station." The waitress pointed to this thirteen-year-old kid who was sitting on a stool at the counter.

"That's Frankie Lymon?" my mother gasped. "I just ordered that little ole boy a meat-loaf-and-gravy sandwich!" Then she walked right over and told Frankie that he wasn't going to see his lunch until he promised to show up at her daughter Ronnie's thirteenth birthday party.

"All right," he laughed. "I'll be there. I gotta eat. Is it okay if I bring my little brother, too?"

"You can bring your brother," she said. "Just make sure *you* come."

When my birthday finally rolled around, I was a thirteen-year-old wreck. All of my cousins were in the living room waiting for my party to start, but I just sat there by the front door waiting for Frankie. I looked all goofy with a big red bow in my hair, and my eyes were caked over with mascara that my mother helped me put on for this special occasion. Whenever the doorbell rang, I jumped four inches. "Oh, God!" I'd whisper. "Is that Frankie? Please, God. Let it be Frankie!" But every time it turned out to be just another cousin, I'd sink down deeper and deeper into the cushions of our green L-shaped couch.

At last my cousin Elaine peeked out the window and screamed, "He's here, Ronnie! Frankie and his brother are coming up the walk." I crossed my legs and pulled myself straight up on the couch while Elaine opened the door. But when she swung it open, it wasn't Frankie at all. Just two boys who looked like him.

"Hi," said the taller one, introducing himself. "I'm Louie Lymon." He must've seen how confused I was, because he was quick to add, "I'm Frankie's brother. And this is our other brother, Howard."

Louie? Howard? I was devastated. It was only my thirteenth birthday and already I'd been stood up by the most important boy in my entire life. The disgrace was more than I could bear. But I didn't want everyone to see me cry, so I ran into the bedroom where I could have a real tantrum in private. Naturally, my mother and every one of my girl cousins followed right behind.

"Oh, Ronnie," my mother said, reaching over to retie my big red bow, which had slipped down around my neck. "You ain't got to carry on like this. For all you know, Frankie might be planning to come around later." She finished tying the bow and started wiping the tears off my cheeks. "And even if he doesn't, you wouldn't want him to hear from his brothers that you spent your whole birthday pouting in your room, would you?"

I shook my head. No.

"Good," she said. "Then come on back out here and take some pictures with Frankie's brother Louie. He came all the way down here for your birthday."

"Okay," I said, and I went back out to join my party. Louie turned out to be a sweet boy, and to this day I treasure the snapshot I have of me cutting my thirteenth birthday cake with the brother of my childhood idol.

I had barely gotten over the disappointment of Frankie standing me up when he finally showed up—unannounced— a few weeks later. Nedra's mother, Aunt Susu, was over to our house, and she was the one who answered the door. "Oh, Frankie," she said after he introduced himself. "Ronnie will be so happy to see you."

When I laid eyes on him I nearly fell over. I couldn't believe this kid was only a year older than me—he looked like a grown man. He walked right over to me, all snappy, holding a long-stemmed red rose. He wore a big white carnation in his lapel, and it was obvious from the way he strutted across the room that he was completely full of himself. He wasn't what I expected at all. "Frankie?" I stuttered.

"I'll just leave you kids alone," Aunt Susu said, walking out of the room.

"You must be Ronnie," Frankie said, leaning forward to kiss me on the lips. "You're even more beautiful than my brothers promised." I could smell alcohol on his breath, which reminded me of my father. I instinctively pulled back, but Frankie hardly even noticed. He just slid right down on the couch and patted the cushion next to him. "C'mon, baby. We do want to get to know each other, don't we?"

It was so confusing. The Frankie Lymon I'd dreamed about was the little boy who sang on the records, a kid so sweet and innocent and real that he made me want to climb inside the radio. But looking at this cocky little midget man sitting in my house, I started to wonder if that kid even existed. Suddenly the whole situation just seemed so uncomfortable, I knew I had to get out of it as soon as I could.

"Make yourself at home, Frankie," I said, getting up from the couch. "I've got to take care of something in the kitchen."

I walked straight into the bathroom and locked the door behind me. I must've waited in there a full hour. When I felt sure he'd be gone, I opened the door, tiptoed down the hall, and peeked into the living room. I breathed a sigh of relief when I saw that the room was empty.

I went in and flopped down on the living room couch, and it was like Frankie had never even been there. I half believed I'd dreamed the whole thing until I looked down at the place where he'd been sitting. That's when I found the long-stemmed red rose that he'd handed me when he walked in. It had gotten pushed down between the cushion and the couch. I tried to pull it out, but it broke apart in my hands. I don't know how long I sat there crying, but it must've been a while, because when I got up the whole room had grown dark.

In spite of how Frankie turned out, I still loved his singing. I played his records and sang along with them until I knew every note by heart. I even made up little routines to go along with every one of them, which I would then practice for hours on end. I put a lot of work into my little rehearsals, but I didn't mind. By the time I got to George Washington High School, I already knew that show business was going to be my life. I wanted to be the Marilyn Monroe of Spanish Harlem, and I wasn't going to settle for anything less.

My rehearsals began as soon as I got home from school. Estelle would be in her room studying, and my mom didn't get home until at least five-thirty, so I knew I had two hours of privacy every day. I used that time to turn our living room into a make-believe auditorium. I'd move the coffee table out to the center of the room as a stage, and I'd twist the lampshade back until it shined out like a spotlight. Then I'd set up my little portable record player in the corner, and, using a big wooden stirring spoon as my microphone, I'd climb up on the table and sing along with every record I had by Little Anthony and the Imperials, the Chantels, and, of course, Frankie Lymon.

I wouldn't stop when the record ended. I imagined an entire audience of people sitting around my mother's couch, and I'd tell them jokes and make dedications—the whole bit. Sometimes I'd even jump down off the coffee table and walk along the front of our couch, flirting with each and every person in my imaginary front row, just like I do in my act today.

At five-thirty my mom would walk in and everything would change back into a pumpkin. I'd go out to the kitchen to help her with the dishes, then I'd do my homework and go to bed. I couldn't wait to get to sleep, because that would bring me that much closer to the next day, when I could set up my auditorium and sing to my imaginary audience all over again. I took my career very seriously, even then. And why not? I knew my time was coming, and I wanted to be ready when it did.

Opportunity finally snuck up to my door when a white guy named Bobby Schiffman walked into King's Donuts and started flirting with my mother. A lot of the regulars at King's tried to date my mom after she split up with Dad, but Estelle and I never paid much attention—until Bobby Schiffman. Bobby was different. Estelle and I loved him from the first day we found out that his family owned the Apollo Theatre. We weren't about to sit back and watch our mom let such a valuable contact pass us by, so we did everything but beg her to go out with him.

"Oh, Mom," Estelle would say. "Bobby Schiffman seems like such a nice man. And so handsome. Don't you think so, Ronnie?"

"Yeah," I'd answer. "And if you married him, I'll bet he'd put us up onstage at the Apollo."

"Oh, that's what you want?" my mother said. "Well, I don't think I have to marry him just to get you that."

By this time Mom wasn't so set against us going into the Apollo anymore. I think she knew how serious we were about singing and she didn't see any point in trying to stop us. Grandma had told her how we would spend hours harmonizing in the back bedroom at her house. And that was true. When I was fourteen, I even organized a little group made up of me, Estelle, Nedra, and two other cousins, Diane and Elaine. We'd sit up in Grandma's back room all afternoon working out harmonies to songs we'd heard on the radio.

We finally brought our little cousin Ira into the group, because he was a boy, and we thought that having him sing lead would make us seem more like Frankie Lymon and the Teenagers. We didn't pay any attention to the fact that he was two years younger than any of the rest of us, or that he was extremely shy. In our minds, Ira made us a legitimate rock and roll group. So naturally, we were thrilled when my mom finally asked Bobby Schiffman to set us up at a Wednesday-night amateur show at the Apollo.

"Oh, singers are they?" he asked with a wink. Bobby was sitting at the counter, but he spun around on his stool to sneak a glance at the booth where Estelle and I were trying so hard to look prim and professional.

"Yeah," Mom answered. "They been rehearsing a little and now they ready to give it a try."

"Well . . ." he said, pausing for effect. "Okay. Anything for *you*, Fifi." That's what Bobby always called my mom. The poor guy never did get to first base with her, but we got our date at the Apollo. And we were ecstatic.

When the big night came, the six of us stood backstage waiting our turn with the thirty or forty other hopefuls who were going to take their shot at stardom that night. The tension was so thick you could feel it on your skin. And if that wasn't bad enough, the only thing the kids backstage talked about was how mean the Apollo audience could be. "If they don't like you, they tear you apart," one of the older kids told us. My mother's cousin Frank was a stagehand at the Apollo that night, and he pulled us aside for a warning before the show.

"If they start to boo," he said, "don't stop and stare. Just keep right on moving off that stage as fast as you can. You don't want to get stuck out there when they start throwing things."

"Throwing things!" little Ira gasped. "What do they throw?"

"Oh, anything," Uncle Frank continued. "Food, paper, pennies. I seen them throw their shoes. And one other thing," he added, looking right at Estelle and me. "Sometimes they don't like the light-skinned singers."

That was all Ira needed to hear. The poor kid just looked out toward that stage like he was staring at a gas chamber. The rest of us were nervous, too, but I think the excitement was stronger than the fear. It was for me, anyway. I'd been practicing for this night too long to get scared off now. But when I looked over at Ira shaking in the wings, I admit I started to have my doubts.

Things didn't get any better once we got out onstage. When the Apollo house band started playing "Why Do Fools Fall in Love," Ira didn't sing a word. He just stood there petrified. After the audience started laughing at our little lead singer, that's when I decided to take over. I just strutted out across the stage, singing as loud as I could. When I finally heard a few hands of scattered applause, I sang even louder. That brought a little more applause, which was all I needed. I moved across that stage in a trance, just working off the energy of those few people who were clapping at me. I knew that they wanted me to entertain them, and that made me feel like a star. After that, it was easy.

The other cousins did their best to keep up with me, and we got through the number without getting thrown offstage. There was even a little polite applause afterward, so I guess we did okay. Ira ran straight into the bathroom to throw up. And it was only when we got offstage that I noticed how much we were all sweating.

"Wasn't it great?" I said, all hyped up. But it was obvious from the looks on their faces that Nedra, Estelle, and my other cousins were just relieved that we got through the number in one piece. I couldn't believe it was over so soon—all I could think about was getting back out onstage. After that night, there was no question that it was where I belonged.

Of course, the next day it was back to school, where I was just a regular person again. My sister and I were popular at George Washington High—she was the valedictorian of her class, and I was on the cheerleading squad. But suddenly just being popular didn't seem enough. I was hungry for something more. I wanted to be the most popular girl of all.

Clothes seemed like the answer. I figured that nice clothes equaled popularity, so I was determined to be the best-dressed girl at GW. Of course, nice clothes cost money, and our family hadn't had much of that since my father left home. So I decided to go out and find an after-school job.

I was fifteen when I started working in the food service department of Montefiore Hospital, and that's where I saw my first dead body. I was in charge of dishing out meals in the geriatric ward. I felt so sorry for all of those old people that I'd always try to sneak a little extra food onto their trays. Mrs. Giardi was one old lady who always had a smile on her face, so I made sure she always got an extra dessert.

I'd been there about a month and a half when I walked into Mrs. Giardi's room to sneak her an extra cup of lemon Jell-O, but what I saw stopped me dead in my tracks. Two large black matrons were standing over Mrs. Giardi's bed, rolling her stiff body onto big sheets of newspaper. I must've gasped out loud, because one of the matrons looked up at me and laughed. "Little girl, you look like you seen a ghost."

Then the other matron chimed in. "You gonna work in the hospital, you better get used to this. This is how we do you when you die."

I looked down at old Mrs. Giardi, who wasn't smiling anymore. I watched as the matrons covered her up with yesterday's sports pages, and all of a sudden I felt sick. I turned around and ran right out of that hospital. And I never went back. Never even picked up my check—Montefiore Hospital still owes me for six days' pay. That was the first and last time I ever had to punch a time clock, but at least I had that experience.

I didn't really care about losing the job. Even at fifteen I knew it was just a matter of time before my singing career took off. And after my success at the Apollo, my mother began to agree that my singing career might be something more than just a childish dream. She and my aunt Susu even agreed to pay for singing lessons for Nedra, Estelle, and me. By this time Ira had retired from the group, and Diane and Elaine had also dropped out. Their mother, my aunt Hermean, was real religious, and she didn't want her daughters singing rock and roll for a living.

And so the three of us—Nedra, Estelle, and me—were signed up for singing lessons. Two afternoons a week we'd take the subway down to the Camilucci Studio at Fifty-seventh and Broadway, where we'd study harmony with old Mr. Camilucci. And that old Italian drove us crazy. We'd walk in and stand around a piano, and then Mr. Camilucci would hit a key and assign each one of us our part. Then he'd have us sing corny old stuff like "When the red, red robin comes bob-bob-bobbing along" over and over and over again, until we were ready to scream.

After a few lessons like that, we finally decided to speak up. "Mr. Camilucci," Estelle said, as he started plucking out our notes for the twenty-fifth time. " 'Red, Red Robin' is great, but we already know that one."

"Oh?" he said, looking suddenly suspicious. "You'd like to learn something else?"

"Yeah," I chirped. "How about some rock and roll? Do you know anything by the Chantels?"

He got a real strange look on his face, like he couldn't decide whether to be annoyed or to just ignore us. Then he finally shook his head and leaned back over the keyboard. "Now," he said, hitting the first note of "Red, Red Robin," "repeat after me, 'When the red, red robin comes bob-bob-bobbin' . . .' "

That's when we knew we couldn't win with Mr. Camilucci. But our mothers were paying him five dollars per lesson, which was a lot of money back then, so we kept going. If nothing else, going to Mr. Camilucci's made us feel like we were part of show business. His studio was right down the street from the Brill Building, which is where all the big music publishers and record producers had their offices.

We used to go into the coffee shop across the street from Camilucci's and fantasize that Clyde McPhatter or Ben E. King might walk in and discover us sitting there. We didn't meet either of them, but we did strike up a friendship with a man named Phil Halikus, who was one of the small-time talent agents that hung around the Brill Building. He was a nice older man who always picked up the tab for our sandwiches and Pepsis at the coffee shop. He'd heard us singing one afternoon when he was scouting talent at Camilucci's studio, and he took an instant liking to us. When my mother came down to pick us up, Mr. Halikus told her how talented we were.

"There's plenty of call for a bright young trio like these girls," he said. "You get them a name and I'll see if I can't line up a bar mitzvah or two. May not be glamorous, but it pays."

Glamorous or not, it was professional work, and we were in heaven. When we told our grandma, she was almost as happy as we were. "You'll be just like the Andrews Sisters," she told us. We didn't have the heart to tell her we had other plans, so we ended up calling ourselves the Darling Sisters for the first few gigs, just to make her happy.

Don't ask me how we came up with that name, but I hated it from the start. I thought it was dishonest. Even then I knew I was going to be somebody in this business, and I didn't want to have a made-up name like Darling. So we dropped the Darling Sisters after about three bar mitzvahs. Then we started calling ourselves Ronnie and the Relatives, which was a name my mother came up with.

We loved getting paid to sing, even if it was just pocket money. But it was frustrating just singing "Red, Red Robin" in three-part harmony for a roomful of little Jewish kids. We'd show up at these bar mitzvahs wearing our fancy party dresses, and we'd do songs like "Goodnight Sweetheart" or "When Your Love Has Gone," anything that was big on the hit parade. The backup band would usually be a three- or four-piece combo that was hired separately, so we never even knew what musicians were going to be playing until we got there.

By the spring of 1961, we'd been doing bar mitzvahs and sock hops for almost a year, and we were starting to get frustrated. What we really wanted was to be recognized as the stars we knew we were, and that meant making records. But whenever we'd talk about our ambitions, Phil Halikus would just try to console us.

"Relax, girls," he'd tell us. "Fame takes time. But don't worry, I've got a lot of contacts in the record business. You'll get your shot soon." We tried to be patient, but after hearing this for six months, we were starting to have our doubts. Then he surprised us.

I was barely awake when Mr. Halikus called over to my mother's house at 7:00 A.M. one morning. "Can you girls skip school today?" Of course we could. "Good. Then get Nedra and Estelle and meet me down at the Wurlitzer Building on Fifty-seventh Street at one-thirty."

"Sure," I answered. "What's going on?"

"Just make sure you're there, honey," he said. "You're going to meet a man named Stu Phillips. And dress nice. This could mean a record deal."

That was all I needed to hear. I was awake, and so was everyone else in the building once I'd finished screaming. "Estelle, wake up. We got a record deal. We're going to be stars!"

Of course, we had no idea who this Stu Phillips was until the three of us met Mr. Halikus outside the Wurlitzer Building that afternoon. "Stu Phillips is one of the biggest producers at Colpix Records," he whispered as we walked into the lobby. "He produced the Marcels' 'Blue Moon,' and that's a number one."

Then Mr. Halikus led us upstairs to the rehearsal studios—a whole row of tiny rooms with a couple chairs and a piano in each one. He had to peek through a few doors before he finally recognized Stu Phillips behind one of them and shoved us in.

"Hi, girls," Stu Phillips said as the three of us crammed ourselves into the rehearsal room. And it was a tight squeeze—the room was barely large enough to hold us, let alone Mr. Halikus, Stu Phillips, and his piano player. But we weren't in there long. The whole audition lasted no more than three minutes. Stu Phillips had us sing one song—I think it was "What's So Sweet About Sweet Sixteen"—and before we even finished he held his hand up and stopped us. "That sounds okay," he said. "I'll give you a shot."

You've heard the expression "walking on air"? Well, for the next two weeks we walked on helium. We were actually going to be recording stars! Up until then, the closest we'd come to making a record was when we went over to the store across from my grandmother's where they had a machine that made

little records of your voice for a quarter. You'd wait three minutes for it to come out, and then it sounded like shit when you
got it home. But this was Colpix Records, the big time.

We especially liked the idea of recording for Colpix after we
found out it was a subsidiary of Columbia Pictures. I didn't
know what subsidiary meant, but I sure knew what Columbia
Pictures meant—movies. And we were convinced that after the
first few hit records, Colpix would put us right into the movies.
We had a lot to learn about show business.

In June 1961, we went to our first recording session at Colpix.
We stood in this gigantic studio that was built to hold an entire
orchestra, which made us feel pretty tiny. The first thing we did
was learn the songs. None of us could read music, so Stu Phillips would take us into his office and play a demo of the song he
wanted us to do. He'd usually ask us whether we liked it or not,
but that was mainly a formality. We didn't have a lot of say
about what material we did. We were just three more rock and
roll singers, and kids at that. And in those days that didn't earn
you much respect.

We recorded four tracks at that first session: "I Want a Boy"
and "What's So Sweet About Sweet Sixteen"—the two sides of
our first single—and "I'm Gonna Quit While I'm Ahead" and
"My Guiding Light," the two songs that eventually came out as
our second single.

I was only seventeen years old, but I tried to handle myself as
professionally as I could once we got in the studio. I made sure
to write all the lyrics out by hand on little sheets of paper, which
I arranged in a neat stack and placed on a music stand. Estelle
and Nedra shared another mike with these two fat ladies, one
white and one black. They sang like they thought they were the
McGuire Sisters or something, and I guess Stu Phillips thought
we needed them to fill out our sound. We were just teenagers,
and none of us had full, church-trained voices like so many of
the other black singers back then. All we knew was the three-
part harmony we'd learned from Mr. Camilucci.

We had another session in the same studio about six months
later, at the beginning of 1962. That's when we did our version
of "Silhouettes," which was already an oldie but goodie then. It
had a simple three-part harmony, and we'd already done the

song a hundred times at sock hops and bar mitzvahs. Great, I thought. Here's one we can do in our sleep. Boy, was I wrong. That was the day I found out that there's a big difference between singing a song at a sock hop and recording it to perfection in a studio.

We worked on that one song forever. It probably wasn't really more than two or three hours, but in those days producers would lay down three or four songs a day, so spending even three hours on one track was pretty extravagant. We just kept singing the verses over and over and over. We'd be in the middle of a chorus that we thought was perfect when all of a sudden we'd hear Stu Phillips shouting over the intercom, "Hold it, girls. Somebody in that modulation is still hitting one note and then changing to another note in the middle of the chord."

We just looked at him, blinking. It was like he was talking in a foreign language. Then we'd start another chorus, only to have him stop us again. "That's better," he'd say. "But let's do one more."

It was always "one more." The engineer would roll the pre-recorded musical track back, and then we'd pick the song up again from somewhere in the middle. I was going crazy having to do it in little bits and pieces like that, so I finally got up the nerve to suggest that we do the song all the way through, from start to finish, which was really the only way I knew it. "Okay, this is take ten," Stu said.

That's when I leaned into the mike and spoke my piece. "Can we take one big one?"

"What?" Stu blasted back over the intercom.

"Let's take a whole one," I repeated.

"No, I don't need a whole one," Stu patiently explained. "When you do the whole one, you lose it by the end. I'm just trying to keep you fresh for the end part."

"Oh," I said, more confused than ever. Then I glanced over at Nedra and Estelle, who looked as bewildered as I felt. Wow, I thought. This is work.

We recorded five more songs before we finished the sessions. Besides "Silhouettes," we did "You Bet I Would," "I'm on the Wagon," "Good Girls," "The Memory," "He Did It," and a

thing called "Recipe for Love." They were all songs that Stu
picked out for us, but if I'd had a say in it, I don't think I
would've chosen most of them.

It's not that I hated them. I just didn't *love* them. And I don't
think they were right for us. I mean, what were three teenagers
doing singing a song called "I'm on the Wagon"? We didn't
even know what it meant. When I sang it I thought it was a song
about a kid's little red wagon.

I did think "What's So Sweet About Sweet Sixteen" was a
great song. I remembered how sad I'd been on my sixteenth
birthday because I still hadn't made a hit record. So I could
relate to that one. I also liked "You Bet I Would," which was
written by a young songwriter named Carole King, though we
had no idea who she was when we recorded it.

When "I Want a Boy" came out in August of that summer,
Estelle and I were so excited we bought about a dozen copies
for all the aunts and uncles. I think those might've been the
only twelve copies sold in the city of New York. The record
went zilch, and we were crushed.

We called Mr. Halikus to ask him why our record wasn't
being played on the radio, but he just told us to be patient. "For
chrissake, girls, don't give up already. A lot of groups don't
make it big until their third or fourth record." He reminded us
how important it was to keep developing our live act, which
turned out to be good advice, even if he was just setting us up
so he could say, "Now, I've got this bar mitzvah for you on
Saturday. . . ."

But we knew that our bar mitzvah days were coming to an
end. They had to. We were a rock and roll group, and real rock
and roll groups didn't play bar mitzvahs every Saturday. We
decided that if we wanted to be taken seriously as rock and
rollers, we had to stop hanging around sock hops and start
moving where the rock and roll crowd went. And in 1961 the
rock and roll crowd hung out at only one place, the Peppermint
Lounge.

During the height of the Twist craze, the Peppermint Lounge
was the "in" place to go in New York. Celebrities used to come
from all around the world and line up around the block to get
in there. And this wasn't just show business people; the Pep-

permint Lounge attracted everyone from painters to presidents.

Since Nedra and I were still underage, we practically needed to disguise ourselves to get past the doorman. That's where having six aunts helped, because they taught us all the tricks to using eyeliner, blusher, and lipstick. It's funny, but as protective as they were in most ways, Mom and my aunts didn't seem to mind grooming us to get through the doors of New York's steamiest nightclub. I guess they knew it was for the good of our careers, and they all had a soft spot for show business anyway. So the night we were ready to go down to the Peppermint Lounge for the first time, Mom and her sisters helped doll us up until they were sure we could pass for at least twenty-three.

My mother even gave us Kleenex to stuff in our bras before we squeezed ourselves into three matching yellow dresses with taffeta and ruffles coming down the front. Then we teased our hairdos until they were stacked up to the ceiling. We were going to the Peppermint Lounge to be seen, and there was no way you were going to miss us in these outfits.

We took the subway down to the Peppermint Lounge, which was at Forty-fifth between Sixth Avenue and Broadway, and got on line in front of the place. Every so often the doorman would walk out of the club to see if any celebrities were waiting, and when he saw us standing there with our wild hair and matching yellow outfits, he figured we must be somebody important. So he walked back into the club and brought out the manager, an older guy who carried an unlit cigar in his hand. As soon as he saw us he said, "What are you doing out here on line? You're already late."

We were still standing there staring when he turned and we walked back into the club. It didn't take us long to figure out that he'd hired a girl group to dance at the club, but they obviously hadn't shown up, so he assumed *we* were them. And we sure didn't correct him. We were smart enough to know that when someone opens a door for you, you walk through it. I took a deep breath and turned to Nedra and Estelle. "Okay," I sighed. "Let's go."

Joey Dee and the Starliters had already started playing when we walked in, and the club was packed solid as we worked our way to the stage. The Peppermint Lounge was set up so you had to squeeze past a long, narrow bar where people stood three or four deep. On the other side of them were little tables packed so close you could barely get through. But with our chaperone leading the way, we inched through the crowd until we made it to the foot of the stage.

"Okay," the club manager said. "You're dancers, so dance."

We probably should have been scared out of our minds, but we weren't. All this guy expected us to do was climb up onstage and dance, and we knew we could handle that. So we hopped up there. And the minute we hit that stage, we knew we were going to be okay. Every eye in the place was on us. They noticed our looks right away, just like I knew they would. With everyone staring at me, it didn't take much effort to get charged up and dancing. Joey Dee and the Starliters played straight through without missing a beat. I think they could tell we weren't professional dancers, but they just laughed and kept right on playing.

Then one of the Starliters, a guy named David Brigati, moved up to the mike and started singing Ray Charles's "What'd I Say?" We did a version of that one in our act, too, and it always went over great at sock hops and parties. So as soon as I heard it, I danced right over to David and started shaking everything I had. After the crowd began cheering me on, he handed me the microphone, almost as a prank. But holding a mike was no joke to me. I grabbed it from his hands and tore through a version of "What'd I Say?" that brought the house down. At the end of the song, the Starliters applauded us right along with the audience.

We were sitting at a table during the break when the club manager walked over, still holding his cold cigar, and offered us a job on the spot. By this time he knew we weren't the dancers he'd hired, but with crowd response like we got, who cared? We would come in every night, do a couple of numbers with the Starliters, and then work the rails the rest of the night, which meant dancing above the crowd on these narrow banisters that circled the dance floor. The pay was ten dollars per girl per night, which sounded like a fortune.

And that's how we got our start at the Peppermint Lounge. We'd go down every night and Twist on these rails until 2:00 A.M. Sometimes we'd Twist so hard our Kleenex would shift, and we'd have to run into the bathroom to restuff it. It was so much fun to look out at the crowd and try to pick out stars like Robert Mitchum or Elizabeth Taylor. I couldn't believe I was performing for the same people who entertained me on the late, late show.

At least once a night we'd get to do a number onstage with Joey Dee and the guys, which was my favorite time of all. I'd basically do the same moves I'd rehearsed so often around my living room couch—except that now the people were for real. It was so much fun, and not at all like working. We'd finish at two or three in the morning, and then we'd take a cab home.

I was still a senior in high school, so I had to get up bright and early for classes every morning. But I was usually so excited after I got home from the club that I couldn't even think of sleep, so some nights I'd take a couple of Sominex to help me relax. I was always on the go in those days. I remember some of the people in the neighborhood started calling me Sputnik, because I never stopped orbiting.

After we started dancing at the Peppermint Lounge, we decided it was time to change our name again. With all the exposure we were getting, we knew it was just a matter of time before people in New York started talking about us. And when they did, we didn't want them talking about a group called Ronnie and the Relatives. It just didn't have that magic. My aunts and uncles were tossing names around one night when my mother pointed out that the Bobbettes and the Marvelettes had both had hits recently.

"There seem to be a whole lot of 'ettes going around," Mom said. "Why don't we call them *the Rondettes?*"

Everyone in the room suddenly sat up. "Yeah," said Nedra's mother, my aunt Susu, "that's a good one. It's got a little piece of all three girls' names in it." We dropped the *d* and shortened it to *Ronettes* soon after that—no one seems to remember why— and that was the name that stuck.

* * *

Right after we got hired at the Peppermint Lounge, Columbia Pictures came down there to make *Hey, Let's Twist*, a teenage dance movie that starred Joey Dee and the Starliters. We were thrilled, of course, because we thought this would be our break, too. The Starliters loved us so much that Joey Dee and David Brigati wanted the three of us to play their girlfriends in the movie. We even went down to the set to meet the casting director, but he took one look at our complexions and walked away.

"We can't use them," he told Joey Dee. "They're too light to play black girls and too dark to play white girls. The audience wouldn't know if they were supposed to be white or black."

We were heartbroken, of course. Losing our chance at movie stardom was devastating—especially after the flop of our first record—and we sank pretty low for a few weeks. We still went down to watch the filming, but it killed us to see the white actresses they'd hired to play the Starliters' girlfriends. The closest we got to being in the movie was when we played dancers in a crowd scene. And that's where we stayed—in the crowd.

Nedra, Estelle, and I finally went to see the movie the day it opened, but it wasn't much fun. While all the other kids in the theater laughed and ate popcorn, the three of us just sat in the last row of the balcony and got depressed. We were probably the only girls in New York who cried all the way through *Hey, Let's Twist*.

3

A Little More Mascara

Our disappointment didn't last long. By the beginning of 1962 we flew down to Miami to open up the Florida branch of the Peppermint Lounge. Joey and the guys knew how crushed we were after losing out on the movie parts, so they offered to let us do the Florida shows with them as a sort of consolation.

It was nice to get away from the New York winter for a few weeks, but I think our mothers enjoyed the vacation even more than we did. I was only eighteen, and Nedra was even younger, so Mom and Aunt Susu had it written into our contracts that they would come along as chaperons.

That was during the days of the civil rights struggles in the South, which was something we never even thought about, coming from up north. But we got a living history lesson one afternoon at a Nedick's hot dog stand. Nedra and I were walking along the beach with our mothers when we decided to stop for a snack. Mom and Aunt Susu were lagging about a block and a half behind, like parents sometimes do, so we went on ahead into the Nedick's and ordered four hot dogs and four orange drinks.

The food was already waiting when our mothers walked in the door. Nedra and I were about to take our first bite when the guy behind the counter looked up at our moms and said the words that made us lose our appetites.

"Sorry, no colored allowed."

We set our hot dogs down on the counter. "What do you mean?" Nedra asked. "You served *us*."

"Yeah . . ." he said, squinting his eyes at us. He must've thought we were just suntanned when he waited on us. But we didn't care what the reason, we were going to set him straight.

"Well," I snapped, "those ladies you just refused to serve happen to be our mothers!"

"Oh?" the guy said, taking our hot dogs back. "I guess that means you can't eat here, either."

"Who wants to eat here?" Nedra said as we got up from the counter. I was so mad I wanted to stay and fight, but I couldn't think of a single thing to say. I just stood there boiling with my fists at my side. Finally I spat out, "You can keep your old hot dogs! We wouldn't eat them if they were the last four dogs in Florida." I realized my insult didn't come out quite as militant as I meant it to sound, and we all started laughing as soon as we got back out on the boardwalk.

The Miami Peppermint Lounge turned out to be as big a hit as the one in New York. In fact, so many vacationing New Yorkers showed up there that sometimes it seemed like we'd never left home. That's probably why it didn't surprise us to see Murray the K backstage on opening night.

Murray "the K" Kaufman was the disc jockey that all the kids listened to back home on WINS. He could make a record go number one faster than anyone in the country, and you knew you'd made it when he booked you on one of the rock and roll shows he staged at the Fox Theatre in Brooklyn. Having him come back to see us was like getting a visit from royalty.

"You kids are fantastic," he said in that way he had of making everything he said seem like the most important thing in the world. "I'd love to get a couple of girls like you for my shows in Brooklyn. Do you ever come through New York?"

We thought he was putting us on. "Are you kidding?" I said. "We live at 149th and St. Nicholas! We listen to you every night." But Murray wasn't kidding—he really hadn't heard of us in New York. We had to go down to Miami to be discovered!

Going to one of Murray the K's rock and roll revues at the Brooklyn Fox was the highlight of any New York kid's week in the early sixties. For two dollars and fifty cents you got to see at least a dozen acts, and these were the top names in rock and roll—from Little Stevie Wonder to Bobby Vee to the Temptations, everybody played these shows.

Murray first put us on the bill at the Brooklyn Fox for his springtime revue in 1962. Actually, we weren't exactly on the bill, at least not as the Ronettes. He only put the top ten or twelve acts up on the marquee, so we were one of the acts listed under ". . . and others." For those first few shows Murray didn't even introduce us as the Ronettes. When he brought us out onstage, he called us his "beautiful dancing girls," which is pretty much all we were at first.

We would come onstage and dance around between the acts just to keep the show moving. Then Murray would come out to introduce the next act, and he'd do some shtick with us. That was usually real corny stuff. One time I was walking offstage backwards when I accidentally bumped into him. It got a laugh, so he did a big take and made his hat fly off. Whenever something like that would happen, he'd say, "Keep it in!" and pretty soon we had a whole act worked out.

Murray also used us as background singers for all the acts that couldn't sing real well. After a while he even started letting us do one or two numbers on our own. We'd do "Twist and Shout" or "What'd I Say?"—anything, as long as it had a fast tempo that we could dance to. That was the key, because the more we shook our behinds in our tight skirts, the louder the kids would applaud.

It was during these shows that the Ronettes' image was really born. My mother always told us to look for a gimmick that would make us stand out from all the other groups, something that made us different. Well, being half-breeds, we were born different, so we figured the thing that set us apart from the other groups was our look. And sitting around for hours on end in our dressing room at the Brooklyn Fox, we had plenty of time to work on our look.

There was nothing back there but mirrors, chairs, and makeup. So we naturally passed the time trying on different looks. Estelle would grab an eyebrow pencil and say, "Let's extend our eyeliner." Then the three of us would have a little contest to see

who could extend her eyeliner the farthest. Then we'd start in
on the lashes. We'd all lay mascara on until our eyelashes were
out to here. Then Nedra would grab a rattail comb and run to
the mirror shouting, "Let's tease our hair!" She'd tease her hair
until she could stack it about three feet on top of her head. Then,
of course, Estelle and I would try to top her.

We'd look pretty wild by the time we got out onstage, and the
kids loved it. They'd clap and make noise as soon as they saw us
walk out. And the louder they applauded, the more mascara
we'd put on the next time. We didn't have a hit record to grab
their attention, so we had to make an impression with our style.
None of it was planned out; we just took the look we were born
with and extended it.

A lot of people have commented that the Ronettes looked
Chinese. Maybe we did, but it wasn't conscious—we never tried
to look like any other race. If we copied anything, it was the
look of the girls we'd see on the streets of Spanish Harlem, the
Spanish and half-breed girls who walked around with thick
eyeliner and teased hair. That's what we saw when we grew up,
so we brought it to our act. Of course, we exaggerated it onstage, because everything onstage has to be bigger than life. But
when people ask me where the Ronettes got their street image,
I always tell them we got it from the streets.

We may have looked like street girls, but I think the audience
could tell that under all that makeup, we were really just three
innocent teenagers. And I think they liked that combination.
The girls loved us because we were different—we followed our
own style and didn't care what anybody thought. And the boys
liked us for obvious reasons. The Ronettes were what the girls
wanted to be, and what the guys dreamed about.

So when the audience started responding to our street look,
we played along. The songs we sang were already tougher than
the stuff the other groups did. While the Shirelles sang about
their "Soldier Boy," we were telling the guys, "Turn on Your
Love Light." We weren't afraid to be hot. That was our gimmick. When we saw the Shirelles walk onstage with their wide
party dresses, we went in the opposite direction and squeezed
our bodies into the tightest skirts we could find. Then we'd get
out onstage and hike them up to show our legs even more.
After a while it got to be so much trouble hiking these tight

skirts up that we finally just cut slits up the sides. That was the Ronettes' look. And we definitely made an impact.

After our first engagement at the Brooklyn Fox, Murray could see our popularity growing. I mean, to have no hit records and still have kids waiting backstage to tear our clothes off made it pretty obvious that we had something special. That's when Murray started using us on his radio show every night.

We'd leave school every day and go straight to his studios in the WINS building on Fifty-seventh Street. He'd tape us doing little promos and sketches that he would scatter through his show. He'd introduce us as his dancing girls, and we'd go, "Ooooh, Murray. Ahhh, Murray." Or he'd have us in a little sketch where we'd play giggling teenagers at the beach. The idea was always that we were these sexy little things, and he used at least one of these bits every night. It was corny stuff, but it was cute then.

It was such a bummer to go back to high school after doing the Brooklyn Fox. Most of the kids at George Washington High did their homework to Murray the K, so they all knew we were the girls who did the comedy bits on his show. Of course, we loved all the attention it brought us, but there was another side to it.

Before all of this, I'd been Veronica, the cheerleader. I was popular and kids would say "hi," and that would be that. After I got famous, the kids still said "hello," but it was a different kind of "hello." It didn't have any realness in it. They might as well have been saying, "Oh, there she is, the radio star." That's when I found out that when you're famous, people can actually turn off to you. You think you're the same person, but suddenly people start acting weird around you. They stare at you and keep their distance.

When they'd stare, I'd start to feel like I really was this strange, different person. It was so horrible it made me want to leave school. Why was I sitting in these classes with all these people who just stared at me? I was supposed to finish out my senior year, but I was ready to drop out.

I hated English and history and math because I didn't see what they had to do with my future. I was going to be a star; what did I need with history? It seemed about as stupid as going to medical school for eight years to be a doctor when you knew you were never going to practice medicine. "Why should I go to school?" I asked my mother. "I'm going to be a star."

"You're never a star without a high school diploma," she preached. That's all I heard my whole last year of school. I ended up going to summer school to make up for all the classes I was failing, and I finally did get my diploma in the middle of the next term, in February 1962. And I have to admit that after I got it, I saw how much sense it made to stay in school. But I still hated my mother for making me go through that. I was really rebelling.

Estelle was different from me in that department, like in so many others. She was valedictorian of her class, and she'd sit in her room for hours with her school books. And when she finished them, she'd go paging through *Glamour* magazine and try to do herself over to look like the pictures in there. We were just two different people.

But we also had a true closeness back then. All of the Ronettes did. There was never any rivalry, and we never fought backstage, unless it was over makeup. If I had a half jar of cold cream, I might switch it with Nedra's full jar. But these were little things. We had blood ties that gave us a closeness that the other groups just couldn't match. The three of us were family, and there just wasn't any jealousy then.

We spent most of 1962 waiting for one of our records to hit. It was a long wait. After "What's So Sweet About Sweet Sixteen" flopped on Colpix, Stu Phillips put our next two records out on May Records, which was Colpix's rhythm and blues label. But it didn't seem to matter what label they were on—nobody was buying our records, period. "I'm Gonna Quit While I'm Ahead" didn't sell any better than our first single.

We couldn't figure out why our stuff wasn't selling, but listening to those songs today, I can see why they didn't make it. Colpix had no idea what to do with us. Stu Phillips just didn't know what rock and roll was—I mean, he had us in the studio backed up by two fake McGuire Sisters. And with the strange songs he picked for us, it's no surprise our recording career was going nowhere.

Thank God for the Brooklyn Fox! Hit or no hit, that audi-

ence made us feel like stars. And by now, Murray booked us on
every show he did at the Fox. Our pay was two hundred dollars
apiece for a ten-day run, which we thought was a fortune. Of
course, every time we needed a new outfit or a few cans of hair
spray we'd hit Murray up for a fifty-dollar advance, and those
added up. By the time we got our paychecks, we'd usually have
about a hundred dollars each left.

But money was never the big thing anyway. We would've
done those shows for free, if only for the chance to be around
all those stars. And when I look at some of the playbills from
those shows today, I'm amazed at the lineup. I still have a
program for one of the shows we did a couple years later, in
September of 1964, when the artists included the Shangri-Las,
Marvin Gaye, the Miracles, the Supremes, Martha and the Van-
dellas, the Contours, the Temptations, the Searchers, Jay and
the Americans, the Dovells, Little Anthony and the Imperials,
and the Newbeats. All that and a movie for $2.50! Can you
believe it?

With all those stars running around, you'd expect the worst
ego battles backstage. But actually there was almost always a
great feeling behind the scenes at the Brooklyn Fox. Everybody
had to do three shows a day, so we all knew we'd be stuck back
in the theater for like twelve hours straight. So everyone tried
to make the best of it. The dressing rooms were all next to each
other on this long hall, so the acts couldn't help but mingle.
Diana Ross would come in to borrow our lipstick, and I remember Little Stevie Wonder loved to play tricks on us. "You girls
sure look great tonight in those red dresses," he'd say, making
light of the fact that he was blind and couldn't have seen our
dresses if they were on fire.

Of course, we didn't get along with everybody. I couldn't
stand the Shirelles when we were just starting out. They were
headliners, and they didn't want to have anything to do with the
other groups. Boy, they were stuck-up. The Shirelles were the
only girl group with their own valet. I mean, to have a valet you
had to be superstars. And they sure thought they were. These
girls would not even come out of their dressing room until they
were ready to go onstage. And then they hardly spoke to you.
They just walked straight out to the stage with their valet wait-

ing in the wings. The Shirelles looked at us like we were little nothings. I just said, "Well, gee!"

Dusty Springfield was another one I'll never forget. She shared a dressing room with us once, and I never saw anyone get so frustrated backstage. She hated being stuck back there all day and night, and she expressed her frustration with dishes. All the dressing rooms opened out onto this long hallway, and at the end of this hall was a big exit door that led to the stage. When Dusty Springfield got upset, she would go out to the hallway and throw cups and saucers at the stage door. By the second show you had to step over piles of broken china just to get to the stage.

After she broke every dish in the place, she'd send her valet out to Lamston's five-and-ten-cent store to buy more. This poor guy would come back with whole boxes of white cups and saucers for Dusty Springfield to throw at the exit door. She'd break dishes for five minutes, then she'd walk back into the dressing room with a big smile on her face. I guess it helped relieve her tension, but we all thought she was nuts. I never could understand the craziness of some performers. Rock and roll came so naturally to me, I didn't understand what all the fuss and frustration was about.

The toughest part about being around all these stars was that we knew we weren't really one of them. All of the other acts that played the Fox had at least one hit record. But even after we'd recorded almost enough songs to make an album at Colpix, most people didn't even know we made records. We wanted our hit so bad we even went to church and prayed for it.

There was a big Catholic church across from my grandmother's house, over by City College. We weren't even Catholic, but Nedra, Estelle, and I were willing to do whatever it took to work our miracle. We trooped into that cathedral and lit candles to the Virgin Mary, touched our foreheads with holy water, and finally the three of us got down on our knees and prayed. I can't say for sure what the other two were praying for, because they were also interested in boys. But I was begging the Virgin Mary, Jesus, and God—and whoever else might have been listening—to please let me have my hit.

4

Pied Piper

For a singer, having the right producer is like an actor having the right director. A good producer knows how to use your voice, and how to get it on record. He has to be able to write songs that work for your sound, or else be smart enough to choose ones that do. For us, Stu Phillips was none of these things. So, at the start of 1963, our New Year's resolution was to get a new producer. And we set our sights high. For our producer, we were going to get Phil Spector.

By 1963, Phil was already a legend. He wrote his first number-one record, "To Know Him Is to Love Him," when he was only eighteen years old, and by the time he was twenty-one, he was already a millionaire. He was only twenty-two when we met him, but he'd already made more top-ten records than most guys twice his age. And these were good records. When you listened to "Zip-A-Dee-Doo-Dah" by Bob B. Soxx and the Blue Jeans, or "Uptown," or "He's a Rebel," or any of the other records he made with the Crystals, you knew this guy could produce rock and roll music like no one else.

Unfortunately, we had no idea how to get in touch with him. All we knew was that his record company had an office at Sixty-second and York Avenue, and that, according to rumors we'd heard, Phil himself lived in a penthouse upstairs from his office.

So with no better plan, Estelle and I just picked up the phone and called over there.

We were sitting in our bedroom one afternoon when we decided to do it. We thought it would be best for Estelle to do the talking, since she was the valedictorian. She picked up the big black phone from the nightstand between our beds and placed it on her pillow. Then she got the number for Philles Records from information, and she dialed it. When the secretary answered, Estelle sat up straight and said, in her most grownup manner, "Yes, I'd like to speak to Mr. Phil Spector."

There was a pause, and then Estelle started to get this panicky look in her eyes. That's when I knew they were actually putting her through. I couldn't stand the suspense, so I buried my head under a pillow. But I still kept one ear out so I wouldn't miss anything.

"Hello, Mr. Spector," my sister was saying. "My name is Estelle Bennett, and I'm one of the Ronettes." I couldn't believe she was actually talking to Phil Spector. I pulled my head out of the pillow to look at her. If this was a joke, I swore I'd kill her. But it wasn't. She was really doing it.

"Yes, we do," she said, and then paused. Agony. "Yes," and then another pause! More agony. What could this guy be saying? And then finally, "Oh, yes. We'll be there. Thank you, Mr. Spector. Oh, okay, *Phil*." She hung up the phone and didn't say a word.

"What?" I demanded. But Estelle just pulled a pillow over *her* head and started screaming into it.

I couldn't take any more of this suspense, so I jumped up on her bed and started shouting, "What'd he say? Estelle! What'd he say?"

Then she stopped screaming and slowly raised her head from the pillow. "Ronnie," she said. "We did it!"

"What? We did what?" I was frantic.

"*It!*" she exclaimed. "We got through to Phil Spector! He wants to meet us!"

"Where?" I yelled. "When?"

"At Mira Sound Studios!" she screeched. "Tomorrow night!"

Then I started screaming again. And she started screaming again. Then we both buried our heads in our pillows and

screamed as loud as we could. We did that for about ten minutes. Then we got on the phone and called Nedra.

We couldn't believe our luck, that a busy man like Phil Spector would agree to audition us, sight unseen. It was only later
that Phil let it slip that he'd seen us at the Brooklyn Fox many
times. He knew exactly who we were all along.

The next night we went down to Mira Sound Studios at
around seven o'clock. Mira Sound was in the back of this real
slummy building on West Forty-seventh Street. I remember,
because we were surprised that a millionaire would choose to
record in such a shabby building.

Of course, we knew Phil was rich. We couldn't stop talking
about it. Since we'd never even seen him, that was about all we
knew about him. We were so naive that our only image of a rich
man came from the TV show "The Millionaire." So all we did
that whole day was joke about which one of us was going to
marry this millionaire.

When we finally walked into Mira Sound, everything was
dark. We expected to find a roomful of musicians, but the place
was deserted. We were almost ready to turn around and leave
when I glanced over to the corner and saw this real little guy
sitting behind a giant grand piano.

"You must be the Ronettes," he said, so softly we had to lean
in to hear him. Nedra and Estelle just looked at him, like they
couldn't believe this weird little man could be Phil Spector. But
I knew who he was the instant I saw him.

He wasn't what some people would call handsome. Even
though he was only twenty-two, he already had a receding hairline, and almost no chin. But he had great eyes. They looked
deep, like he could see right into you. I remember just staring
at him and thinking how cute he looked sitting there in the dark
all by himself, like a sad little boy who got stuck inside with his
piano lessons while all the other kids were outside playing. I
thought he was adorable.

"I'm just going to have you sing some songs," he said, getting
up from the piano and walking to the other side of the studio.
I loved the way he walked, with one hand stuck in his pocket.
"But I want you to stand over there." He pointed to a group of
music stands over in the corner.

Oh, no! He wasn't going to ask us to read music. I nearly freaked. But then Phil said, "You don't have to do anything special. Just sing something you know." It was almost like he had read my mind.

We walked over to the empty music stands, cleared our throats, and launched into our best three-part harmony from Mr. Camilucci's:

> "When the red, red robin comes
>   bob-bob-bobbin' along . . ."

Phil sat back down behind his piano, smiling. He let us go through two whole verses before he stopped us. "That's great, girls. But I'd like to hear you do something for yourselves now. Just sing me the kind of stuff you might sing when you're goofing around at home."

He didn't have to ask me twice. One thing I've never had trouble doing is singing. I went right into Frankie Lymon's "Why Do Fools Fall in Love." But I hadn't even finished singing "Why do birds sing so gay" before Phil jumped up, knocking the piano bench down behind him.

"Stop!" he shouted. "That's it. That is it!"

I was shocked. I hadn't figured out yet that this kind of drama was typical for Phil. I was sure I'd done something wrong until he said, "*That* is the voice I've been looking for!"

He was practically yelling. I didn't know whether to keep singing or to run out of the room. Then he walked over and asked me, real sweet, "Do you know any other songs?"

Well, we sang him every song Frankie Lymon ever did. Then we started in on Little Anthony. And Phil sat there the whole time, smiling and tapping his fingers. After a while he joined in on the piano. We gave quite a little concert. I'll never forget that night.

After we finished, it was obvious he didn't want us to leave. "Hey," he said. "You guys must be hungry." He didn't even wait for our answer, he just popped up from behind the piano and started walking toward the door. "C'mon," he said, waving after us like a Pied Piper. "Let's go get some pastrami on rye."

We followed him out to the street, where a long black limousine stood waiting at the curb. He bounced into the backseat, and we followed right behind him. He seemed delighted by our company. And though we were all too shy to say so, the three of us were getting a kick out of him, too. "Let's get the sandwiches to go," he said. "Then we'll bring them back here so you guys can sing some more songs."

We were supposed to be there for an audition, but this was turning into quite a night. The chauffeur drove us over to the Carnegie Deli and parked the car. Phil climbed out to pick up the food, but just before he went in, he turned to me and said, "Hey, Ronnie. Would you like to come in with me to pick up the sandwiches?"

I was so shy I couldn't even bring myself to answer, let alone walk into the restaurant with him. I just shook my head no, and he went in alone.

When we got back to Mira Sound, we all ate pastrami and potato salad while Phil played us a tape of his latest record. It was Darlene Love singing "(Today I Met) The Boy I'm Gonna Marry." When the song ended, Phil ran back into the control room and played it again. And again. And again. It was so entertaining, the way he ran all around the control room like Charlie Chaplin. He knew he had an audience, and he did everything he could to keep us laughing.

I already knew I liked him that first day. And I knew he liked me, too. It really was love at first sight on both our parts, even though I hardly said three words the whole night. I didn't have to say anything else—we communicated in other ways. Every time Phil put that song back on, I wondered if he wasn't trying to tell me something. Because it sure did speak to me. I couldn't stop thinking that today I really had met the boy I was going to marry.

Of course, before our relationship could go any further, personally or professionally, Phil had to meet my mother. We were still too young to sign our own contracts, so getting my mother's consent meant everything. We told him how protective my mother was, and that if he planned to keep us out rehearsing songs all into the night, he had better get on Mom's good side—and fast.

So, a week later, Phil showed up at our apartment at 405

West 149th Street carrying flowers and a big bottle of expensive wine. That was an exciting night for me. Not just because Phil was coming, but because I was going to cook a complete dinner by myself for the first time. I tried to get my mother to sit down with Phil in the living room while I cooked, but she spent most of the night bothering me in the kitchen. It was "Ronnie, you're going to burn those peas," or "Ronnie, watch out those rolls don't rise too high" the whole night. Mom even complained when I tenderized the meat. "Ronnie, you don't give a rich man tenderized steak. A rich man wants a filet mignon." I finally had to throw her out of the kitchen.

When we sat down to eat, Phil put his big bottle of wine in the middle of the table and poured my mother a glass. I kept my eye on her the whole time, trying to figure out what she thought of Phil. My mom was a shrewd woman—you couldn't just waltz in there and sweep her off her feet by promising to make her daughter a star, so I figured Phil would have a tough time getting her to trust him. But he was so charming and funny that she liked him right away. Mom later admitted that watching Phil sitting at the table making jokes reminded her of my father, who sat at that very same table cracking jokes and telling funny stories when we were kids. Phil didn't know it, but he had zeroed right in on my mother's soft spot.

After dinner, Estelle and I went into the kitchen to do the dishes while Mom and Phil talked business. As soon as he got her alone, Phil started raving about my voice. "Mrs. Bennett," he said, "that girl of yours can sing. I just hand her a song and she flies with it. A lot of singers will worry a lyric to death, trying to get it just so, but not Ronnie. She just jumps in and attacks it—and it doesn't even matter whether she's even got the words right. You don't notice. When that girl wants to sing, there's just no stopping her. She's obsessed with music."

He paused for a few seconds. "And I understand that obsession, Mrs. Bennett. I really do. Because I'm the same way." Then he went quiet to let what he'd just said sink in. When he started speaking again, he leaned forward, like he was going to let my mom in on a great secret. "Your daughter's dream is to be a real singer, Mrs. Bennett. Give her to me. I'll make her dream come true."

Then he sat back and added, almost like a postscript, "The other two girls are okay, but it's Ronnie's voice that I want."

"I'm glad you like my daughter's voice," Mom said. "But the Ronettes is a group. If you think you going to bust that up to get Ronnie . . ." Now it was Mom's turn to pause. "Well, uh-uh. You ain't."

From the way Mom sat there shaking her head, it was obvious she wasn't kidding. "Now, if you want to see about taking on all three Ronettes as a group . . . well, then we can talk." Phil didn't argue the point. And from that moment on, it was clear that any discussion of the Ronettes included all three of us.

They spent the rest of the evening discussing another touchy area—our contract with Colpix Records. Even though Colpix had long since lost interest in us, we were technically still signed to the label. Before Phil could take over our career, he and my mother had to plot out what they called "The Great Escape."

Phil knew that if he approached Colpix and offered to buy out our contract, they'd never let us go, thinking that if Phil Spector wanted us, we must be better than they thought. But if my mom walked in and told Colpix that we were tired of the music business, they'd probably let us go without a peep. And that's just what they did.

My mother prepared a whole story about how the three of us wanted to leave the business and go back to school. She told them that Nedra and Estelle wanted to go to secretarial school, and that I planned to go into nursing. It sounded right, since that's probably about what we would've done if Phil hadn't come along when he did. The story worked, and Colpix let us out of our contract within a week.

Phil finally signed us in March of 1963. And once he had us, we became his obsession. He wouldn't record us for a few months yet, but he rehearsed us every single night of the week. These rehearsals always went the same. We'd meet Phil at around six or seven o'clock at an apartment that belonged to one of his arrangers, a man named Arnold Goland. After we got there, Arnold usually disappeared. Phil always said we'd have more privacy at Arnold's, and we had no reason to doubt him.

What would usually happen is, Phil would bring in a song for us to learn—"Why Don't They Let Us Fall in Love" by Jeff Barry and Ellie Greenwich was the first one I remember practicing with Phil. We'd work on the harmonies and background vocals for an hour or so. Then Phil would send Nedra and Estelle home so he could work with me on the lead vocals in private. And it was during this private time that our romance began.

Since I didn't read music, the only way I could learn a song was to go over and over it until I knew it by heart. So it would just be me and Phil sitting there, and he'd strum the song over and over on his guitar while I read the lyrics from a piece of paper. And there was something very sexy about that. I'd be looking into his eyes while he played guitar, and all of a sudden I'd feel like kissing him. Or he'd hear me hit a note in a certain way, and he'd suddenly realize he was getting hot.

After a few rehearsals like that, it was getting pretty hard to contain ourselves. Finally, one night after Estelle and Nedra had left, I was right in the middle of a verse when Phil stopped strumming long enough to ask, "Would you mind if I kissed you?"

Just like that, he came out and asked. I can't say that I was surprised, because I'd been waiting for those words since the first day we met. "No," I told him. "I don't mind." Then he set down his guitar—which I still remember because of how carefully he laid it back in its case—and he leaned forward and kissed me. It was a nice kiss, more romantic than sexual, because that's the way we were then. But I could tell by the gentle way he did it that kissing me really meant something to Phil. I know it meant something to me, because I couldn't stop thinking about him after that night.

And that's the way our rehearsals went from then on. We'd rehearse a little. Then we'd kiss a little. Then we'd rehearse a little more. Then he'd take me home. It all seemed so romantic and almost perfect in its way. By the time we finally got into the recording studio that spring, we were already completely in love.

When Phil was finally ready to record "Why Don't They Let Us Fall in Love," he flew my mother and me to California for the session. But for some reason, Nedra and Estelle followed us a few days later by car. They drove out with Bobby Sheen, who was the lead singer of Bob B. Soxx and the Blue Jeans, one of the other groups Phil had under contract.

It took them five days to get across the country in Bobby's brand-new 1963 Chevrolet station wagon, and they were all miserable by the time they got to California. Nedra and Estelle were furious at Bobby because he had insisted on driving straight across the desert without stopping at a gas station so they could fix their makeup. By the time they climbed out of his car in L.A., they had mascara running down their faces in streams that looked like black tears. But they forgave him pretty quickly, and we ended up staying with Bobby and his family in this big old three-story house they had in L.A.

None of us had ever been out west before, but we didn't see much of California on that trip. We spent most of our time at Gold Star Studios on Vine Street in Hollywood. We thought we were there to record "Why Don't They Let Us Fall in Love," which we assumed was going to be our first single. It was only later that we found out that Phil had no intention of recording our first record at these sessions. The real purpose of that trip was to give him a chance to hear how we sounded in the studio. We thought we were old pros after our Colpix sessions, but during those first few days at Gold Star, we found out how little we really knew about professional recording techniques.

For one thing, we had no idea of how to pace ourselves in the studio. On our first day at Gold Star, Phil asked us to go through the song once, and we tore into it like there was no tomorrow. When we finished, all the guys in the studio were impressed, and some of them even applauded. Then Phil's engineer, Larry Levine, came out of the control booth, barely able to hold back a grin. "That was great, girls," he said. "But you didn't have to go all the way through the whole thing—we were just checking your mikes for balance."

We were pretty embarrassed for a minute, until Phil got us off the hook. "If you think *that* was good," he said, his voice booming out over the intercom from the control booth, "wait'll you hear how they sound when we start checking their volume levels." Everyone in the studio cracked up at that, and we joined in the laughter.

I think the reason Phil loved our enthusiasm so much is because it came close to matching his own. I never stopped being amazed at how fanatical Phil was about every detail of what went on in the studio. His musical fluency was amazing. He could play any instrument—he could walk into the studio and show the drummer what he wanted him to do, then he could walk over to the guitarist and show him exactly the chords he wanted to hear. He had such control in the studio. And I don't know about other women, but that was an instant turn-on for me. I love knowledge in a man, and Phil was a genius. If I wasn't already in love with him before we walked into the studio, I would have fallen in love with him anyway.

And I did love the guy. From the first minute I saw him, I couldn't wait to have his kids. He wasn't conventionally handsome, but the Rock Hudson type never impressed me anyway. I thought Phil had a great body. He had a great tush, the cutest one I'd ever seen. He wasn't very tall, but he was the perfect height for me. As little as I am, it hurt my neck to kiss a tall guy. But Phil was so small that when we walked together, I fit him like a glove. Phil and I really were a perfect match.

5

Wigs on the Ceiling

When we returned from California, the Ronettes went right back to work. Even though our Colpix singles had all flopped, we were always in demand as a live group. By 1963, all three of us were out of high school and playing with rock and roll variety shows like Clay Cole's Twisterama Revue. The following we developed at those shows—along with the fans we made at Murray the K's Brooklyn Fox revues—were all that kept us going before we met Phil.

Even before we ever had a hit record, we had a hard core of fans who followed us from show to show, and for some reason, a lot of them seemed to be gay men or lesbians. I'm not sure why. Maybe it was because we were half-breeds, and the gay crowd sensed that the Ronettes were outsiders just like they were. Whatever the reason, there was something about our style that spoke to a lot of gay people, because they've always been there for us. Even today I meet gay guys who saw the Ronettes at the Cafe Wha or the Bazaar in the Village, and they can still name every song we did at a show that happened twenty-five years ago.

In that long stretch before "Be My Baby," our live shows were the only place our fans could hear us. Even after Phil recorded our first song out in California, he refused to release it. When I asked him when "Why Don't They Let Us Fall in Love" was coming out, he answered without missing a beat.

"Never," he said.

I was shocked. I thought it was a pretty good record. But Phil just shook his head. "It's a good song," he told me. "But it's not a number-one record."

By this time I really believed that Phil actually could predict a number-one song, and I thought that was fantastic. "I'm still working on your first million-seller," he teased, "and it's almost finished. If you're a real nice girl, I might let you come over to my house to hear it."

I'd never been in a penthouse before—Phil's or anyone else's. So naturally, when I walked in I couldn't resist peeking into all the closets and poking around behind all the closed doors. I opened one door and was surprised to find a bedroom where six or seven pairs of women's shoes were scattered all over the floor. When I asked Phil who they belonged to, he nearly turned pink.

"Will you stop snooping around where you don't belong?" he snapped. I think it was the first time I ever saw Phil lose his temper.

"Okay, honey," I said. "I'm sorry." He must've noticed the hurt look in my eyes, because he softened his tone immediately.

"Those are my sister Shirley's shoes," he explained. "She stays here sometimes when she's in New York. Now," he said, changing the subject, "why don't you go into the other bedroom and watch TV? Jeff and Ellie are going to be here any minute to work on the song, and we don't want to be disturbed."

Phil was still very hush-hush about our relationship at that point, and he didn't want his writing partners to know I was there. I didn't complain. I was too thrilled. I thought it was the greatest thing in the world to be sitting in the bedroom while my boyfriend wrote my first hit record in the next room. But what did I know? I also believed those were his sister's shoes spread out all over the floor.

If I had any doubts, I was too busy listening to what was going on in the living room to worry about them. I put my ear to the wall and tried to hear what Phil, Ellie Greenwich, and Jeff Barry were singing. It was hard to hear the words over Ellie's piano playing, but when they came around to the chorus, I could hear all three of them loud and clear. "Be my, be my baby," they sang. "Be my baby, now." I thought it was catchy, and I couldn't help wondering if that was what a number-one record sounded like.

Phil and I rehearsed that song for weeks before he would let me fly out to California to record it. But when that morning came, I knew the words to "Be My Baby" backwards and forwards.

I got up really early so my mother and I could catch the plane. Since I was going to sing lead, Phil wouldn't need Estelle and Nedra to do their backgrounds until later, so they stayed behind in New York for a few more weeks. I remember the morning I left, Estelle stuck her head out from under the sheets and said, "Don't forget to fill out the airplane insurance forms when you get to the airport." Airport insurance was a big thing with my family. Whenever one of my uncles would drop me off at the airport, it was always straight to the insurance stands.

My mother and I got in a cab, and I sang "Be My Baby" all the way out to LaGuardia. I wanted to be so perfect, I couldn't rehearse it enough. I even made my mother wait in the airport bathroom with me while I sang through it a few times more. We must've stayed in there a little too long, because by the time we got out we'd missed our plane.

Then my mother did something I'd never seen her do before. She sat down and sighed. Right there in the airport waiting room, she just let out a big sigh like she was real tired all of a sudden. "Ronnie, sit down here with me," she said, patting the brown cushion of the airport couch. "I think you're at the age where you can go out there and sing 'Be My Baby' all by yourself now, so I don't think I'm gonna go all the way out there to California with you this time." Then I kissed her good-bye and got on the next plane all by myself.

When I landed in California, Phil picked me up at the airport in his big limousine and drove me straight to Gold Star Studios. Gold Star's Studio A was old and really tiny, but that was the only place he ever recorded anymore, because he knew he could get sounds out of that room that he couldn't get anywhere else. It had something to do with the acoustics. The room was so small, the sound seemed to bounce off the walls, creating a natural echo that made every song recorded there sound fuller.

And Phil loved that, because he was always experimenting with ways to make his sound as big as possible. Instead of having one guitarist playing rhythm, he would have six. Where someone else might use one piano, Phil would have three. He'd have twin drum sets, a dozen string players, and a whole roomful of background singers. Then he'd record everything back on top of itself to double the sound. Then he'd double it again. And again. And again and again, until the sound was so thick it could have been an entire orchestra. That's what Phil was talking about when he told a reporter that his records were like "little symphonies for the kids."

Watching Phil record the background music for "Be My Baby," I finally understood what he meant when he stopped me that time and said, "That's it! That's the voice I've been looking for." He knew from the first second he heard me that my voice was exactly what he needed to fill in the center of this enormous sound. Phil had been trying to construct this giant wall of sound ever since he got started in the record business, and when he heard me, he knew my voice was the final brick.

I was always surprised at how much Phil used me when he had singers like Fanita James and Darlene Love around. When I'd hear them singing with those great big gospel voices, I'd start to wonder what was so special about my little voice. But I have to give Phil credit. He loved the way I sang, and he knew exactly what to do with my voice. He knew my range. He knew my pitch. He even knew which words sounded best coming out of my mouth. He knew that "Be My Baby" was a perfect song for me, so he constructed the whole record around my voice from the ground up.

It took about three days to record just my vocals for "Be My Baby." I was so shy that I'd do all my vocal rehearsals in the studio's ladies' room, because I loved the sound I got in there. People talk about how great the echo chamber was at Gold Star, but they never heard the sound in that ladies' room. And, between doing my makeup and teasing my hair, I practically lived in there anyway. So that's where all the little "whoa-ohs" and "oh-oh-oh-ohs" you hear on my records were born, in the bathroom at Gold Star.

Then, when I finally did go into the studio, I'd hide behind this big music stand while I sang, so Phil and Larry Levine wouldn't see me with my mouth all popped open when I reached for a high note. I'd keep the lyric sheet right in front of my face, and then, after I finished a take, I'd peep out from behind my music stand and look through the window to see how Phil and Larry liked it. If they were looking down and fooling with the knobs, I'd know I had to do it again. But if I saw they were laughing and yelling "All right!" or "Damn, that little girl can really sing!" I'd know we had a take. Since my approach to each song was completely up to me, watching Phil and Larry react afterward was the only real feedback I ever got.

Recording at Gold Star in those days was like one big party. Phil always got the best musicians in town to play at his sessions, guys like Hal Blaine, Nino Tempo, Leon Russell, Barney Kessel, and Glen Campbell. Jack Nitzsche did all of our early arrangements, and the guy was a genius. Then there was Larry Levine, who engineered all our songs. Phil had so many good people working for him that it really was a joy to go into work.

But the biggest fun of all came when it was time to lay down the background vocals, because Phil always invited everyone in the whole studio to join in. If you were standing around and could carry a tune, you were a background singer in Phil's wall of sound. And everybody Phil knew seemed to show up the day we did the backgrounds for "Be My Baby." Darlene Love was there, and we had Fanita James from the Blossoms, Bobby Sheen from Bob B. Soxx and the Blue Jeans, Nino Tempo, Sonny Bono—who was Phil's gofer in those days—and Sonny's girlfriend, who was a gawky teenager named Cher.

I have to be honest—the first time I saw Cher, I thought she was a hooker. It was in a hotel room where I was supposed to meet Phil for a rehearsal. She and Sonny were already in the room sitting at the piano when I walked in. And when I saw this skinny young kid with her long black hair and thick mascara, I just assumed she was a call girl from the hotel. Then Sonny introduced her as his girlfriend, and I was so embarrassed, I just had to laugh. After a few minutes I could tell that she was really just a sweet kid, and we got to be friends.

We would meet in the bathroom at Gold Star to tease our hair. Sitting over the sink, we would share black eyeliner and gossip. We were about the same age, and we both had stars in our eyes, so it was only natural that we would hit it off. I had fun with Darlene and Fanita and the other girls who sang for Phil, but I never felt like I could talk to them the way I did with Cher. I was probably closer to her than to anyone outside of my family in those days. And as time went on, Cher and I began to see that we had a lot more in common than just bangs and makeup.

Sonny always acted extremely jealous of Cher. And when I got out to California, I started to notice that Phil could get pretty possessive of me, too. Neither of them liked for us to go off on our own. But Phil seemed to trust Cher, so she and I spent a lot of time together while Phil and Sonny worked in the studio. We'd go shopping together, or we'd spend the day at the movies. Other days we'd just drive around in Cher's little red MG, looking at all the strange sights of Hollywood.

As soon as we finished "Be My Baby," I flew right back to New York, where the Ronettes were scheduled to start a two-month tour of the East Coast with Joey Dee and the Starliters. One of our first stops was Wildwood, New Jersey. I'll always remember that town, because that was where we heard "Be My Baby" for the first time. It was one of those moments that changes your life forever.

Nedra, Estelle, and I were sleeping late in our motel room on the Saturday morning after our first show in Wildwood. In those days all three Ronettes would share one big bed, and Mom or Aunt Susu would usually sleep in the other one. By the time I woke up that morning, Mom had already gone out to get breakfast, so I walked over and turned the TV on to find "American Bandstand," which we woke up to every Saturday, just like every other teenager in America. You would turn it on even if you were still half-asleep, because you didn't want to miss the latest records.

Even though I was barely awake, I could hear Dick Clark talking about how this next record was guaranteed to be the hit of the century. I couldn't wait to hear what this thing could be. Then I heard "boom-ba-boom-boom"—the drumbeat that starts off "Be My Baby." Even though I was sitting up in bed, I was convinced that I'd fallen back asleep and was only dream-

ing that Dick Clark was playing our record on "American Bandstand." But if I was dreaming, Estelle and Nedra were having
the same dream, because they sprang upright in bed and started
staring at the TV, same as me. After that I nearly passed out
right there in that motel room.

We sat there for about a minute watching all those happy
teenagers dancing to our record. Then Nedra and I ran out to
the terrace to tell Joey Dee and the guys, who were all swimming around in the pool.

"Hey, guys!" I yelled. "Get up here. Dick Clark's playing our
record!"

It was like we couldn't really believe that this was happening
unless we had witnesses. Joey and the guys ran up the stairs just
in time to catch the end of our song. Then they hugged us, and
we hugged them. And then we all laughed and sang and enjoyed what it feels like to be on top of the world.

A few minutes later Phil was on the phone. He was as surprised as we were to see the record taking off so fast—or so he
said. He told us the Ronettes would have to leave Joey Dee's
tour immediately so we could get back to New York to promote
the record. Of course, Joey Dee wasn't very happy to hear that.
But he didn't want to stand in our way, so he finally did let us
out of the tour.

"Be My Baby" hit the charts in the last week of August 1963.
After that, the thrills only got bigger. When we showed up at
the Brooklyn Fox for our first show after "Be My Baby," we
took one look at the marquee and had to pinch ourselves. There
was *our* name, spelled out in letters three feet tall—*the Ronettes*!
Now we knew we were big-time, because Murray the K didn't
put just anybody's name up in lights. When we saw him backstage, Murray kissed each one of us on the cheek and told us
how happy he was. "Maybe now you girls will stop hitting me up
for cash advances every two days!"

The other acts at the Fox were just as happy for us—even the
Shirelles! Shirley Alston actually called us into her dressing
room. The Shirelles were the biggest girl group around, so for
us, this was like being called in to visit the queen.

I remember how eager we were to finally see what went on in
a star's dressing room. The Shirelles had a little bar set up in the

corner, with shot glasses, a bowl of ice, and a whole row of liquor bottles all lined up on it. For some reason it shocked the hell out of us to see alcohol in a dressing room. The Shirelles also had a portable record player set up, and the record spinning when we walked in was "Be My Baby." Shirley surprised me by saying right out how much she liked the record. "Especially the part where you go '*Be my little bay-bee,*' " she told me. I nearly collapsed! That was the first time any of the Shirelles had ever been nice to us. Things were changing all over.

A few weeks later, Phil came backstage after one of our shows and told us he had a surprise. He was with this guy who wore a three-piece suit. Phil introduced the guy by saying, "This is one of my accountants." Then he added, a little too casually, "Oh, and I think he's got something for you girls." Then this accountant reached into his briefcase, pulled out an envelope, and handed it to me. Inside was a check for fourteen thousand dollars! It was our first royalty check from sales of "Be My Baby."

"Not bad for a few hours' work, huh?" Phil said, making a joke about all the weeks and months we put into that record. I held the check in my hand for a few seconds, staring at it like it wasn't real. Then I handed it to my mother. It's not that I wasn't thrilled to get it—I was. That check was more money than any of us had ever seen in one piece at one time. But Mom took care of all our financial matters, so naturally the check went straight to her. She deposited the money when we got paid, and she wrote the checks whenever we needed something. I guess we weren't very sophisticated financially, but money was never anything we worried about. As long as we had money for lipstick or a new dress when we wanted one, we were rich.

Phil was so excited about giving us the check that he could barely keep still. As far as he was concerned, that royalty check was the greatest gift he could have given us, and he insisted we go out and celebrate. So after our show, Nedra, Estelle, and I all piled into Phil's limousine and went to an all-night coffee shop downtown, where we each had a cup of coffee and a piece of pie. But when it came time to pay the check, Phil pulled one of those little tricks that was so typical of him. He handed the waitress a hundred-dollar bill, knowing full well she wouldn't be able to change it at that hour. When she told him so, he turned and asked us, "You girls don't have any cash on you, do you?" Then we each chipped in a dollar and paid the check.

It wasn't the last time he pulled that hundred-dollar-bill bit on us, either. That was the strange thing about Phil. For a millionaire, he sure could be cheap. There were plenty of times when we took the subway home from rehearsal because we'd handed all of our money over to Phil, so he could take a cab home. Our mother always got pissed off when that happened. "*He's* the millionaire," she'd say. "You girls are barely out of high school."

"Be My Baby" turned out to be a huge hit. It hit number one on the *Cashbox* top 100, and number two in *Billboard*. It was one of those songs the deejays loved to play, and they're still playing it today. That record is a rock and roll classic, and no matter how many horrible things I went through later, at least I can look back and say I made a record that's going to be around long after all of us are dead. And that's a nice feeling. Spooky, but nice.

"Be My Baby" was a tough record, but it had a sweet side to it, just like the Ronettes. It was the kind of song a street kid would like. And a lot of them did. After that record, the Ronettes were bigger than ever with the kids on the street. In fact, we sometimes wondered if we weren't getting a little *too* popular.

One night the black and Spanish gangs in Harlem nearly had a riot over us outside the Apollo Theatre. We had come back to play the Apollo as headliners, right after we made it big. We didn't know anything about any trouble until a security guard came backstage before the show to tell us that the black kids and the Puerto Ricans were fighting over us in the alley out back. We ran over to a window, and sure enough, there were two gangs of kids—one black and one Spanish—facing each other off in the alley. There were maybe twenty kids on each side.

One member of the black gang would yell, "The Ronettes are black!" Then a couple of the Spanish kids would get mad and start kicking him, saying "No way. The Ronettes are Spanish." We were amazed that two gangs of kids were actually fighting over our skin color! The funny thing is, they were both right.

Nedra *is* half-Spanish, and my sister and I *are* half-black. Of course, we weren't about to go out there to settle the argument.

The security guard finally walked out and broke it up, and when he came back in, he told us he'd never seen anything like it. "They was about to have a riot," he said. "And we ain't never had no riot here. We've had lines goin' all round the block, and fistfights, and James Brown. But we ain't never had no riot."

But even without a riot, it was already a rough night for us, because we were scared out of our minds to be playing the Apollo. We'd managed to slip by as kids on amateur night, but now here we were, three light-skinned girls trying to pass ourselves off as headliners. What made us think we could go on after established acts like the Impressions, Garnet Mims, and—especially—Patti LaBelle and the Blue-Belles?

With her big gospel voice, we knew Patti LaBelle could tear the roof off that place. And that's exactly what she did. Patti usually closed her set with "You'll Never Walk Alone," which was always a show-stopper. And naturally, it sounded spectacular that night. When Patti hit the last refrain, the part where she goes, "You'll nev-VERRR," she must have held that note for about two minutes. The people in that theater went nuts—every wig in the place hit the ceiling. And now these three little half-breeds are supposed to walk out on that stage and sing, "Be my little bay-bee"? I was so sure those kids were going to boo us right out of Harlem that I freaked out.

I ran down the back stairs of the theater in a panic, and I didn't stop until I hit the ground-floor lobby. I was so hysterical, I could hardly breathe. I finally made it over to this fountain they had in the lobby, and I sat there for four or five minutes trying to catch my breath.

From where I sat, I could hear the applause for Patti LaBelle booming through the theater like a thunderstorm. But instead of making me more nervous, the applause actually seemed to calm me down. A few seconds later, Nedra came running down the stairs looking for me. "Come on, girl," she said. "We're on!"

I got up and walked back up the stairs, knowing with each step that we were walking out to stand in front of a few hundred tough Harlem street kids who had just paid two dollars each to see us. I knew these kids were going to get their money's worth—one way or another. When we finally got to the edge of the curtain offstage, I turned to Nedra and asked her right out, "Do you think we can pass for black?"

"It's too late to worry about that now," she said, walking out toward the hot lights that were already burning up the stage. "Besides, Ronnie. We *are* black." Then she gave me a wink. "*And* Spanish. And probably a whole lot of other things we don't even know about. So let's go. We got enough kinds of blood to make everybody happy."

I had to smile, and that grin was about the only thing that got me out onto that stage. Of course, once I started singing, the rest was easy. I got through "Be My Baby," and the kids loved it! As we stood there drinking in that applause, I felt so emotionally exhausted I could've used an oxygen tent. But we'd done it. We'd earned an ovation from the audience at the Apollo Theater, and that meant something. When the street kids applauded us at the Apollo, it was like we were getting our wave—from that moment on, we knew we could pass in the black world.

6

Fools Fall in Love

By the fall of 1963 our lives were turned upside down. All the things I'd ever dreamed about were finally coming true. We had appeared on Dick Clark's "American Bandstand." People from all over the world were calling to ask for interviews with us. And, best of all, you couldn't turn on your radio without hearing "Be My Baby." I was in heaven. My only complaint was that so many great things were happening so fast, it was getting hard to appreciate all of them. I wanted to slow down the clock so I could enjoy every single minute. But it doesn't work that way.

My family was happy for us, of course. My grandmother didn't live to see the Ronettes make it, but my mother and all the aunts and uncles were full of pride for us. My uncle Charles even wanted to throw a big party to celebrate our success. At least that's the way it started out, until someone in my family got the idea that the party might turn a profit if they invited the public and charged admission. "We raised them from little girls," one of my uncles said. "And now that they made it, why shouldn't we all share in the profits?"

Unfortunately, there weren't any profits to be made that night. The party was a disaster. My family rented a midtown ballroom called the Carlton Terrace, and they put up a few signs advertising what they called a "Gala Halloween Masquerade, with a special guest appearance by the Ronettes." They thought just having the Ronettes show up at an event like this was enough to bring people in. But they were wrong. Nobody even knew it was happening. There were maybe three people from outside the family who showed up. It was kind of funny, really. I remember my uncle Charles standing at the door in his pirate costume, waiting for the crowds of people to show up. It was embarrassing. That was the first time I saw how our being famous could bring out the worst in my family.

I never did get used to how my family changed after we made it big. It reminded me of how the kids in high school reacted to us after we started doing Murray the K's radio show, except that now it was our own cousins, uncles, and aunts who were treating us like we were somehow different than they were.

My dad finally saw the Ronettes in the fall of 1963, a few months after "Be My Baby" came out. We were on the bill at a rock and roll revue in Philadelphia, and Dad had a lot of relatives in that area, so one night he came up from Florida to surprise us. We had no idea he was even there until Estelle spotted him in the audience.

We usually did only two or three numbers when we toured with one of these rock and roll revues, and we'd just finished doing our second song, which was our own version of "The Twist." I was about to go into "Be My Baby," our finale, when Estelle crossed the stage and whispered in my ear.

"First row, seventh seat," she said.

I glanced down to the front row, and there he was. I was so excited to see my daddy that I nearly dropped the mike. He looked so happy, like a guy who had front-row seats at the circus. He was laughing and telling everyone around him that we were his kids. "Those are my girls up there," he told anyone who'd listen. "My two little girls."

The house band had already started pounding out the opening drum beat to "Be My Baby" when I waved my hand to stop them. I had a little speech to make, and I didn't want anything to upstage it.

"We . . . uh, don't usually do dedications," I said, my voice starting to choke. "But . . . well, the Ronettes have always been a family act. So, my sister Estelle and I would like to dedicate this next number to our favorite guy in the whole world. He's sitting right there in the front row."

Then the drum beat started up again.

Boom-ba-boom-boom.

"This one's for you, Daddy," I said. And the whole place went into hysterics. It was like magic.

When Dad came backstage after the show, he was crying like a baby. He wrapped one arm around Estelle and the other around me, and we were so happy to see him that we didn't even care that there was alcohol on his breath. "I'm so proud," he kept saying. "I'm so, so proud of you both."

"Oh, come on, Dad," I said. "What are you talking about? We got it all from you."

When he heard that, he cracked the biggest smile I'd ever seen. And that made me happy. I tried to talk to him some more that night, but he'd had so much to drink that he couldn't hold a real conversation. I finally just hugged him good night and made a promise to visit him every time I got down to Florida.

I kept that promise, too. After our reconciliation in Philadelphia, I'd drop down and see my dad every couple years. He kept right on drinking until he died of complications from his alcoholism in 1978. He never did realize his dream of playing drums in a Harlem jazz club, but he lived long enough to see his daughters sing rock and roll. And in a small way, I think that gave him peace.

One of the things that happens when you have a hit record is you start hearing from old friends you haven't talked to for years. One of the old friends who came calling after "Be My Baby" was Frankie Lymon, the boy who got me started in the first place. I hadn't seen Frankie in a long time, but I'd heard stories—that he was still drinking, that he'd gotten into drugs, that he'd become a junkie. But I was home when he called our house, and he sounded perfectly normal to me.

"Ronnie," he said. "I'm so glad to hear about your record, and I want to come and congratulate you in person."

I still had a soft spot for Frankie, so I told him to come on over. My sister wasn't around that day, but my mother was in the house with a guy we called Duke, a neighborhood barber who Mom used to date sometimes. When I told them Frankie was coming over, they agreed to hang around in the kitchen while he was there. My mother even helped me clean up the living room before Frankie showed up.

I still had a big crush on him, and I wanted to make a good impression. So I put some potato chips and dip out on the table, and my mother set up a little bar with a bottle of Canada Dry ginger ale, a fifth of J&B scotch, and a set of her best drinking glasses.

When Frankie came to the door a half hour later, he was wearing fresh-pressed black pants and a button-down shirt with horizontal red, blue, and green stripes. He was a very cool individual. I took one look at him and thought, God, I still love him.

He walked in, and we sat there on the couch talking over old times for about a half hour. Everything was really nice. And then I made the mistake of offering him a drink.

"Thanks, Ronnie," he said, reaching for the J&B with one hand and grabbing one of my mom's tall glasses with the other. He filled the glass halfway to the top with straight scotch and drank it down like Seven-Up. Then he poured himself another. And another. I was amazed as I watched an entire fifth of J&B disappear in less than twenty-five minutes. And I didn't touch it myself, because in those days my mother would have killed me if I'd even had a drop.

As I watched him get drunker and drunker, I felt nothing but pity. Here was Frankie Lymon, my all-time idol, and he hadn't made a record in three years. He was washed up at twenty! But what made it even sadder was that he couldn't stop talking about *my* voice.

"You know, Ronnie, I really love the way you sing on your record," he slurred. I just sat there huddled in the corner of my mom's L-shaped couch, watching my childhood hero drink himself silly. And, of course, once he started drinking, he couldn't keep his hands off me. He'd lean over, swaying, and try to grab hold of my arm. I'd pull it away, but he'd just wait a few seconds and then try again. After a while, I didn't see any point in trying to stop him.

"You're the one with the real talent," I said, trying to steer the subject back to him. I don't think I'll ever forget how you sang, 'Why do birds sing so gay.' "

But Frankie was in no mood to talk about his own career, so he kept going back to my singing. "I love your record, Ronnie," he kept repeating. But every time he said it, the words came out sloppier than the time before. "That vibrato kills me," he said. "Where did you ever learn that?" I couldn't believe my singing idol was asking *me* where I got *my* voice!

"From you, Frankie!" I told him. "I wouldn't even be a singer if it wasn't for you and your records." I was on my feet by now, practically shouting to get through to him. "It's *all* yours. The phrasing, the vibrato, everything. I got it all from you, Frankie. From you."

But he wouldn't listen. He just got up, shook his head, and then stumbled off to the bathroom. He came back a few minutes later, more obnoxious than ever. He walked right over and pressed me down against the couch. He didn't say a word, but he reached down and tried to pop the buttons of my shirt apart. I put a stop to that before he got to the second button.

"Mom!" I called out, loud enough to be heard in the kitchen. "Duke! Frankie's leaving now."

I couldn't take it anymore. I thought Frankie and I might have had a little romantic evening. Okay. I even fantasized that he and I might start up a regular girlfriend-guy kind of thing. But all Frankie wanted was to climb on top of me and leave. And I couldn't do that.

Duke finally walked in, took one look at Frankie straddling me on the couch, and figured out what was going on instantly. "Come on, man," he said, pulling Frankie gently to his feet. "It's time for you to go home."

Then, with his hand on Frankie's shoulder, Duke calmly walked him to the front door. Just before he left, Frankie turned and stared back at me with this awful look on his face, like he'd just been betrayed but couldn't figure out why. "What's going on, Ronnie?" he asked. "Aren't we going to have another drink?" He seemed so hurt and confused, but there was nothing I could do to help him.

"So long, Frankie," Duke told him, closing the door. "There ain't nothin' left to drink in there." And then Frankie was gone.

I hated so much having to throw him out, and I felt bad about it for years. But what else could I do?

I never saw him again. When I read in the papers a few years later that Frankie Lymon had died of a drug overdose at the age of twenty-five, it didn't really surprise me. That boy was hungry for love, but when he didn't find it in any of the regular places, he started to believe it didn't exist. So he turned to drinking and drugs as a way to ignore the pain. But the pain never did go away.

I didn't understand any of it back then. I wouldn't figure out Frankie's problem until much, much later. And by then it was too late to save him. I barely figured it out in time to save myself.

After "Be My Baby" went through the roof, Phil was hot to do a follow-up. He wrote "Baby I Love You"—again with Ellie Greenwich and Jeff Barry—and in the fall of 1963, he called me in New York. "We've got another hit for you. How soon can you be in California?"

I would've left that minute, except for one thing. The Ronettes were leaving the next day to tour with Dick Clark and his Caravan of Stars.

"Don't go," Phil told me as if a tour with Dick Clark was no big deal.

"But, Phil," I tried to explain. "This is *Dick Clark*. He needs us for this tour."

"So what?" he said, and I could tell from his voice that he was getting more pissed by the second. "I need you, too. And it's more important that you record a follow-up hit right now than go driving around the country in some broken-down bus with Dick Clark."

"Okay," I sighed. I knew there was no arguing with Phil once he got his mind set on something. I figured he'd work out the details somehow. I never guessed that he already had. "Should I tell the other Ronettes we're not going on tour?"

"Why? The Ronettes can still do the tour without you. We'll just get your cousin Elaine to fill in while you're in the studio."

I have to admit it was a good plan. Elaine had been with the Ronettes at the very beginning, when we did amateur night at the Apollo. And with our family resemblance, she could have passed for any one of us. So that's how it was settled. Elaine stepped in for the first couple of weeks of the Dick Clark tour, and I rejoined the show like clockwork a few weeks later.

Of course, since Nedra and Estelle were on tour while I recorded "Baby I Love You," we ended up recording that one without the other two Ronettes. But to tell the truth, the way Phil worked, it didn't sound a whole lot different from our other records. I always recorded my lead vocal alone anyway, and when we went to lay down the backgrounds for "Baby I Love You," Phil didn't seem to mind that Nedra and Estelle weren't around. As far as he was concerned, the other Ronettes were just two more background singers, and he already had plenty of those. That's how it was with all of the Ronettes' records—if Nedra and Estelle were around, Phil would add their voices to the mix. If they weren't, Darlene Love and Cher would do the backgrounds with whoever else happened to be around. I've never told anyone this, but it's true—Nedra and Estelle didn't even appear on some of the records that had our name on them.

We didn't think all that much about it at the time. As long as Nedra and Estelle appeared at our live shows and continued to share the credit and the money, who could complain? It never occurred to us that this all might be part of some plan Phil had to separate me from Nedra and Estelle so he could have me all to himself. But that thought would cross my mind plenty of times in the years to come.

One record that did feature all three Ronettes—and just about everyone else who worked for Phil—was Phil's Christmas album, *A Christmas Gift for You*. Phil is Jewish, but for some reason he always loved Christmas. Every year he would spend weeks designing his own special Christmas card, which he would send to everyone in the business. In 1963 he took that idea one step further and recorded an entire album of Christmas music, with contributions from all the acts on his Philles label. All of the groups got to do three or four songs each. The Ronettes did "I Saw Mommy Kissing Santa Claus," "Sleigh Ride," and "Frosty the Snowman."

We worked on that one forever. Phil started recording it in

the summer, and he didn't leave the studio for about two months. We'd start recording early in the evening, and we'd work until late into the night, sometimes even into the next morning. And everybody sang on everyone else's songs, so all of Phil's acts really were like one big, happy family for that one album.

While he was recording it, Phil told everyone that this Christmas album was going to be the masterpiece of his career. And he meant it. We all knew how important this project was to Phil when he walked into the studio on the last day of recording and announced that he was going to add a vocal himself. The final song on the record is a spoken message from Phil, where he thanks all the kids for buying his records and then wishes everyone a Merry Christmas, while we all sing a chorus of "Silent Night" in the background. A lot of people thought the song was corny. But if you knew Phil like I did, it was very touching.

But then I always did have a soft spot for Phil's voice. There was something about his phrasing and diction that drove me crazy. It was so cool, so calm, so serene. Phil wasn't a singer, but when he spoke he put me in a romantic mood like no singer could. He was the only guy I ever met who could talk me into an orgasm.

Of course, he wasn't doing *that* back then. Not yet, anyway. Phil and I were still just sweethearts in those days. We spent lots of time together, and we were very romantic, but we still hadn't slept together. Maybe that's why we were so romantic.

A Christmas Gift for You finally came out in November of 1963. But in spite of all the work we put into it, the album was one of Phil's biggest flops. It was reissued as *The Phil Spector Christmas Album* in the early seventies, and nowadays people talk about it like it's one of the greatest albums in rock and roll history. But nobody bought it when it first came out.

President Kennedy had been shot a few days before it was released, and after that people were too depressed to even look at a rock and roll record. And they stayed that way until well into the New Year of 1964, when—thank God—four long-haired English guys finally got them to go back into the record stores.

7

John, George, Ringo, and Mom

We didn't expect much when we went to England for our first British tour in January of 1964. The Rolling Stones were our opening act, but they were just starting out then, so we had no idea what kind of crowds would turn out to see us. We were actually scared that the English kids wouldn't know what to make of us—three half-breed girls from Spanish Harlem. Turns out we had nothing to worry about. We got standing ovations everywhere we played. If anything, the British fans liked our music even more than the kids back home.

I can still remember sitting on the bench at Heathrow Airport with my mom and the other Ronettes while we waited for the guy from our English record company to come pick us up. We must have been quite a sight in the Heathrow waiting room—three black American girls sitting with their legs all crossed the same way, our three identical, enormous hairdos piled a foot or so over our heads. When our young chaperon finally showed up, he was all smiles.

"I was afraid I might not recognize you," he said when he saw us. "But something tells me you're the Ronettes." He said his name was Tony King, and then he explained that Decca Records—our British label—had assigned him to watch over us while we were in London. "My job," he told us, "is to make sure you don't get bored while you're here." And we were about to find out that this guy took his job very seriously.

On our first night there, he took us to a party where we met the Beatles. It was at a guy named Tony Hall's house, in Mayfair. Tony Hall was a big promotions man for Decca, so he knew everyone in the business. When the Beatles heard he was throwing a party for the Ronettes, three of the Fab Four made sure they were there to meet us.

George, John, and Ringo had already arrived when we got to the party. The Beatles hadn't been to America at that time, so we didn't know their music. But we sure knew who they were. All anyone talked about in England was the Beatles. That's why we were so shocked when they came up and introduced themselves as fans of *our* music.

"You've got the greatest voice," George told me. "We loved it the first time we heard you." The guys had just seen us on an English TV show called "Sunday Night at the Palladium," and they couldn't stop raving about it. "You were great," John Lennon told me. "Just fuckin' great."

Naturally, we all hit it off right away. It was obvious that these guys listened to a lot of records, because they knew as much about American music as we did. Or more. The Beatles loved all the girl groups, and they knew every Motown song ever put out. They kept telling us how much they loved our long black hair, and how our whole look blew them away. It was obviously quite a thrill for them to spend an evening with us. And we weren't exactly having a bad time ourselves.

Then somebody put on some records, and the Beatles asked us to teach them all the latest American dances. So we showed them the Pony, the Jerk, and the Nitty-Gritty. Every time we'd start to dance, John would come over and say, "I don't know if I've got this one yet, Ronnie. I may need some extra instruction." It didn't take me long to figure out that he liked me. After Estelle started getting the same signals from George, we met in the ladies' room to compare notes.

"Estelle," I said. "I think George really likes you."

"I know," she said. "And John's going bonkers over you. Isn't it great!" Estelle had a guy waiting for her back in New York, and I was already seeing Phil by that time. But we were young

and in a foreign country, so we decided to forget our boyfriends back home and have some fun.

When we got out of the bathroom, Tony Hall's wife, Mafalda,
offered to take me on a tour of her house. The Halls had a
beautiful place—there were antique vases and fine art in every
room. I tried to appreciate all of it, but every time Mafalda
pointed out a painting or a sculpture, John would run in and
make a joke about it to crack me up. Mafalda finally threw her
hands up and laughed. "I can see I'll get nowhere as long as this
one's around. Why don't you just take over the tour, John?"

"Thanks, luv," he snickered, and that was all the encouragement he needed. John grabbed my arm and said, "C'mon! Let's
go explorin'!" Before I knew what was happening, John
dragged me upstairs to this long hallway where the bedrooms
were. Then he started walking down the hall, jiggling all the
door handles, hoping to find an empty room.

John finally found one door open, so we walked in. We could
tell it was a bedroom, but it was so dark we didn't even notice
that George and Estelle were already in there, sitting on the
bed.

"Oops! Sorry, guys," I said. Then I turned to leave, but John
was already back out in the hallway, jiggling more door handles. We finally found an empty bedroom at the end of the hall,
a huge room with a cozy little window seat that looked out over
all the lights of London. It was breathtaking. I walked into the
darkened room and sat down, staring out the window at this
fairy-tale land of lights and towers that seemed to go on forever. "Oh," I sighed. "It's beautiful."

Then John snuggled in next to me. "You know," I said, "if
someone had told me a year ago that I'd be sitting here today
looking out at all of London, I would've said, 'You're nuts.' "

"If a year ago someone had told *me* that I'd be looking out a
window at London, I'd have said, 'You're nuts,' too," John answered. "But 'ere we are, eh?"

I liked talking to John. He was the first guy I'd ever met who
knew how strange it was to go from being a nobody to the
biggest thing in the country overnight. "What's all this like for
you?" I asked.

"Well, there's a draft, and this window seat is killing me bum," he joked. Then he put on a fake voice like some romantic guy from the late show. "Ah, but the view from here is smashing," he said, looking right at me.

"That's not what I meant," I continued, trying to ignore his teasing. "I mean being famous."

"Oh. I see. Serious stuff." He got up and grabbed an ashtray from the bedside table. "I'll need a smoke for this, then."

He carried the ashtray back to the window, and we sat there for a long time, smoking and talking. He told me about the days before he made it big, how he used to sit around coffee shops with the other Beatles while their manager went out and tried to get them a record contract. "We'd sit there with our jam butties and tea, saying, 'When we get our record contract, everything's going to change. We'll have limousines and chauffeurs, and we'll never have to eat another jam buttie as long as we live!' Then we got our record contract, and you know what 'appened?"

"Nothing really changed," I answered in all my twenty-year-old wisdom.

"Nope. Turns out we were right—everything did change. We got our limousines and our drivers, and now we've gone right off jam butties. If I even think of them I want to heave up." He was laughing, but I got his point. Things *do* change when you get famous, and there's nothing you can do about it. Still, neither of us would've changed our lives back to the way they were for anything in the world.

I felt pretty close to John right then, like he understood all the things I wanted to know. I knew he was one of these heavy brain people, just like Phil. And I could also tell John liked me for more than just my voice. When he leaned over and started kissing me, I have to admit he made me forget about Phil for a few seconds. But just a few.

We kissed for a couple of minutes on that window seat. And for me, that was a pretty big deal. I know it might seem hard to believe now, but I hadn't done much more than kiss a guy on the lips up until then, and that included Phil. Romance was everything, and sex was still a mystery. But the way things were going on that window seat, it didn't look like it was going to stay that way for long.

As we kissed, I could feel John's breaths getting shorter, and so were mine. Before long, we fell into the same rhythm, and it felt great. Then John started moving his hands around in places I didn't even know I had. I didn't resist when he slid his hands down around my waist and pulled me up onto my feet—but I panicked in an instant when I saw where he was trying to move me. We were only about a foot and a half from Tony Hall's big king-sized bed, and I knew that if I didn't decide what I wanted to do pretty soon, there wouldn't be any decision to make. That's when my thoughts turned to Phil.

I'd been faithful to him so far, and I wanted to stay that way. John was a great guy. But I loved Phil, and that's all there was to it. John was still trying to move me over to the bed when I dug my feet into the rug and stopped short. I guess I caught him by surprise, because he lost his balance and ended up plopping down on the edge of the bed.

"Do you think we could go back down to the party?" I asked. I knew it sounded corny, but I couldn't think of what else to say. John didn't seem too upset, though, because after we went back downstairs, we danced and had a great time for the rest of the night.

Estelle and I went out on double dates with John and George a couple more times before we left London. They'd take us to these romantic white-tablecloth restaurants, but once we got there all they'd want to talk about was American rock and roll.

"Tell us about the Temptations," George would say. Then John would ask, "What's Ben E. King really like?" So we'd just go down the list, telling them stories about all the acts we worked with at the Brooklyn Fox. And as we'd talk, John and George would sit there like they were hypnotized.

We went out one last time, but my mom came along that night and it was a disaster. What happened was, John and George were making conversation with my mom before we left the hotel. Then, out of politeness, John invited her to come along, never dreaming she would take him up on it. Estelle and I walked into the room just in time to hear Mom give her answer. "Dinner? Oh, that sounds like fun. Let me get my purse." It was enough to set our teeth to grinding for half the night.

There we were at this fancy candlelit restaurant in London with John Lennon, George Harrison, and our mother. It was terrible. How can you say anything with your mother sitting around? And the worst part was that she didn't say a word the whole time. She just kept staring at us through the whole meal.

When we left the restaurant, I got into a limousine with John, and Estelle climbed into a little two-seater sports car with George. My poor mother didn't know which way to turn. It suddenly dawned on her that as much as we loved her, there were times when we just didn't want her around.

It wasn't until I started writing this book that my mom finally confessed what she went through that night. "I was so used to you being little," she told me. "I didn't like to think that these big grown men were really liking my little girls. But I stood in that parking lot and I didn't know which car to get in. I saw this grown man leaning up against Estelle, and another grown-up man had his arm around you. And I thought, 'Well, what kind of a life am I going to have now?' That was the hurtingest night of my life."

Mom stood there in the middle of the restaurant parking lot for a half minute before she finally shrugged her shoulders and walked up to a London cabbie. "Taximan," she told the driver. "Take me to the Strand Hotel."

On January 6, 1964, we left London for Harrow, which was the first stop on our cross-country tour of England with the Rolling Stones. We rode in the same bus as the Stones, but unlike with the Beatles, we didn't warm up to those guys for a long time. Or, I should say, they didn't warm up to us, because we tried our best to be friendly to them. But no matter what we did, we couldn't get these guys to talk to us. It was weird. We'd do a show, and then afterward we'd be looking around for the guys, and they'd have gone off somewhere on their own. We couldn't figure out why they were avoiding us.

Finally, after about three days of this, I went to their manager, Andrew Loog Oldham, and asked him why the boys were ignoring us. "Hey, I know this is England," I told him, "and I hear that people over here are supposed to be kind of cold. But you guys could at least say hello once in a while."

Andrew looked at me with a kind of sideways grin, like he

was trying to decide whether to give me an honest answer or
not. Then he finally admitted the truth. "Darling, the boys are
your biggest fans. We'd all *love* to talk to you. But we got a
telegram just before the tour started that forbids us from frat-
ernizing with you."

"A telegram? From who?" I asked. But the truth is, I already
had a pretty good idea who sent it.

"From Phil, darling," Andrew explained. "He was very specific, too. We aren't to speak to you before a show, or
afterwards—or there'll be dire consequences."

"Andrew," I interrupted. "That may be the way Phil feels,
but Phil's not here. You tell the Rolling Stones that if they
don't *start* talking to us, there'll be dire consequences all right—
from us."

Andrew just chuckled and walked away. He was in awe of
Phil, like a lot of people we met in England. But I think he got
the message, because that night the Stones came back to our
dressing room after the show carrying a little birthday cake for
Nedra. It was always hard to have a birthday on the road, and
Nedra was especially depressed being so far from home on her
eighteenth birthday. But I don't think she ever forgot the night
the Rolling Stones dropped in to sing "Happy Birthday." It was
the beginning of a friendship that would last for years.

We had a few days in London before we had to fly back home
after the tour, so we naturally wanted to take advantage of the
time and go to as many nightclubs as we could. After all those
years of my mother and grandmother telling me what I could
or couldn't do, it was great just to go out to a nightclub and stay
out until I got tired, which never happened before dawn.

One night, Tony King, our young chaperon, invited Estelle
and me to meet him and George Harrison at a club called the
Crazy Elephant on Germyn Street in the West End. We had so
much fun that night. I remember that the song "Mockingbird"
by Charlie and Inez Foxx had just come out, because the deejay
kept playing that record over and over. George and I sang
along, trading off the verses, just like Charlie and Inez did on
the record. When the place finally closed at dawn, the four of
us stumbled down to George's flat for breakfast.

What a feast we made! George didn't have eggs or toast or

anything normal in his kitchen, but his cupboard was filled with canned stuff—peas and potted meats, and every kind of soup in the world. So we opened every single can in his cupboard and made this enormous breakfast. And then we couldn't stop laughing as we tried to eat this crazy breakfast of potted ham, pickles, corn, and turkey noodle soup. We made quite a mess that morning, but it was one of the nicest days I ever had.

When Phil showed up in London at the end of January, I was glad to see him. But I was also a little sorry, because I knew we wouldn't have nearly as much fun with him there. He hated going to clubs, and there was no way I could go out without him. But as it turned out, we still had a good time after Phil got there—it was just a different kind of fun. He'd brought a brand-new song over to England, and we ended up having a blast working it out in our suite at the Strand.

When Phil loved a song as much as he loved "(The Best Part of) Breaking Up," he could work on it for days without ever getting tired. He spent hours working out the harmonies with Nedra and Estelle, and he'd jump up and down every time he heard something he liked.

My mother was in the room when we worked out my lead part, and Phil kept telling her how he wanted the record to sound like Ella Johnson, who was this blues singer from my mother's time. Every time I'd sing a verse, Phil would turn to my mom and say, "How's that, Mrs. Bennett? Is that how Ella would've done it?" When I made up the part that goes, "Oowee, baby . . . come on, baby," Phil liked it so much he jumped up on the bed and started bouncing around like he was on a trampoline.

"Yes, yes!" he shouted. "And then we'll do the false ending. This is perfect."

After a few hours of this, the front desk called upstairs to ask if we could kindly keep the noise down. Phil was so insulted that anyone would dare to interfere with his creative process that he grabbed the phone right out of my hand. "Who complained?" he demanded to know. "I happen to be rehearsing the Ronettes' next hit record up here. And I demand a chance to face my accuser! Who complained?" Naturally, the desk guy refused to tell him who called to complain, so Phil slammed the phone down. We were sure he was going to be in a bad mood for the rest of the day, but Phil had this way of surprising you. "I guess rehearsal's over," he said with a smile. "Let's go get something to eat."

Phil never came out and said it, but I could tell he didn't like the idea of us spending too much time with the Beatles. I don't think his ego could stand the competition. The Beatles were leaving to start their first U.S. tour in a few days when John asked me if we wanted to fly back with them on their chartered jet. I didn't have the nerve to ask Phil if it was okay, so I had my mom make the suggestion.

"You know, Phil," she told him. "It might be good publicity if the girls went back on the jet with the Beatles."

"No," he told her. "I've already bought their tickets." And that was all he said. Nedra, Estelle, Mom, and I were on a flight back to New York the very next day.

Beatlemania hit America when the Fab Four landed at JFK on February 7, 1964, just a few days after we returned from England. My mother and I watched the whole thing on TV. We were amazed at how many kids showed up at the airport screaming and carrying banners. But what surprised me even more was something that happened after the plane landed.

The jet was already on the ground when the cameras zoomed in on the door that was about to open up to give America its first glimpse of the Fab Four. But when that hatch finally did swing open, who do you think was with them? I almost fainted when I looked at the TV and saw Phil Spector following the Beatles out of their plane.

I wanted to strangle him! *We* couldn't fly back with the Beatles, but there *he* was, standing in front of all the cameras after the Beatles got off their plane. Phil had found a way to squeeze into the Beatles' spotlight, and he wasn't about to share it with anybody—not even us. That's when I first realized how badly Phil really wanted to be a star himself.

Beatlemania was even crazier in America than it had been in England. I recently saw some old news clips of the mob waiting outside the Beatles' hotel, but those films don't even begin to show what it was really like. The crowds were lined up practically the whole way from JFK to the Warwick Hotel. It was incredible.

The day after the Beatles landed, Murray the K was on the phone, trying to see if we could get him in to see them. "You gotta get me into the Warwick, honey," he said, and I almost dropped the phone. The top disc jockey in New York was calling, asking *me* to get *him* in somewhere. But Murray was smart. John Lennon had left special instructions with the front desk to let us up—so Murray was able to slip through hotel security with Nedra, Estelle, and me. We also brought Nedra's boyfriend, Scott Ross, who worked with Murray at WINS Radio.

The scene in the Beatles' suite was amazing. They had an entire floor of the Warwick at their disposal, and there was food everywhere you looked. Gigantic plates of finger sandwiches and huge trays piled high with alcohol, fruit juice, Coca-Cola, and just about anything else you could think of to drink. When we walked in, the first thing John Lennon did was make a crack about why they had so much food. "We're prisoners up here," he explained, "so they have to feed us well."

And with that mob surrounding the hotel, the Beatles really were like prisoners. They couldn't leave that place without hours of advance planning, so somebody had to see to it that at least they had all the comforts of home. And they did. There were portable record players in every room, and 45 rpm records scattered everywhere around the floor. In every single room there was a television set playing with the sound turned down, all of them set to different channels. It was like a circus. There were all sorts of people running around—roadies and managers and assistant managers, and a whole lot of people like Murray the K, who were just up there trying to collect their little piece of the Beatles.

We'd barely had a chance to say hello to George and John before Murray started into his act. He flipped his tape recorder on and started asking dumb questions and making bad jokes about their hair. Then he started bragging about how he was the only guy allowed up to see the Fab Four. That's when he started calling himself the fifth Beatle.

The Beatles' attitude was like, "Sure, Murray. Anything you say." But they were only putting up with him because he was a

big New York disc jockey, and they knew we had worked with
him. But they thought it sucked that he called himself the fifth
Beatle, and they couldn't wait to get rid of him. Murray kept
pestering the guys until George finally gave me the eye, as if to
say, "Let's take a few pictures with this guy and get him out of
here."

"I think it's time to go, Murray," I told him. Murray had us
snap a few pictures of him goofing around with the Beatles, and
then he left. Things went a lot easier after that. Estelle and I sat
on the floor with John and George, playing records and talking
all through the afternoon. And the Beatles had every record
you could think of up there, including a few that hadn't even
come out in the stores yet. "Where'd you guys get all these?" I
asked.

"People give them to us," John said, like he couldn't believe
it. "I love America. People here just bring you anything you
want."

We sat there with John and George until it got dark outside.
That's when things started to change. A lot of the people who'd
been hanging around during the afternoon had already left,
and as I looked around, I noticed that there seemed to be a lot
more young girls in the suite than there were when the press
was hanging around earlier. You didn't have to be a genius to
figure out that a whole new kind of scene was about to start.

John gave a signal to Mal Evans, the Beatles' road manager,
and he started walking around, kicking out anyone who didn't
belong there. When he came up to our friend Scott Ross, I
spoke up for him. "Don't worry, Malcolm," I explained. "Scott's
with us."

John shot me a look and said, "We don't know him, Ronnie.
He's got to leave."

"Oh, that's okay," Scott said, "I was about to go anyway."

Nedra and Estelle got up with him, and Estelle walked over
to me. "I think we better get out of here, Ronnie," she said
quietly. She sensed that something strange was in the air, and
she didn't want to stick around to find out what it was. But I've
always been a little more bold. If weird things were going to
happen up there, I didn't want to miss them. "I want to stay,"
I told her.

"Are you sure?" Estelle asked.

"Sure," I answered. "What's the worst thing that could happen?"

After Nedra, Scott, and Estelle left, I noticed that people seemed to be flocking into one of the bedrooms. It seemed kind of strange, but I barely had the chance to think about it before John walked over and grabbed my hand. "C'mon," he said. "Don't you want to see what's so interesting?" Of course I did. In fact, I was dying to get a look at what it was the Beatles didn't want any strangers to see.

The first thing I noticed in the bedroom was how crowded it was. There were so many people in there that I couldn't even see what was going on at first. Someone was standing on a chair taking pictures, but I couldn't see what he was photographing. When people saw that I was with John, they kind of moved aside, and that's how I got my first clear view of the naked girl on the bed.

I moved in for a closer look, and it was the most amazing thing I'd ever seen. This girl was lying on the bed, and one of the guys in the Beatles' entourage was having sex with her—right in front of all these people.

The girl looked young. She couldn't have been much older than me, and I was only twenty. She was a cute kid, with dark brown hair. And from the look on her face, she didn't seem to mind being used as entertainment at a Beatles party, even though none of them were even taking part. I guess it was enough to just be in the same hotel suite as them, as if that gave her something to tell her grandchildren. I felt sorry for her. I couldn't see myself doing that for anybody—I didn't care how famous they were.

These two just kept going at it, having sex every which way, doing just about every pose for the guy with the camera, who just kept snapping away. I have to admit I was fascinated by the whole thing. I was still a virgin, so this was educational for me. I knew about regular sex—intercourse—but I didn't know the first thing about doing sixty-nine, or any of these other variations. This was 1964, when you couldn't even get films with that stuff in them—and here was an actual girl having naked sex in every different position! That was a scene I'll never forget.

I stared like a wide-eyed little kid, which is what I was. I mean, I was a girl who kept my underwear on when I went to bed. I still do. So every time this girl took a new position, my jaw dropped a little lower and I gasped, "Wow . . . oh, wow!" a little louder.

My comments must have been louder than I thought, because John started to get a little embarrassed after a while. Finally, after I let loose an especially loud "Oh, my God," John leaned over and whispered, "Uh, Ronnie. Could you do that a little quieter, please?"

John had sat down on this big stuffed chair, which was the only real seat in the room. Then he pulled me down on his lap, and I continued watching the show from my ringside seat. That's when I realized how aroused John was getting. He couldn't very well hide his excitement with me sitting on his lap. I may have been dumb back then, but I knew when it was time to get up off a guy's lap. So I did.

Then I walked out of the room with John following close behind. "Let's go have something to drink," he said. I was all ready to leave the hotel, but for some reason I didn't particularly mind staying, either. As strange as that whole situation was, I was never the least bit nervous around John. I felt secure around him. And I also knew I could walk away if things got out of hand. Which they hadn't. Yet.

We went into John's private bedroom, and I could see instantly that he was trying to recapture the atmosphere we had in London. He even pointed to a big window that looked out over the Manhattan skyline and asked, "Do you remember the window in London?"

It was dark in his room, so I walked over to the window and sat on a straight-backed chair. I could see the flickering lights of Times Square and Broadway in the distance, and I tried to point them out for John. The city looked so beautiful from up there. I would've been perfectly happy just sitting there, but I could tell John was already too worked up for sightseeing. He stood behind my chair and let his hands fall down on the back of my neck. It felt so good that I had to remind myself that I couldn't be doing stuff like this.

"John," I said, trying desperately to find my best no-nonsense voice, "I've got to tell you something."

"Not now, luv," he said, as he slipped his hands under my unbuttoned collar.

"Oh, no," I insisted, "I'd better tell you now."

"I know all about you and Phil," he interrupted. "I just thought you and I might have something, too." He went on talking about what a great relationship he and I could have, but I wasn't listening very closely. My eye just kept drifting over to the king-sized bed that was less than four feet away. I mean, I did have a mother who warned me about these situations.

And in all honesty, I knew my feeling for John wasn't a sexual attraction. I loved his sense of humor, and I loved the way we could talk all night. But I was so head over heels in love with Phil that I knew it just wasn't going to happen between me and John.

I stood up and John's hands fell onto the back of the chair. "John," I told him, "I think we've got a great friendship. I love telling you stories about all the groups, and I love hearing all about your music. But sometimes a guy can seem more like a brother than a boyfriend. And that's the way I think of you."

After I spoke my mind, he just stood there staring at me with a blank expression. "I adore you, John. I really do. But not the way you want." Then I gave him a little wink and said, "I'll see you." And I was very sincere. Then I walked out.

I was already in the hotel hallway when John slammed the bedroom door shut. I got such a chill as I left that place that I didn't bother looking back. I was just glad to get out of that suite.

The next day John called my house acting like nothing had happened. "We're going to make an escape today, and we want to get some real New York food. Where should we go?" I knew this was John's way of apologizing, so I played along.

"I know just the place," I told him. "If you don't mind coming up to Harlem."

"We'll be there."

That night the Beatles picked us up in a limousine for a feast of ribs and chicken at Sherman's Barbecue on 151st and Amsterdam in Harlem. And they loved it. Sherman's is just a little takeout counter today, but back in 1964 it was beautiful, with lots of tables and a great big jukebox in back. But for the Beatles, the best part of all was that they could eat in peace.

They may have been mobbed at the Warwick, but very few of their fans followed them into Harlem.

In fact, the Beatles were no big deal up in Harlem. The people at Sherman's were not exactly Murray the K's crowd. They took one look at these four guys with their long hair and funny clothes and went back to their chicken. If anything, they might have thought the Beatles were dorks. But you can bet Sherman never forgot that day. Every so often I still go into Sherman's for takeout, and whenever I do, Sherman comes out from the kitchen to say hello. "I remember you!" he always says. "You're the little girl that brought the Beatles!"

I had my last brush with Beatlemania when the guys played Shea Stadium in 1965, and it nearly killed me. Literally. I went with Nedra, her boyfriend, Scott Ross, and a guy named Jerry Schatzberg, who was a big fashion photographer we used to see at all the nightclubs in those days. Jerry later became a success-ful Hollywood director, but even then he was a real stylish guy who always drove a big Bentley limousine, which is the car we took to Shea Stadium.

After the show, the Shea Stadium parking lot was like a mob scene, with kids hanging around everywhere, trying to catch a glimpse of their idols. The Beatles were nowhere around when we climbed into Jerry's Bentley, but a couple of the kids rec-ognized Nedra and me, and that was all it took to start a near riot. The fans knew that the Ronettes were friendly with the Beatles, so when they saw us getting into a big English limou-sine, they assumed the Beatles must be in there with us. None of them seemed to notice that Jerry and Scott looked nothing like John, Paul, George, or Ringo.

Some kid yelled, "It's them!" And we had just enough time to slam the doors shut before the kids were climbing all over our car, screaming and yelling and bouncing it back and forth. Within a few seconds there were teenagers hanging from every square inch of that Bentley—on the fenders, the hood, even on the roof over the passenger compartment! It was amazing. There were at least a hundred teenagers screaming outside our car, and every one of them was determined to do anything they could to stop us from leaving. There were so many of them packed around us that none of them could even see into the car. But that didn't stop them from trying to break the windows open for a better look.

They were pounding on the windows with their fists, and the ones on top of the car were kicking at the glass with their heels. Being trapped in a car while a mob of kids tries to beat their way in is about the most terrifying thing you can imagine. We looked out the window and all we could see were fists and feet. It reminded me of the little sparrows who kept throwing themselves against the door in that Alfred Hitchcock movie *The Birds*.

The kids were already getting tired of trying to pound their way in when some of them started rocking the car back and forth. We were afraid they were going to tip the whole car over. And they probably would have, if the car hadn't been a Bentley. Jerry put his foot on the gas pedal to try and get us the hell out of there, but with all those kids pressed so tight against us, the car wouldn't even budge.

"Jerry," I shouted. "Hold your foot on the gas! Just keep pushing through."

"You'd better believe I will," he said. He held the pedal down to the floor, and with the engine racing away, we finally lurched forward about six inches. That was enough to shake some of the kids off, which gave the car a little more power. Jerry didn't let up, and we kept rolling forward through the crowd in slow motion with the engine groaning under the strain. We finally wedged our way out of the parking lot and into the street, where the last kids finally gave up and fell back. Maybe they saw another limousine that looked more like it might have the Beatles in it. I don't know for sure, because once we got that car out of the parking lot we pointed it toward the city and drove away from Shea Stadium as fast as we could.

Whoever named it Beatlemania sure knew what they were talking about. Those kids who chased after the Beatles really did act like maniacs. After that day, I'd had a little taste of what it must have been like to be a Beatle, and it was scary as hell.

8

Beauty and the Beast

After the Ronettes got back from England, Phil and I grew closer than ever. By early 1964, I knew he wasn't perfect. I knew he had a temper, and that he could be jealous around other men. But I figured I'd seen him at his worst, and it wasn't really all that bad. Besides, I knew Phil's romantic side, which is something most people never saw.

To understand how romantic Phil was, all you have to do is look at the titles of the songs he wrote for me: "Be My Baby," "Baby I Love You," "Born to Be Together." And even though he wrote them with writers like Jeff and Ellie, Barry Mann and Cynthia Weil, and Vinnie Poncia and Pete Andreoli, Phil couldn't have made those songs any more personal if he'd sent them as love letters. Which is really what they were.

It was so romantic. I was twenty years old and my boyfriend was telling me how much he loved me by writing hit songs, which I would then sing back to him. People always ask me how I got such a raw sensuality in the records I made with Phil. Well, it's not hard to sound sexy when the man you love is standing five feet away from your microphone.

My romance with Phil lives in those records. And you can actually trace our entire relationship through the songs we did together. He courted me while we rehearsed "Be My Baby," we fell in love when we recorded "Baby I Love You," and we made love after we listened to "Do I Love You" for the first time. I'll never forget that night.

It was in June 1964. Phil had just gotten the test pressing of "Do I Love You," and he wanted to come over to my house to play it for me. I told him I'd cook dinner, and then I asked my mom and sister to get lost for the evening, which they did. They both knew how much Phil meant to me, and he was one guy my mother trusted completely.

After dinner, Phil and I went into my room to play our new record. I sat on the bed while Phil set the record up on my little portable record player. Then he moved over and thumped down next to me on the bed. He was so excited as he waited for the needle to hit those first few grooves that I could feel him bouncing up and down on the mattress. And when that slow horn intro came on, we naturally squeezed closer together in anticipation. The horns gave way to that driving drum beat—a slow, pulsing sound that made me feel warm all over. Then my voice came on, sounding all low and kind of sleepy, like I'd just woken up from a long night of grown-up sex.

"Do I want you for my baby?" I was asking from the record. "Do I want you by my side?" The words might not seem so romantic now, but the way they sounded on that record that night! I looked over at Phil sitting on the edge of the bed with his ear cocked toward the speaker and his hands folded on his knees. I watched as a tear began to form in his eye, and I reached up to wipe it away. That surprised him so much he turned to me, startled, like he was coming out of a trance. Then he smiled a little half smile, like he was embarrassed that some-one caught him crying, and I just had to kiss him. It was a big kiss, a great, long mixture of spit and sweat and salty tears.

After that, he paused for a minute, like he wasn't quite sure what to do next. That's when I took control. I pressed my whole body on top of his, and we both slid back onto the mattress like we were one person. I didn't have any idea where to go from there, so I just followed my body, which was moving right along with the beat of the record. The only thing I knew for sure was that I didn't want to be a virgin anymore.

Phil and I made love for the first time listening to that record. And every two minutes and fifty seconds, Phil would reach over from the bed and lift the needle back to the beginning of the record. We must've played that song fifty times, because we made love on that mattress until late into the night.

My mother and Estelle still hadn't come home when we finally took a break, so Phil got up and walked into the kitchen. He came back with two glasses of wine. "For our toast," he said.

Then he put the record back on, and we made a silent toast and listened to it all over again. It was the first time I'd ever had a drink, and I didn't really like the way it tasted. But I figured there had to be a first time for everything.

When I heard Mom and Estelle come in a few minutes later, I walked into the living room to meet them so Phil would have a chance to get himself together. I guess the glass of wine made me a little clumsy, because I stumbled as I walked into the living room.

Maybe it was also the wine that made me feel so emotional when I saw my mother. "Oh, Mom," I cried. "I love him. I really do."

She must have looked pretty surprised, because Phil walked in a second later and tried to make excuses for me. "Oh, Mrs. Bennett," he said. "I think Ronnie had a little too much wine tonight."

"No," I argued. "It's not the wine. I do love you. I do."

"Now, Ronnie," my mother said, lecturing me. "Don't start moving too fast. You haven't even started anything yet, and you're trying to overlove this man already." I disagreed, but I didn't say anything. Phil just smiled. I'm pretty sure he was enjoying this little scene.

A few minutes later Estelle and I walked Phil out to 149th Street to find a cab. My sister and I usually went out to the street with Phil, because he was afraid to stand alone in our neighborhood, especially that late at night. When we finally got a cab, Estelle took a step back while Phil and I kissed good night. As he got into the cab, I noticed that he was still carrying the test pressing of "Do I Love You" in his hand.

He glanced down at it, and then he looked up at me. "I think this one's a hit," he said.

"So do I," I whispered. And then I watched the cab pull off into the dark.

After that night, sex became a solid part of our relationship. Phil and I would go to a hotel and rehearse for a few hours, then I'd call my mother and say, "We're still rehearsing." Then we'd make love. Sex with Phil was the greatest thing in those days. I'd never experienced it before, and certainly not in high-class hotels with room service and no parents around. And Phil was very good in bed. Excellent. Sometimes I wouldn't get home until six in the morning.

Thank God my mother chose to look the other way. I guess she knew Phil and I were pretty serious by that point. Besides, there wasn't much she could've done to stop us even if she'd wanted to. I was almost twenty-one, and Mom knew better than to try and stop me from getting anything I wanted as badly as I wanted Phil.

But it was only after Phil and I started making love that I found out just how insecure he really was. That's when he first started joking about his looks, saying how the two of us reminded him of Beauty and the Beast. I never saw Phil as a beast, and I was always telling him how handsome I thought he was. But he never listened. And I know a lot of it had to do with his hair loss.

Phil first started losing his hair around the time we met. In fact, there's a picture that was taken when he signed us in March of 1963, which also was the first day I ever saw him wearing a toupee. It was so obvious if you knew him, but he still went to great lengths to hide the fact that he wore wigs, even when we slept together.

After we'd do our foreplay, he'd get up from the bed and make sure all the lights were out. That way I couldn't watch him when he took his hair off. Then he'd stumble into the bathroom in the dark, so he could rub this acetone solvent all over his head. It was the smelliest stuff in the world, but I guess it was the only thing he could use to get the toupee glue off his scalp. When he came back to bed, the smell of that acetone could've killed a horse, but Phil tried to pretend it wasn't there. Only it was impossible to hide. Like rubbing alcohol or marijuana, it was a smell that just wouldn't go away.

That whole game of hiding the toupee was one thing I knew I'd have trouble with in our relationship. I remember lying in bed one night, thinking about how I'd have to have a long talk with him about it before we got married. We never did get around to having that talk.

Through this whole period, Phil still insisted on being secretive about our relationship whenever we went to a hotel, which I thought was silly. He was my producer and my boyfriend. What did we have to hide? But that was Phil's way, and you just didn't question it. There was one time, though, when all his damn secrecy almost got me arrested.

We had been making love one afternoon at the Delmonico Hotel when Phil got a call from his office. There was some emergency, and he had to rush back there. So he jumped into his clothes and left me in the room to take a shower. I left a few minutes later, but as I was walking through the lobby, two well-dressed men walked up on either side of me and grabbed both of my arms.

"What's wrong?" I asked.

"Please understand that we want to get this over with as quickly as you do," one of them said. "So if you'll come into our office quietly, everything'll be just fine."

"Did Phil forget to pay the bill or something?" I asked. They just looked at me like I was strange.

When we got into their office, they told me I could call my lawyer. When I asked them why I'd want to do that, they both got real angry. "We've already called the New York Police Department. We're holding you for prostitution."

I was stunned, of course. But the way Phil and I were sneaking around that hotel, I couldn't really blame these guys for jumping to conclusions. I mean, one minute Phil goes running out of the room, and five minutes later I walk down the hall wearing my thick Ronette mascara in the middle of the afternoon. What else were the house detectives going to think?

I tried to explain who I was, and I even offered to call Phil to prove my story. I got him on the line and started telling him what happened, but he insisted on talking to one of the detectives. I felt sorry for the guy, because I knew what he was in for. Sure enough, even after the detective put the phone to his ear, you could still hear Phil shouting all the way across the room.

"You stupid, incompetent bastard!" Phil yelled.

"Excuse me, Mr. Spector," the guy said. "I don't have to listen to that kind of language. If there's been some mistake—"

"*If* there's been a mistake?" he interrupted. Phil could tell the guy was weakening, so he really laid it on. "That's *my wife* you've got in there! And if you lay one more grubby hand on her, I'll sue you, the Delmonico Hotel, and the New York City Hotel Commission. And then I'll personally arrange to have you killed."

Then Phil hung up. The detective was speechless. His partner muttered a few apologies, and I was out the door in less than thirty seconds. I took a limousine all the way home to Spanish Harlem, and it didn't cost me a cent. The Delmonico picked up the tab.

That summer, my mother and sister and I moved out to the suburbs. We rented a big house in an area of Long Island called Flushing Estates. We didn't like the suburban life very much, and we moved back to New York a few months later. But I'll never forget that house, because that's where we lived when the Rolling Stones showed up for scrambled eggs.

This was in June 1964, during the Stones' first trip to America. They hadn't even recorded "Satisfaction" yet, so they were still pretty unknown over here. But Phil always liked them, so he let them sleep in the offices of Philles Records on York Avenue when they first got to New York. The only problem was, Phil's secretary would kick them out as soon as she opened the place up every morning. Since they didn't know anybody else in New York, the guys would usually end up on our doorstep.

My mother was always nice to our rock and roll friends, especially the Rolling Stones, who usually looked like they could use a good meal. Whenever Mick or Keith came around, she would say, "You boys just come on in here and sit down. Would you like me to make some eggs?" Their answer was always the same: "Yes, Mrs. Bennett. If it's not too much trouble."

Then Aunt Helen or Aunt Susu would come over and help cook breakfast for them. They were so far away from home, I guess they just needed to be around a family sometimes. They'd hang around with us all day, playing records or watching TV. At night we'd take them into Manhattan to see us perform.

One of the big thrills of that trip for Keith and Mick was meeting James Brown. Mick Jagger was the biggest James Brown nut I'd ever met. When we were on tour in England he kept us up half the night asking questions about James Brown. What was he like offstage? Where did he learn to dance? How much did he rehearse? I finally had to tell Mick, "Enough already. I don't even know James Brown. I'm a Ronette, remember?"

Keith and Mick finally got to meet their hero when I took them backstage one night when he was headlining the Apollo. They were standing there like scared teenagers when James Brown walked past them on his way to his dressing room. They introduced themselves, he shook their hands, and that's all there was to it. I don't think James Brown even knew who these weird English guys were. But Mick and Keith were practically shaking.

We all spent a lot of time hanging out at Ondine's in those days. Ondine's was a very exclusive East Side club, on Fifty-ninth Street. Bob Dylan used to come in, and all the English groups would drop by when they were in town. The house band was led by an unknown guitarist from Seattle named Jimi Hendrix, and I used to get up and sing with him all the time. We always had so much fun at Ondine's that we often wouldn't leave until dawn.

In fact, that's what finally made us move back into the city. We were spending so much time at Ondine's that it seemed stupid to take a cab all the way out to the suburbs every morning at dawn. That's when I used some of my Ronette money to rent an apartment at 173 Riverside Drive, at Eighty-ninth Street. It was a beautiful place with more than enough room for Estelle, my mother, and me.

The night we moved in, I looked out the window and stared down at Riverside Drive. As I watched the cars whizzing past, I thought back to those hot summer nights when Dad drove us down Riverside Drive to cool off. I remembered how I used to stare up at the tall buildings and wonder what kind of people lived in those apartments up there. That's when I pulled the window open and waved down at all the cars below. Maybe it sounds silly, but I thought there might be some ten-year-old kid looking up at me from the backseat of her daddy's car. And if there was, I wanted to let her know we weren't really all that different up here.

9

Thunderstorms

The year 1964 was a great one for rock and roll—as long as you were English. You were okay if your name was the Beatles, or the Dave Clark Five, or Herman's Hermits. But if you were American, you couldn't get arrested. The British Invasion turned most of the great rock and roll acts from the Brooklyn Fox into overnight has-beens. It was very sad. If you were an American act in the early sixties, you either became a dope addict and killed yourself, or you waited out the decade and went back on the road as an oldies act in the seventies.

But the Ronettes were lucky—1964 was actually our biggest year ever. "Baby I Love You" was still on the charts in January, and we had three more songs in the top forty that year: "(The Best Part of) Breaking Up," "Do I Love You," and "Walking in the Rain." We probably made more live appearances in 1964 than any other girl group, except maybe the Supremes. We also did every major TV show that featured rock acts, from "Shindig" and "Hullabaloo" to England's "Ready, Steady, Go." And I loved every minute of it.

Even so, I could tell that the pressures were starting to get to Nedra and Estelle. They loved being Ronettes, but it wasn't the same for them. They had steady boyfriends and they were always talking about settling down and starting families. I wanted kids, too, but show business came first.

You also have to remember that Nedra and Estelle stood in the background while I got to bask in the spotlight. I was the one who flew out to California and sang lead on all our records. I was the one the deejays wanted to talk to. And I was the one our producer was in love with, which meant I got preferential treatment in all kinds of other ways that drove them crazy.

When Phil picked up takeout food for the three of us, he would always tell Nedra and Estelle to save the carton on the bottom for me, because it was the one that stayed the warmest. I knew that was just Phil's way of flirting with me, but it was still hard for them to take, especially Estelle. All through our childhood she'd been treated like a little queen, but now, with Phil, *I* was suddenly the princess. I don't think it was easy for her to adjust, but I have to confess I loved playing the part.

After a while, the grind of being a Ronette just started to get to Nedra and Estelle. I guess it was inevitable that jealousies would start coming out backstage. "Ronnie," Estelle once said to me after a show, "do you think you could hike your skirt up any *higher* out there? The guys in the first three rows spent more time watching your panties than they did watching us."

I have to hand it to Estelle, she knew exactly how to get to me. She knew that I took special pride in going as far as I possibly could with my audience. It's still true today. When that spotlight comes on and it's just me and the audience, something happens to me, and I just let the feeling take me. If that means making a sexy movement with my hips or hiking my dress up a little more, so what? It's not called rock and roll for nothing.

But this was one issue where Nedra and Estelle thought they had me, so they refused to ease up. One day they even dragged Estelle's boyfriend over to our apartment to help them argue the point. His name was Joe Dong, and he really pissed me off that day.

"I have to agree with Estelle," Joe said, talking like some kind of expert. "I think you girls could stand to be a little more classy. Just look at the Supremes."

"But we don't do their kind of act," I told him, trying to hold in my temper. "They've got a style of their own, and it's not rock and roll. Rock and roll is exaggerated—bigger than life. That's why the kids pay three dollars to see it."

"But they're not paying three dollars to see you pull your dress up," he said. "That's just vulgar."

"Vulgar?" I shouted, getting carried away. "Joe Dong, you don't know the first thing about what it's like to be out there on that stage! So how can you walk into my house and insult me like that? Get out!"

Then Estelle tried to step in. "Ronnie, Joey was just trying to offer a little constructive criticism."

"How? By comparing us to the Supremes?" They really had me going now. "The Supremes wear long, tight gowns and sing about *where-did-their-damn-love-go* in high-pitched voices. That's not sexy. That's Las Vegas!"

"Well," Joe continued, "would it be so bad to do an act where the people listened to your music instead of wondering what you'd be like in bed?"

"What's wrong with their wondering what we'd be like in bed?" I yelled. "When people come to see us, we want them to feel something. They're supposed to fall in love with us. Don't you get it? This is rock and roll. If they want to fantasize that they're making love to us—that's great. Because I know that when I stand in front of that audience, I'm making love to them!"

That shut them up, just like I thought it would. Nedra and Estelle turned all funny looking, and Joey just said, "Well, I think I have to go now." The argument was over, but I don't think I ever forgave Nedra and Estelle for siding with him that day.

Even though we were starting to have our differences, our little family squabbles never really grew into anything major. Part of the reason was that I hardly even saw the Ronettes after Phil started recording us. I was the lead singer, and Phil Spector wasn't content to share me with anyone, not even my own family.

For some reason, Phil's jealousy seemed to get worse whenever we got to California. I remember going out to lunch with Phil and Herb Alpert, who is a very good-looking guy. When we sat down at the table, Phil made sure he put himself between Herb and me. Every time I said a word, Phil would lean in front of me so Herb Alpert wouldn't have a chance to look at me. It didn't matter that Herb was always a perfect gentleman. To Phil, any man was a threat.

I found that out when I made the mistake of going out to get a hamburger with Sonny Bono. I was at Gold Star with Nedra one night, and I was starving. Sonny usually went out and brought us back stuff when we got hungry, like a bag of Fritos and maybe a couple of Pepsi-Colas. But that night Phil was busy in the mixing booth, and nothing else seemed to be going on, so Nedra and I jumped in the car with Sonny and went out for hamburgers to a drive-in called Stan's.

We were only gone for about a half hour, but when we got back to Gold Star it looked like the earthquake had struck. There wasn't a soul in the studio, but all the music stands had been knocked over, and there were pieces of broken glass everywhere. A long, thin ribbon of recording tape stretched the length of the room like a streamer of shiny brown confetti, and our feet made a squishing sound when we walked on spots where the carpet was still wet from soaking up an entire pot of coffee—or what had *been* an entire pot of coffee before Phil threw it across the room. And it must have been Phil. Who else could've caused this much damage in such a short time?

Cher was the first to see us. "Watch out, guys," she warned. "Phillip is having a fit." But it was too late to get away, because Phil was waiting for us in the hallway.

"Where the fuck have you girls been?" Phil shouted. Nedra and I just stood there staring at the veins throbbing up and down on his head, too scared to say a word.

"It was my fault, Phil," Sonny explained. "I just took the girls out to get something to eat."

"You're damn right it was your fault," he said to Sonny. "You should know better." Then he turned back to me. "And *you* should know better than to leave here without telling me."

"But I was with Sonny," I stuttered. That only made Phil even angrier. He grabbed my arm and pulled me into the studio, where he could yell at me in private.

"What made you think it was okay to go out and get hamburgers with Sonny?" he hissed. "You really amaze me sometimes, Veronica. You just fucking amaze me." Then he turned and walked away. He didn't say anything else about it, but I knew he would still be steaming for the next few days.

And it wasn't just men Phil was jealous of. He didn't like to share me with anyone, Cher included. One time she found me sitting alone in my hotel room waiting for Phil to come back from the studio. "Honey, I know you're in love with the guy," she told me. "But nobody can blame you for playing hooky every once in a while. Let's get out of here."

"But Phil likes me to be here when he gets back from the studio," I tried to explain. I shouldn't have bothered. It's impossible to argue with Cher about anything. She just kept saying, "*I'm* going dancing at the Purple Onion. Are you coming?" Finally I said yes.

We went into the Purple Onion, a big dance club on the Sunset Strip that really was painted purple, and we hit the dance floor. We ran into Darlene Love when we got there, and the three of us just went crazy. We danced and made fools of ourselves for hours. And it was great. Until Phil found me.

He was so pissed at having to come down to the Purple Onion to get me that he walked right out onto the dance floor and dragged me off. Oh, well, I thought. That was fun while it lasted.

You might wonder how I could stay with a boyfriend who treated me that way. But Phil wasn't always like that. There were other times when I could tell he absolutely idolized me. Sometimes after we'd finish a session at Gold Star, Phil would take me for a moonlight drive up Laurel Canyon into the Hollywood Hills. Then we'd park the car on Mulholland Drive and make love high above the city, with the lights of Hollywood spread out like a blanket at our feet. "You're my little nugget of pure gold," he would whisper. "My precious music box."

He could be so sweet when we were alone that I'd completely forget all his horrible moods. I'd close my eyes and think of all the good things that had happened since I met Phil. He found me when I was still a teenager, and one by one, he made all of my dreams come true. And he was still making them come true every single day. If I had to put up with a little craziness for that, I could deal with it.

But I had no idea what real craziness was until Darlene Love finally told me Phil's best-kept secret. It happened in the spring of 1964, on what must have been the worst day of my entire life.

I was doing background vocals at Gold Star that afternoon with Darlene and some of the other singers when Phil's mom dropped by for a visit. Bertha Spector was a tiny woman—a real Jewish-mother type—and very protective of her son. She used to walk right into the studio, no matter what was going on. Some days she even brought a bowl of chicken soup for Phil, which he hated. He finally came up with a plan to outsmart her.

We were on a break from recording when the studio watchman buzzed Phil from the front door to warn him that his mom was on the way back with his tray of soup. Phil immediately had Sonny Bono lock the studio door and turn the red light on so she couldn't come in. Then we waited.

About ten minutes later, Phil had Sonny check the door to see if Mrs. Spector was still waiting in the hallway with his soup. She was. "Okay, let her in," Phil said. "I'm a fucking millionaire and my mother still brings me homemade soup."

Darlene and I watched the whole thing from a corner of the studio, and we were cracking up. I asked Darlene if she didn't think Phil looked cute when his mom handed him his soup spoon. "Cute?" she said. "You really think Phil is cute?"

"Yeah," I answered. "Don't you?"

"Not the way you do, girl," she said. "You really are hung up on this guy, aren't you?"

"Hung up?" I repeated. Then I was quiet for a long time, until I finally decided to confess my deepest fantasy. "I'm not hung up, Darlene. I'm in love. And one day I'm going to marry that man."

Darlene just shook her head and said, "I don't think so."

"Why not?" I demanded.

"Well," she sighed. "You're gonna have to find out sometime." She looked around for a more private spot, which didn't exist at Gold Star. Then she pointed to the ladies' room door. "Come on," she said. "In there."

I'll never forget the next five minutes. I walked into the ladies' room and took my usual place at the sink, right in front of the big mirror. Then Darlene blurted it out.

"Honey, this guy is married."

When you're in a car wreck, people talk about how everything goes into slow motion. Well, the same thing happens when somebody tells you the man you love is married. I just stared into the mirror, trying to make sense out of it. I thought of all the great fantasies that had come true in that bathroom—how I'd practiced all my hit songs there; how I fixed myself up at that sink the first time Phil took me out to eat on the Sunset Strip; how I rehearsed for my first appearance on "American Bandstand" staring into this very same mirror. Only now when I looked in it, all I saw was a strange girl standing there with tears running down her cheeks.

Then I leaned forward and began throwing my guts up all over the sink. I didn't even make it to the toilet, I just let everything inside me go right down that sink basin. Darlene had no idea I would be so startled by her little revelation, but I was in shock.

Darlene turned the faucet on and splashed water around, trying to get as much of it as possible on my face without actually having to touch me, because I was such a mess. I just stood there and watched the water and vomit go circling down into the drain hole, and I remember thinking that my life was going right down there with it.

Married?

I stood there clutching the sink until I felt like I might be able to stand up and walk away. Then I heard that word in my brain, and I sank down and grabbed the sink once again.

Married!

I kept turning the word over and over in my brain, hoping that if I said it often enough I might discover some new, less painful meaning for it that no one had ever thought of. But no matter how many times I repeated the word, it still felt like I was getting slapped with a big, wet rope every single time I said it.

Married. Married. Married.

Darlene tried her best to comfort me, but what could she do? "Who is it?" I asked her. "Give me a name. Give me a face." I couldn't understand how this wife could've avoided me all this time. "I've never met her."

"Not many people have," Darlene told me. "Her name is

Annette, but Phil never talks about her. I don't think he even sees her anymore. She just lives up there in that penthouse he's got in New York."

The shoes. Suddenly all I could think of was that collection of shoes that I'd seen at Phil's house, the ones that supposedly belonged to his sister. Those were *her* shoes! His wife's. So it was true.

Phil had kept it so well hidden, but I knew that everyone who worked for him must have known about her. Nino Tempo and Sonny. And Larry Levine, our engineer. But none of them had ever bothered to tell me. Suddenly I felt betrayed and completely alone.

"I've got to get out of here," I told Darlene.

"What should I tell Phil?"

"Tell him I got sick," I said. "That I had my period. Tell him anything you want. But I've got to go now."

"Okay, sweetie," she said. "But I want you to call me if you need anything. Anything at all, okay?" I nodded quietly and walked out of the studio, all alone. I went back to the hotel, locked the door, and cried for about seven hours straight. I never talked to Phil about it. As far as I know, he never even suspected I knew.

I felt terrible for a few days, like somebody had died. But my strategy for getting past the grief was to pretend nothing had happened. I was angry and hurt, but in those days I didn't know how to show those emotions. I didn't know how to say "Don't fuck with me!" Besides, Phil couldn't deal with being confronted any better than I could deal with confronting. In that way we really were a perfect match for each other.

I also had my career to think about. It's not like Phil was just an unfaithful lover. He was also my producer. If I put an end to our relationship as lovers, Phil would never record me again. And for a girl singer in the sixties, your producer was your lifeline. Without Phil, it would've been back to Colpix for the Ronettes. Or worse. If I said bye-bye to Phil, I would've been saying bye-bye to my career. And I had a sister, a cousin, and lots of other relatives depending on me for a living.

The way I saw it, my choice was simple. I could keep my mouth shut and hold on to my career, my relationship, and my family. Or I could confront Phil now and throw it all away. And I was no fool. So I pretended I'd never heard of Phil's wife. I pretended to Phil. I pretended to my sister. I even pretended to myself. And I was good at it—after a few days I had myself convinced that nothing had really changed between me and Phil. And by that time, most of the pain had passed.

Of all the records I did with Phil, "Walking in the Rain" is still my favorite. It was also the only song I ever recorded in one take. The way it usually worked was, I'd come in at the start of a session and sing a song through once, just to give the musicians a feel for it. Then I'd leave while they laid down the musical tracks. A few days later, Phil would have me come back to add my finished vocals, which we usually did late at night. Unlike Phil's other artists, I always recorded alone. Phil liked to concentrate on my voice completely, so I almost never put my vocals on a record while anyone but Phil and Larry Levine was there.

The night we did "Walking in the Rain," though, Barry Mann and Cynthia Weil were there, too. They had just written the song with Phil, and they were still working on the lyrics right up until the minute I recorded it. They wanted to find a better line to rhyme with "Johnny, no, no, he'll never do." They had "Bobby, no it isn't him, too," which everyone knew sucked. But nobody could come up with anything better, so they finally just left it the way it was.

When it came time for me to record, Phil said, "Go on into the studio. I've got a surprise for you." I stepped in and stood at my usual spot behind the music stand. "Okay, Ronnie, just listen to this." I put the headphones on as Phil reached over to flip the tape on.

Everything was quiet. Then all of a sudden I heard a low rumble, like there was thunder coming in from every corner of the room. It was the intro to the song, but Larry and Phil had mixed the sounds of a real thunderstorm in with this beautiful melody. It was absolutely perfect. I closed my eyes and I was in a whole other world.

I started singing on the downbeat. I thought I'd just do a rough take to get a feel for the song before we recorded it. But

I was really into it, and I kept singing all the way through the whole song. When I finished, I opened my eyes and found myself standing in complete darkness.

"What happened?" I asked. I couldn't see Phil or any of the other guys in the glass booth, and I started to wonder if they'd even heard my rehearsal take. Then Phil's voice came out over the speaker.

"That's the one," he said. "We can go home now."

"You were recording that?" I asked. Then I walked straight into the booth, feeling a little confused. "But that was just a rough one," I said. "Let me try it one more time. I know I can really feel it now."

"Oh, you felt it," Phil said. "Listen for yourself. Play it back, Larry." And when I heard it played over the speakers, I had to agree with Phil. It was a perfect take. And that's the take you hear on the record today.

Then I looked back out at the dark studio. "But what happened to all the lights?"

"That was Phil's idea," Larry said. "He shut them off to help put you in the mood. And it sure worked, didn't it?"

I looked at Phil and Larry and Barry and Cynthia. They were all grinning so wide I thought their faces would crack. I didn't have the heart to tell them that I'd had my eyes closed the whole time, anyway. I hadn't even noticed the lights were off.

It became a kind of tradition with Phil to have me sing in the dark after that. But the truth is, I never knew whether the lights were on or not. I'm still like that today. Once I put the headphones on, everything else disappears.

"I'm tired of paying for hotel rooms," Phil announced one afternoon as we got into his Rolls after a recording session at Gold Star. "Maybe we should get a house."

I thought he must be joking. "I'd love that! When can we start looking?"

"Why not today?" he asked, with a little smile. Then he leaned forward and told George Brand, the chauffeur, "Let's go see if we can't find a house, George."

He obviously had the whole thing set up beforehand, because George knew exactly where he was going. He steered the big limousine through Hollywood and into Beverly Hills by way of the Sunset Strip. We wound up and down the curling streets, past giant mansions with yards the size of golf courses, until we finally came to a narrow little street called La Collina Drive. Then George drove up a hill and parked the car in front of a big house with a fountain out front.

"I understand this place might be available," Phil said as he got out of the car. "Let's take a look."

By this time I knew Phil had the whole thing set up, so I wasn't surprised when the lady who was showing the house came out to the driveway and offered to take us inside. It's hard to describe exactly what it's like when a little girl from Spanish Harlem sees her first mansion, but it's not a bad feeling. The place was like a palace. There were twenty-three rooms, and the whole house was furnished like a big castle, with lots of old paintings in gigantic wooden frames. There was antique furniture everywhere, and huge four-poster canopy beds in all the bedrooms. Even the ceilings were amazing, with murals on them that were painted in Europe in the 1400s, or so the lady said. It was like nothing I'd ever seen.

"What do *you* think?" Phil asked me as we walked back to the car. "Could you be happy in a place like this?"

"Yes," I told him. "As a matter of fact, I think I could."

I was trying to play it cool, but inside it was midnight on New Year's Eve. I mean, it isn't every day that the love of your life asks you to settle down with him. And if Phil wanted me to live with him, could marriage be far off? Of course, we still hadn't discussed his divorce, but with Phil moving out to California, it was pretty obvious that he was finally cutting all ties with his New York past. As far as I was concerned, that Beverly Hills mansion was all the proof I needed that Phil was mine at last. And only mine.

We got in the car and drove back down the wide, tree-lined streets of Beverly Hills. As I stared out the window of the Rolls at the pink stucco palaces with their endless driveways and perfectly manicured lawns, I thought I must be in heaven. "Wow," I said to myself. "This is where I want to die."

10

Fatal Mistakes

By 1965, the Ronettes were already on the way out. We only had two songs even break into the top hundred that year, "Born to Be Together" and "Is This What I Get for Loving You?" The biggest reason for our slump was Phil, who had already started to lose interest in us as far back as April of 1964. That's when he recorded us doing "Chapel of Love," and then refused to release it as a single. We thought it was such a great record that we practically begged him to put it out.

"No," he told us. "It doesn't sound like a hit. Forget about that one." Then the Dixie Cups' version came out and it was a smash! It was so depressing.

But that was Phil's way. He was always recording songs that he refused to release. Between the middle of 1965 and the end of 1966, we recorded a whole string of unreleased songs, including "Paradise" and "I Wish I Never Saw the Sunshine," which were two of the greatest records we ever did. Or they would've been, if Phil had only put them out. But he didn't, and those fantastic tracks just sat on his shelf for years, while the Ronettes' career dwindled away to nothing. Phil finally put a few of these things out on some oldies albums that came out in England in the seventies, but that didn't do the Ronettes any good in 1965.

Phil always had an excuse whenever he held one of our songs

back from release. "The backgrounds aren't right," he'd say, or "The fade-out still needs a little work." And then he'd file it away, and we'd never see or hear the tape again. We assumed Phil was just being a perfectionist, but I can see now that he had other, darker reasons for abandoning the Ronettes.

For one thing, Phil didn't want to see me get too big. I was just a little girl from Spanish Harlem when I met him, but he knew I had the potential to become a star even then. So he did everything in his power to help me make that happen. And it worked. Then he fell in love with me, and that was his fatal mistake.

Once I'd made it big, Phil was too insecure to let me keep growing, because he was terrified that I might one day outgrow him. So he tried to reverse the whole process and slow everything down so that I would stay a dependent little kid from Spanish Harlem. And I let him do it. I didn't see what was so wrong with sitting back and letting my millionaire lover tend to my every whim. I didn't think I had to grow up. Ever. And that was *my* fatal mistake.

Even after the Ronettes' slump began in 1965, I didn't get too concerned. Phil had just scored the biggest smash of his career with "You've Lost That Lovin' Feeling," by the Righteous Brothers, and he was still as hot as ever. So I figured it was just a matter of time before he turned his attention back to my career.

It wasn't like he could ignore me. I'd practically been living with him since he moved into the mansion on La Collina. Whenever I came out to California, that is. Which actually wasn't that often in 1965, since the Ronettes had personal appearances booked solid throughout the year.

And I was having so much fun onstage with the Ronettes, I didn't have time to worry about our failing recording career. I still had my audience, and I could tell by their applause that they still loved me. Before long, though, I think Phil even grew jealous of them.

We did one of our biggest shows ever in late November, when Phil put us in *The Big T.N.T. Show*, which was a concert he produced in Hollywood that was being filmed for release as a movie. Phil was the orchestra leader for a lineup that included some of the biggest names in rock, including Ray Charles, the Byrds, and the Ike and Tina Turner Revue. Of course, Phil had to be in complete control whenever he produced anything, and this show was no exception.

When the technicians asked us to do some of our act during rehearsal, we ran through our routine just to give the camera guys a basic idea of what we did. We didn't give them a full performance, because we wanted to save that for the show. But Phil was in charge—and he wanted to make sure everyone knew it—so he stopped us in the middle of the rehearsal and started barking out orders at us like we were in the chorus or something.

"Hold it, girls," he commanded. "You're just walking through it. I'd like you to start again, and this time, I want you to do it just like you're going to do it tonight."

That was ridiculous. We'd been doing the same basic routines ever since we started at the Brooklyn Fox, but our act always changed a little bit each night, depending on the audience response. The only thing you could be sure of was that we never ever did exactly the same show twice. But Phil insisted, so we went ahead and played our entire act to this empty theater.

"That wasn't so hard, was it?" he called out after we finished. "Do it *exactly* like that tonight."

That night we did our act the same way we always did it—flat out crazy. I shimmied around the stage and danced wherever the feeling took me. The crowd was up for grabs, but I think it was too much for Phil.

The director and all the cameramen told us how exciting it was, and the other acts all said the nicest stuff. But Phil hated it. He came up to me after the show, steaming mad. "What did you think you were doing out there?" he shouted. I hated it when Phil got like that, but I knew the only thing I could do was humor him until the mood passed.

"What's wrong?" I asked. "Was there something wrong with our routine?"

"It was all wrong," he snapped. "It looked completely different tonight than it did this afternoon."

"But there was no audience then," I explained. "You know I always play the house."

"*Play the house?*" he exclaimed. "You were all over the place.

Out of control." That was a big thing with Phil. If I lost control in front of a crowd, he hated it because that meant that I was out of *his* control.

"And on top of everything else, you came in off key!" He could only ever criticize my singing for technical reasons, because he knew I didn't read music, so I couldn't argue. "Don't bother coming to the party after the show," he ordered. "I don't want to see you there!"

I went straight back to my hotel room and cried. I suppose I could've gone to the party anyway, but I never even considered it. I just couldn't go against Phil's wishes in those days. I was like a little Japanese geisha girl walking five paces behind her master. Phil couldn't control what I did once I got out onstage, but that wasn't a problem he had in our personal life.

Of course, he dominated me most of all in the recording studio. After the hamburger incident with Sonny Bono, I knew Phil didn't want me getting too friendly with the other singers and musicians at Gold Star. He never really came out and said so—he didn't have to. He had more charming ways of getting me to do what he wanted.

Once when I was doing backgrounds with a bunch of people at Gold Star, this big fat singer named Olla got me laughing. She was always saying something that cracked me up, and this time I was doubled up with laughter when I happened to catch a peek at Phil, who was smiling at me from behind his glass window in the control room. "Ronnie," he said, waving me into the booth. "Come on in here."

When I got there, Phil pulled up an old wooden stool and motioned for me to sit down on it. Then he turned back to work at the mixing board. "Uh, Phil?" I asked. "What was it you wanted?"

"Nothing, really," he admitted, looking a little embarrassed. "I just felt like I could use some inspiration in here."

It was such a sweet thing to say, and so flattering. Up until then, Phil had always tried to keep up the illusion that our relationship was purely professional. But by inviting me to sit next to him in the control booth, he was admitting to the whole world that I was someone special. I sat straight up on that rickety old stool and felt like a queen.

From then on I always sat in the booth with Phil. He seemed to really enjoy having me in there with him, and it made me feel like a privileged character. Phil would make jokes about whoever happened to be standing on the other side of the glass, and they were especially funny because no one could hear them but me and Larry Levine.

And I also got to watch Phil at work, which was always a thrill. He would sit there in his booth with the speakers blasting so loud I thought he must have been going deaf. But then he would hear something in the mix that no one else could, and he would motion for Larry to stop the tape. One time I saw him point to the end violinist in a row of ten and say, "You. Sounds like you're a little flat. Check your A string." The guy checked his tuning, and Phil was right. It was amazing.

A lot of people have asked me how Phil created his wall of sound, but to understand Phil's sound, you have to understand Phil. The wall of sound was really just a reflection of his own personality, which was very extravagant. When Phil made a record, he might start out with the same basic tracks as everyone else—drums, guitars, bass, and vocals. But then he'd always add in more sounds, because he wanted his records to be as extravagant as he was. He didn't have any use for a record unless it was at least ten times bigger than life. Phil was one guy who believed that *more* is more.

When he walked into a recording studio, Phil was always looking for a new rule he could break. He wasn't afraid to try anything. I remember there was this little meter on the tape machines that told you how loud the volume was, and it had a needle that would go into the red zone whenever the sound got too loud or distorted. Well, everyone in the record business lived in fear of making that needle go into the red—but not Phil. Sometimes I think he was only really happy when he was in that red zone.

After being in the studio with Phil for a time, it was only natural that you'd get caught up in his madness. Everyone who worked for him did. With Phil as our inspiration, we'd try to push ourselves as hard as he pushed himself. When I'd sing a lyric, I'd close my eyes and try to feel the truest emotion I could find. And I'd keep pushing myself until I got there. Then Phil would add that sound to the sounds of all the other singers, musicians, and engineers. And the result would be a wonderful combination of textures and personalities and genius that people started calling the wall of sound. You can say what you want about Phil Spector, but no one who was there at Gold Star can ever forget the music we made. No one had ever heard anything like it before, and they'll never hear anything like it again.

As much as I loved hanging around the booth with Phil, it wasn't long before I started to miss being out in the studio with the crowd. But the first time I tried to leave the booth and join in on the fun in the studio, Phil made it clear that my place was with him and only him.

"Where are you going, Ronnie?" Phil asked when I got up from my stool.

"I'm just going out to sing a few of these backgrounds with the guys."

"No, no, no," he said. "I don't want you doing that anymore."

"But, Phil," I argued. "Everybody sings backups."

"Not you, Ronnie," he said. "Your voice is too distinctive. It comes right through."

"Well," I suggested, "maybe I could just go 'oooh,' real low." But Phil wouldn't budge. So while everyone else was laughing and joking and smoking cigarettes, I'd sit there watching them in silence from behind my glass wall.

If 1965 was a slow year for the Ronettes' recording career, 1966 was like death. We only had one record out the whole year, "I Can Hear Music," and that one barely got on the *Billboard* chart at number 100. It stayed there exactly one week. It was demoralizing.

But I never gave up hope. Phil still brought me into the studio every few months to record a new Ronettes song— sometimes alone, and sometimes with Nedra and Estelle. But then he'd just file it away with our other unreleased records. After a while I started to wonder why he even bothered having me come down to the studio.

And it wasn't just the Ronettes he was hurting. By 1966, Phil's perfectionism was ruining every artist on his label. Every time he made a record, he'd find some flaw that nobody else in the whole world could hear, and he'd refuse to put it out. And if he released a song that didn't make it to the top of the charts, he'd get depressed for months. Sometimes longer. Finally, he made one record that flopped so bad, it actually sent him into retirement.

"River Deep, Mountain High" was a song that Phil recorded with Tina Turner in March of 1966, and it was a great record. Phil captured the rawness in Tina's voice and made it a part of his wall of sound, and the result was a record that sounded tremendous. It should've been one of Phil's biggest hits, but it turned out to be his biggest failure.

He did everything he could to push "River Deep, Mountain High," but the American deejays just wouldn't play it. I guess they all thought Phil had gone too far with that one. It was a huge hit in England, but in this country, it barely got on the charts.

Phil was crushed. He was so depressed he didn't go near the studio for months. He just moped around his mansion, playing pool all day. I was spending a lot of time with him in those days, but there was nothing I could do to cheer the guy up. I hated seeing Phil depressed like that, but I figured it was just a matter of time before he got inspired again. And I was determined to stick by him until his dark mood passed.

Thank God I still had my live shows with the Ronettes to take my mind off Phil's depression. Even without a recent hit, we were still popular enough to get a booking at Manhattan's Basin Street East, a classy nightclub that was just starting to book rock and roll acts. We opened there in July of 1966, and I'll never forget that night. We did a great show, and the crowd loved us. But it's not what happened onstage that sticks in my mind.

I was sitting in our dressing room backstage when one of the waiters came back and told me there was a lady out front who wanted to talk to me. I asked him who it was. "She didn't say," he told me. "She just said to tell you she was a good friend of Phil's."

I was curious, so I followed the waiter out to a table in front where this pretty young blond woman was sitting with a guy in a suit. The waiter pulled a chair out for me, and the woman stood up and held out her hand.

"I'm Annette Spector," she said, shaking my hand. "I've heard so much about you."

At first I didn't even realize who she was. *Annette Spector?* I'd blocked that name out of my head the first time I heard it, so I just assumed this girl was one of Phil's cousins. Then she said, "I wanted to introduce myself and let you know there are no hard feelings." That's when I figured it out.

Annette had been divorced from Phil for about six months—or so I found out through the grapevine—so I thought it was nice of her to make the effort to meet me. Even so, I couldn't think of a single word to say to her. Which is too bad, because looking back, I'll bet we could have had one hell of a conversation.

I think Annette sensed how tongue-tied I was, because she introduced her companion—he was some kind of lawyer or something—and then offered me a drink. I was glad she did, because at least that gave me an excuse to say something.

"Oh, no, thanks. I'm about to go on," I stammered. "And I never drink before a show." *Oh, no,* I thought. Now she'll think I'm some kind of drunk who can't wait to get bombed *after* my act. "Actually," I added, "I never drink after a show either." That still didn't sound right, so I finally told her, "To tell the truth, I don't drink at all."

By this point Annette and her friend were both smiling, so I said a quick good-bye and stood up to get the hell out of there. But as I was walking back to the dressing room, something made me spin around for a last look. "Annette," I blurted. Then, in a whisper, I said, "Thanks."

Richard Pryor was our opening act that night, but he was still a young unknown then, and I honestly don't remember much about his act. In fact, I don't remember much about *our* show that night, either. I guess I was just happy to get through it.

We had a second memorable night during our run at Basin Street East. It happened a few nights later. We'd just finished our show when our tour manager, a nice old guy named Val Irving, told us he had some important news. "Sit down, girls," he said. "I got a telegram today, but I didn't want to tell you about it until after the show, because I thought it might throw you off."

That's me with my sister Estelle when I was about one year old. My dad thought I was going to be a boy, so I got stuck with the nickname "Butchie" until I was twelve.

A family photo of all the aunts and uncles who used to watch me sing on the weekends at Grandma's house. That's my mother in the top right corner, with Nedra's mom—my aunt Susu—sitting just below her on the arm of the couch. Next to Aunt Susu, going clockwise, is my aunt Hermean; my grandmother, Susie Mobley; my aunts Hattie, Oretha, Helen, and Grace; and my uncles Charles, Cecil, Roy, Ray, Arthur, Clarence, and Maceo. (Courtesy Beatrice Bennett)

I had a little identity crisis when I was twelve years old—I couldn't figure out whether I was white or black. One time I even tried darkening my skin with suntan lotion. It didn't work.

*H*ere are the Ronettes—Nedra, me, and Estelle—with Murray the K, the biggest deejay in New York in those days. We'd do his radio show every night, then we'd be depressed because we had to go back to high school the next morning. (Courtesy Randal C. Russi)

Killing time backstage at the Brooklyn Fox Theatre. Sometimes we'd stage little contests to see who could tease their hair the highest or extend their eyeliner the farthest. (Courtesy Art Charles)

Still goofing around backstage at the Fox Theatre. In the days before we hit, the headliners at the Fox knew us only as "Murray the K's dancing girls."

*O*nstage with Clay Cole and the Capris at one of Clay's Twist-erama Revues. After three flop singles on Colpix, shows like these were all that kept us going. (Photo by Lillian Wright)

*T*he day we signed with Phil Spector, in March 1963. Phil wanted to sign me alone, but my mom wouldn't let him. "Uh-uh," she said. "The Ronettes is a group." (Photo by Popsie; courtesy Kevin C. Dilworth)

*A*n early publicity pose—Nedra, me, and Estelle. Everyone thought we must've been the toughest girls in New York, but we were really three naive teenagers who just borrowed their look from the girls on the streets of Spanish Harlem. (Photo by James J. Kriegsmann)

*P*hil gives me a few last-minute pointers at Gold Star Studios before we record "Frosty the Snowman" for the Christmas album in 1963. (Photo by Ray Avery; courtesy Michael Ochs Archive)

A quiet moment at Gold Star in 1963—that's me on the left. The Ronettes were family, and our blood ties gave us a closeness that none of the other groups could match. (Photo by Ray Avery; courtesy Michael Ochs Archive)

*P*hil could be so much fun in those days. I think he loved our enthusiasm because it came close to matching his own. (Photo by Ray Avery; courtesy Michael Ochs Archive)

When the Rolling Stones were the opening act on our first English tour, Phil didn't even want them to speak to us. But when they came to New York a few weeks later, my mom fixed them scrambled eggs. (Photo from New Musical Express; courtesy Danny J. Williams)

With Phil and George Harrison at Decca Records in London, 1964. I'm next to Phil, Tony Hall is standing on the far right next to George, and the guy in the center is Tony King, our chaperone in London. We'd never even heard of the Beatles before we went over to England, but they sure knew about us.

At the height of our popularity in 1964. So many great things happened so fast, it was hard to appreciate them one at a time. (Courtesy Michael Ochs Archive)

Phil and Veronica, the ultimate rock and roll couple. I was so dazzled by what Phil could do that I just stood there while he built his wall of sound around me. Nobody told me that the spotlight wouldn't always burn so bright. (Courtesy Kevin C. Dilworth)

"A telegram?" Estelle asked.

Then Nedra added, "Is it good news or bad?"

"It's from the Beatles' manager, so I guess that makes it good news," he said. When I heard that, I did sit down. If this was from the Beatles, we knew it had to be big. "The Beatles are doing a tour of the U.S. next month," Val explained. "And they just wanted to know—"

Then he stopped cold and pretended to yawn, just so he could drive us crazy. It did.

"Val!" Estelle screamed, as I reached over to strangle him.

"Okay, okay," he said, laughing. Then he spit the rest out, real fast. "The Beatles just want to know if the Ronettes are available to be the opening act on their U.S. tour."

You never heard three girls scream so loud. We shouted and giggled and danced around until we made such a racket that the Basin Street stage manager finally had to come back and tell us to shut up. "Please, girls," he said. "There're still people out front."

"Oh . . . sorry," I apologized. "We were just celebrating. We just got invited to go on tour with the Beatles." I tried to contain myself, but as soon as I said those words out loud, Nedra and Estelle started screaming again. I finally just gave up and joined them.

Opening for a Beatles tour was probably the greatest thing that could happen to any group in the sixties. That's what finally got the Ronettes on the cover of *Ebony* magazine. I couldn't wait to tell Phil, so I called him in California as soon as I got home that night. But even though I thought it was the greatest news in the world, all Phil could say was, "Hmmm."

"What's wrong, Phil?" I asked.

"Nothing's *wrong*," he said. But he obviously had something on his mind. "We can talk more after you get back out here."

"But, Phil. This is the Beatles."

I expected to at least hear an argument of some kind, but Phil just ended the conversation with a statement that really confused me. "Ronnie," he said, very slowly. "We've got to think about your career."

"Okay, Phil," I said. "I'll see you next week."

I didn't give it much thought after that. You could never

predict Phil's reaction to anything, so I'd given up trying to second-guess him. When I got out to California, I didn't even bring up the subject of the tour. In fact, neither of us mentioned it until Phil took me down to Gold Star. And that was a surprise, because I knew Phil hadn't been to the recording studio in months.

I followed him into a storage office and watched as he started shuffling through a few boxes of old recording tapes. He still hadn't said a word when Larry Levine poked his head in to say hello. They made a little small talk, and I was just starting to get bored when Phil revealed what this whole game of going down to Gold Star was all about. "Oh, by the way, Larry," he said, trying to sound casual. "Can you see about booking us some studio time in August? I'd like to get started on Ronnie's next record."

Larry said he'd look into it, and then he left. That's when I spoke up. "But, Phil," I said. "I'm supposed to be on tour with the Beatles in August."

"Ronnie," he said, reaching into another box of old tapes, "you've got to ask yourself, do you want to do another live tour, or do you want to get back in the studio and make another hit?" Phil was trying his best to sound casual, which only made me realize how important this really was to him.

"But, Phil, this isn't just any tour. This is the Beatles."

"That's even more reason to skip it. Nobody's coming to those shows to see you. Those concerts are nothing but a freak show. Ask the Beatles. They'd be the first to admit it. But do what you want. It's your career." Then I watched as Phil flipped through the same box of tapes for the third time. That's when I saw that his hands were shaking. Obviously, something about this tour was upsetting Phil so much he couldn't even talk about it. And I had a pretty good idea what it was. Or who.

His name was John Lennon.

Naturally, I'd never told Phil about my little encounters with John, but I always had a feeling he knew anyway. I don't know how he could've, but Phil always seemed to have a radar about those kinds of things. And there wasn't anything I could deny, because Phil never accused me. But I still got the feeling I was being tested.

"And I'll tell you something else," he continued, looking me straight in the eye. "I'm not going to stick around and watch you throw your career away doing live shows for the rest of your life. If you want to make records, fine. I'll be here for you. If you don't, that's fine, too. Just don't expect anything else from me."

His voice cracked a little as he said that last part, and that's when I saw how afraid he was that I might go off with the Beatles and leave him behind. He was trying so hard to pretend he didn't care, but I knew he was scared to death of being left all alone. And I knew what that was like. I felt like that myself sometimes.

Phil had made his ultimatum—"Them or me." That might've sounded harsh to someone else. But to me it was a declaration of his love. The guy wanted me, all or nothing at all, and he wasn't going to settle for less. That's when I realized that John Lennon didn't matter one bit. And neither did the Beatles. I had to choose between going on a tour and being screamed at by a million people who didn't care who I was, or staying home and being adored by the one man who could give me more love than a million people ever could.

For me, that was no contest.

The Ronettes did go on tour with the Beatles, but my cousin Elaine stood in my place, the same as she did for part of the Dick Clark Caravan of Stars tour. The tour turned out to be such a circus that no one even noticed the switch. Except the Beatles. And they were pissed, or so my mother told me.

"We ride in the Beatles' jet with them," Mom told Phil and me when the tour stopped at Dodger Stadium in Los Angeles. Phil had invited her to dinner at the mansion, but he regretted the invitation as soon as she got there, because Mom just couldn't stop talking about the Beatles. "Oh, Ronnie, John's so sweet," she told me. "And he's always asking about you. 'Where's Ronnie?' he says. 'Where's the voice?'"

Phil shot my mother a look that said, "Enough already." But Mom ignored Phil's signals, probably because she was having so much fun needling him. "Ronnie," she continued, "did you know the Beatles had monitor speakers set up in their dressing rooms so they could hear you onstage? And when you didn't come, John said, 'It's too bad. I love that voice. I would love to rest in peace with that voice.' "

That was all Phil needed to hear. He tossed his napkin on the table and walked out of the dining room without saying another word. Now it was my turn to give my mother a look. Mine said, "Gee thanks, Mom. Thanks a lot."

Phil was worried that I might regret missing the tour, but what he didn't know is that I'd already spoken to Nedra. And from what she told me, I was glad I hadn't gone. "It's no fun, Ronnie," she said. "Those kids who come to see the Beatles are just crazy. They scream through the whole act—they don't listen to a single thing. You'd hate it."

When Nedra described the tour that way, all I could think of was that nightmare we'd had in the Shea Stadium parking lot, when those Beatles fans almost killed us in Jerry Schatzberg's Bentley. All of a sudden I began to wonder if, by keeping me home from that tour, maybe Phil had actually done me the biggest favor of all.

11

Gross Pictures

*A*ugust 1966 was probably the darkest month of my life. No matter how miserable I might have been with the Beatles, nothing could have been worse than the month I spent with Phil in his mansion. He was still bummed out over the failure of "River Deep, Mountain High," and I found out that Phil was hell to be around when he got depressed. He'd lock himself away in his second-floor study for days on end, only coming out to eat or sleep.

I never knew exactly what he did in there all day. Sometimes I'd hear him talking on the phone, doing business. Other times he'd just sit there playing his records in the dark. He was definitely developing into a depressed case.

But what really put Phil under was when he got the news that his friend Lenny Bruce had died of a drug overdose. Phil loved Lenny's sick sense of humor, and the two of them hung out together all the time. Even after Lenny's career hit the skids, Phil always stuck by him, which I thought was great. But there was also a creepy side to the way he idolized Lenny.

Phil worshiped the guy, even when he was still alive. He hung a giant picture of Lenny right over our bed. I'm not talking about an eight-by-ten headshot—this was a huge blown-up poster of Lenny Bruce, looking hungover, with big bags under his eyes. Lenny wasn't a bad-looking guy in his heyday, but this picture was taken a long time after that. Phil always fell asleep before I did, so I spent a lot of nights lying in bed with Lenny Bruce staring down at me from the wall. And that sure didn't make it any easier to sleep.

Phil never even told me that Lenny had died—I found it out by accident one night when I couldn't sleep. Phil had been locked up in his study most of the evening, but I happened to be wandering past when he finally opened the door. When I looked at him, I couldn't help but notice that his eyes were all red, like he'd been crying.

"What's wrong, Phil?" I asked.

"Nothing," he said, trying to act normal. "What are you doing still up?"

"I don't know," I said. "I just couldn't sleep."

"Well, go on back to bed," he commanded. Then his mood changed, and he spoke a little softer. "I'll bring you in a snack." Phil loved to make me grilled cheese-and-tomato sandwiches late at night. That was his specialty.

"Thanks, honey," I said as he turned and headed downstairs to the kitchen. I started back toward our bedroom, but when I noticed that Phil had left the door to his study open, I couldn't resist tiptoeing in for a peek. I wasn't really allowed in there, but I thought I'd just slip in and try to find something to read. Phil never let me have magazines in the house, but I thought he might have a copy of *Cashbox* lying around that I could sneak out and read before bed.

There weren't any magazines in plain sight, so I pulled open the top drawer of his antique mahogany desk. The only thing in there was a small stack of black-and-white photographs. I picked one up out of curiosity, but I wished I hadn't as soon as I saw it.

They were photos of Lenny Bruce, dead. He was lying naked in front of a toilet. He had gotten really fat, and his stomach was all bloated up. At first I thought they were fakes, that they were part of some sick joke that Phil and Lenny had cooked up. Then I noticed the hypodermic needle lying on the floor next to Lenny's body. He was dead, all right.

They were gross pictures, but I have to admit I couldn't take my eyes off them. I sat down in Phil's chair and studied the pictures one by one. I was still sitting like that when I felt something small and flat go whizzing past my head.

I didn't know what it was, but it sure startled me. It bounced off the wall and down onto the floor before I recognized it as half of my grilled cheese-and-tomato sandwich. That's when I looked up in terror to see Phil standing in the doorway. He was dead silent. As he stared at me with his stone face, I thought he looked a little bit like Buster Keaton, and I almost started to giggle. Almost.

He was about to throw the other half of the sandwich at me, but he tossed it straight to the floor instead, plate and all. My body tensed like a cat's as Phil walked toward me. He looked so pissed that I was sure he was finally going to let loose and hit me. But all he did was rip the photos out of my hand. I was so scared, I flinched anyway. Then he turned his back to me and tossed the pictures into the drawer where I'd found them.

I was still shaking when I finally found the nerve to speak. "Phil," I said. "You never told me about Lenny. What happened?"

Then came the yelling. "I don't fucking believe you! You break into my private area. You snoop around in materials of a highly personal nature. And then you have the nerve to stand there asking me questions that are *none of your goddamned business!*"

I knew there was no talking to Phil when he started shouting, so I walked into the bathroom. I locked the door behind me, but I shouldn't have bothered. Phil locked himself back up in his study, and I didn't see him again for the rest of the night. I sat on the toilet for a long time, waiting for the shaking to stop. When my emotions finally caught up with me, I started crying. And then I couldn't stop. I stayed in the bathroom for a couple of hours, and when I finally went to bed, I pulled the covers way over my head so I wouldn't have Lenny Bruce staring down at me in my sleep.

Phil never mentioned Lenny or the pictures again, but I was still dying to know what he was doing with those photographs. I later heard a story that they were police photos that Phil had bought from the sheriff's department for five thousand dollars. And knowing Phil, it was probably true.

*   *   *

In the fall of 1966, the Ronettes left for an extended tour that included a series of concerts at U.S. Army bases in Germany. After that terrible month with Phil, I was glad for the chance to go back on the road for a while. It wasn't so much that I wanted to get away from him—I just needed a break from being cooped up in the house. I was still so attached to Phil that I hated going a day without hearing from him.

And I rarely did. For all his craziness, Phil was a very attentive boyfriend. He always wrote me nice long letters when I stayed at my apartment on Eighty-ninth and Riverside. And when he wasn't writing, he was on the phone.

Phil was a wizard at keeping track of me while I was on tour. He always knew exactly where to reach me at any moment of the day or night. No matter where I was—I don't care what time zone—I'd hear the phone ring and I'd know it would be Phil. My mother thought he must have owned stock in the telephone company.

Whenever the Ronettes checked into a hotel in Germany, there would always be a message waiting for me from Phil. I'd run up to my room and call him, and we'd talk for a couple hours until I got sleepy. Sometimes he wouldn't even want me to hang up—I'd just leave my phone off the hook all night while I slept. In the morning I'd pick it up and there would be Phil, yawning and saying, "Good morning, baby. Did you sleep well?" It was just like we were sleeping together, except that I was in the middle of Europe and he was in Beverly Hills.

Estelle hated the way we kept the phone tied up, so she was always giving me lectures. "Ronnie, can't you see that Phil's just trying to keep tabs on you so you don't spend the night with anyone else?"

"So what if he is?" I said. "I don't even want to sleep with anyone else. You're just jealous because your boyfriend doesn't care enough to call you long distance." And that's really how I felt. It never occurred to me to question Phil's obsessions, or my willingness to go along with them. If I had, I might have realized how dangerous they were becoming.

The GI's in Germany loved us. In fact, we were so popular that we actually started a riot at an army base in Gelnhausen. It was a real disaster. The army had us playing in a mess hall that was too small to hold all the men who wanted to see us, so they added a second show for officers only at a place called the Moonlight Lounge. We did our first show in the mess hall, and the guys were packed in like french fries. But they loved it. Our dancing always drove guys a little crazy, but we had no idea what a powerful effect it could have on a roomful of men who weren't having sex.

One guy actually had an orgasm right in front of the stage! It happened during "What'd I Say?" That was our encore number, so we always went really wild on that one. I was shaking around pretty good up there when I looked down and saw this soldier lying on the floor, rubbing himself through his dungarees. Then I did a quick bump, and all of a sudden his body tensed up and he got a real blissful look on his face. Oh, my God, I thought, he's coming! I'd never seen that response to our act before. It was something.

The guys were still screaming for a second encore when five MP's met us backstage to escort us to our second show at the officers-only club. We took one look at these five MP guys with their big pistols strapped at their sides and we broke out laughing. "This is the first time we ever needed an armed guard to get offstage," I joked. But none of them laughed.

"If you think *these* guys are wild," one of them said, "just wait until you see the little situation that's developing over at the officers' club."

When the MP's drove us over to the Moonlight Lounge in their jeep, we saw what they were talking about. There were about thirty or forty enlisted guys crowded around the front of the place, and they were going ape. These were the guys who couldn't get seats for our first show, and now they were getting really pissed because the MP's told them that this show was off-limits. By the time we showed up, most of the officers were already waiting for us inside, but the mob outside refused to go away. They were shouting and shoving each other around, and after a while some of them even started throwing rocks and beer bottles at the front of the club. That's when the MP's went into action.

"I think you girls better get in there and do your show now," one of them suggested. "And if I were you, I'd get it over with as fast as I could."

The Ronettes did one of the worst shows of our career that night. It was hell. The officers sat there trying to pretend nothing was going on outside, but we could hardly even hear ourselves over the sound of all the rocks and beer bottles that kept crashing up against the front of the place. We tried to get through the act, but we were so scared we could barely remember the words to "Baby I Love You." We had only done about three songs when one of the MP's gave us the signal that it was time to go. "Thanks, everyone," I blurted into the mike. And then the three of us ran off the stage.

The MP's had a big truck waiting for us by the stage door. "Don't worry," our MP said. "It's bulletproof." And he wasn't joking. When we drove back around the front of the place, we could see a whole battalion of MP's arriving to break up the mob with riot shields, night sticks, and machine guns. I was still too scared to speak, but Nedra finally made us all laugh when she glanced out the window and said, "And we thought the Apollo was tough."

Germany turned out to be the Ronettes' last tour. We never made any big plan to split up, but after we got back to the U.S., it just seemed like the natural thing to do. Phil hadn't recorded us in months, and the other two Ronettes were getting sick of waiting for him. Nedra made plans to marry Scott Ross and start her own family as soon as we got back from Germany, and Estelle was just as anxious to settle down with her boyfriend, Joe Dong.

Phil and I weren't married yet, but by the start of 1967 I was spending more time at the mansion than I was at home in New York. My mother still thought I was living in hotel rooms when I went out to California—or at least that's what I told her. And she never questioned it. But I knew she wasn't stupid—it was just a matter of time before she stopped looking the other way.

I mentioned it to Phil one night after dinner. We were sitting in the kitchen, which is where we usually ate. "I can't remember the last time I talked to my mom," I said.

"So?" he said. "Pick up the phone and call her."

"I'm afraid to," I explained. "Because if I do that, she'll ask me where I'm staying. And I can't lie to her anymore. But if I tell her the truth, I don't think she'll like it."

"Don't worry," Phil told me, picking up the phone in the pantry. "All you have to do is to tell her we got married last weekend."

"You don't know my mother, Phil. She'd *never* believe that story."

"Well, then," he said, dialing my mother's number, "we'll have to convince her." When my mother answered, Phil said a quick hello and then tried to pass the phone off to me. "Go on," he whispered, holding his hand over the receiver. "Tell her." But I wouldn't touch that phone.

"I can't," I told him.

"Okay." he said. "If you won't tell her, I will." He turned and spoke directly into the phone. "I've got some great news, Mrs. Bennett. Your daughter and I were married last week."

There was a long pause, and I knew she didn't buy it for a second. She started asking him all kinds of questions, and the more answers he gave, the more incredible his story grew. "The service was performed by two practicing rabbis," he said. "There were no witnesses. That's right. It was an obscure Hebraic ceremony. Very ancient."

After hearing that, my mother insisted that Phil put me on the line. "Hi, Mom," I said, trying to sound cheerful.

"What is this story Phil's tellin' me about two ancient Hebrews?" she asked.

I didn't want to lie to my mother, but it was all so weird. Here I was, standing in the pantry with Phil on my left side and a big jar of mayonnaise on the other, and my mother talking in my ear. I didn't know what else to do, so I finally just told her, "It's true, Mom. Phil and I really did get married last week."

"You did, did you?" she said. "Well, I guess I'm gonna have to come out there myself to see about this marriage. And you better hope it is for real, because if it's not, I'm going to carry you right on back to New York. I didn't raise no daughter of mine to live with no man."

It was obvious she hadn't believed a word of it, but Phil just stood there smiling like a clown when I hung up the phone. "I don't see what's so funny, Phil. She's coming out here to check on us."

"I know," he said. "And I'm going to pay for her ticket. First class. And I'll have my limo pick her up. And I'll have him drive her straight to this twenty-three-room mansion. Once she gets a good look at this place, she won't ask any more questions."

"Not my mother," I insisted. "When she finds out we're not married, she'll kill you and me both."

But it was all a big game to Phil. "Okay then, let's make it a bet. A hundred dollars says that when your mother sees the way you're living, she won't give a shit whether we're married or not." I took the bet. And that's where we let it sit until my mother flew out the next weekend.

I could tell Mom was going to be trouble the minute she climbed out of the limousine. She didn't wait for George Brand to open her door, she just shot out of that car and walked straight into the house. The first thing she said to me was, "Where's the ring?" She only had to look in my eyes to know that I'd been lying the whole time.

Just then Phil walked down the stairs. "Hello, Mrs. Bennett," he said.

"I don't see no ring on my daughter's finger, Phil."

"We're having one specially designed," he started to say, but she was no longer listening.

"Take me to your closet, Ronnie."

I didn't know what she had on her mind, but I knew better than to argue. We walked up to my room while Phil waited downstairs. When we got to the closet, Mom slid the door open, took one look inside, and then slammed it shut.

"These are the same clothes you brought out here from New York. If you're supposed to be married to this man, how come he hasn't bought you one single new dress?" I started to make up an explanation, but she cut me off. "Don't even bother, Ronnie. You're not married to this man and I know it." Then she grabbed my wrist and pulled me back downstairs. I don't think I ever saw her so mad. "Come on, girl," she said. "I'm carrying you home."

Even Phil was surprised when he saw my mother pulling me back down the stairs. He tried to speak up, but she wasn't listening. "You ain't got no right!" she told him. "You ain't got no right to keep my daughter in this house."

"But we're married—" he argued.

"Stop your damn lying, Phil," she said. By this time she'd let go of my wrist and was standing right in Phil's face. "No two Hebrews married you and Ronnie. You just using her and you know you're not supposed to do that! Now get out of my way, because I'm carrying my daughter out of here tonight!"

"What about her clothes?" Phil asked, trying anything to stop her.

"Throw them out the fucking window," my mother said. I was shocked. This is a woman who almost never swore. Then she turned to me. "Go upstairs and get whatever clothes you need, because I'm calling a taxi right now."

I was so scared I did exactly what she said. I tried to get dressed for the plane ride, but I was shaking so hard I almost couldn't get my dress off the hanger. When I got back downstairs, my mother was still shouting at Phil.

"Why you got her out here, anyway?" she said. "You ain't making no records with her."

"We've been rehearsing," Phil said.

"Rehearsing? For three months?" Then she stopped shouting long enough to give Phil the eye. "Don't bullshit me, mister. I know better."

When Mom saw me coming down the stairs, she reached up and grabbed my arm and started pulling me to the door. "Let's go, Ronnie."

I looked back at Phil, who was standing by the stairs with his face all twisted and desperate. "Ronnie!" he called out. "Don't go."

I hated to leave him like that, but I knew there wasn't any other way. This was my mother, and I had to go with her. Besides, I knew that no matter how hurt Phil acted, this kind of scene appealed to his sense of drama. That's why I knew he wouldn't give up, even after the taxicab pulled up the driveway. And he didn't. As my mother dragged me out to the taxi, Phil ran right ahead and tried to intercept us. When Mom refused to stop, he finally reached into his pocket and pulled out a thick stack of five-hundred-dollar bills. "I've got money, Mrs. Bennett!" he said, tossing the bills around her feet. "Take it. It's all yours. Just leave my wife here!"

Mom stepped right over those five-hundred-dollar bills and got in the cab. She'd known Phil long enough to spot one of his stunts, and she wasn't so impressed by this one. But Phil had gone too far to stop now. He dropped down on his knees and kneeled in the pile of money, crying, "Leave me my wife! Take the money, just leave me my wife!"

"Take us to the airport," she told the cabbie. As we headed down the driveway, Mom stared straight ahead and ignored Phil's pitiful crying. I was still trembling when I peeked back through the rear window and caught a glimpse of Phil carefully gathering up his money before it started blowing all over the yard. Mom didn't say another word until after we landed in New York. And neither did I.

I didn't really want to leave Phil, but I could see my mother's point. The way things were going, he might never marry me. I knew he loved me, but after the way his first marriage turned out, I don't think he was anxious to go through another one. So he was sitting on the fence. By taking me away, my mother was telling Phil to get off the fence or give me up.

"Phil must've called here a hundred times," Estelle told us when we walked into our apartment in New York. "He said he's flying right out to get you back."

Mom knew he'd do it, too. So she decided to hide me out at different relatives' houses all over Harlem. I'd stay for three days with a cousin here and two nights with an aunt there. The plan was to keep me hopping so Phil wouldn't ever be able to track me down. But after a few days of that I started to go crazy. I was used to living in a twenty-three-room mansion in Beverly Hills, and now all of a sudden I was sleeping on couches in a different little apartment every night. It was like spending a vacation in hell.

There wasn't a thing to do at any of these places I stayed. I didn't have that much to do in California, either. But having nothing to do in Beverly Hills is a far cry from having nothing to do in Spanish Harlem. That's the first time I realized how much I really depended on Phil. Now that he wasn't around, I didn't see any purpose in anything. I'd spend my day sitting around an aunt's house watching soap operas and "Let's Make a Deal" on TV. A lot of my cousins and other relatives were drinkers, so after a while I even started drinking with them.

It was strange at first. My cousin Diane was pouring shots from a great big bottle of gin, and she asked me if I wanted one. I was so bored sitting around the house that I said, "Why not?" I'd always wondered what alcohol was like, and this seemed like a good time to try it out. So I took a drink.

It was stronger than I ever imagined, and it made my mouth burn. I hated the taste. But I found that after I drank a whole glass of gin, I felt a little better about sitting around and waiting for nothing. After two glasses I actually started to enjoy watching "All My Children." And four glasses made me go to sleep, which was best of all.

Once I started drinking, I completely stopped caring about how I looked. I wore the same clothes day after day, and I didn't even bother combing my hair anymore. None of my relatives even noticed. They treated me like a freak to begin with—I was their odd little relative from Beverly Hills. All they wanted to do was brag about how they were helping me snag my millionaire by hiding me out until he married me. Not once did anyone ever talk about Phil without mentioning money in the same breath.

Mom and Estelle weren't much better. The Ronettes weren't bringing in any income anymore, so I was the family's last chance. "I sure hope Phil comes to his senses and starts you singing again," Mom told me one day. "That, or marries you. But if he don't do one or the other, we're going to have to get rid of this nice big apartment." It was the first time I realized how important money had become in my relationship with my family.

Things were getting so bad with my relatives that I thanked God when Phil finally showed up to rescue me. He came to Spanish Harlem in the back of a long black limousine. He stopped at my mom's apartment on Eighty-ninth and Riverside first, but when he didn't find me there, he drove out to my old neighborhood and parked in front of my aunt Hermean's house. As soon as he pulled up, every kid in the neighborhood came running out to the curb to take a peek at his car. Phil rolled down the window when he recognized my cousin Ira, who was the same kid who sang with us when we did amateur night at the Apollo Theatre, except now he was about nineteen years old.

"Come here, Ira," Phil said. "I'm trying to find Ronnie."

"I'm not supposed to tell you where she is," Ira told him.

"But I know Ronnie would want to see me," he said. "I've been in an accident." Then he swung the door open and pointed to his leg, which was covered in a cast that stretched from his knee down to his toes. "I'm in a lot of pain, and I really need to see her. Please."

Ira finally gave in. I was asleep on my cousin Elaine's bed when he brought Phil to the door. My aunt Hermean refused to let Phil in the house, but I could hear him shouting all the way in the bedroom.

"Ronnie!" he called. "Are you in there?"

I stumbled out of the bedroom, not sure if I was dreaming or awake. But when I saw Phil standing there at the doorway, I sure hoped he was real. I felt like a complete wreck in my wrinkled shirt, with my hair going out every which way. But Phil gawked at me like I was Jackie Kennedy. "Oh, baby," he said. "I've missed you." In that moment, I fell in love all over again.

I was running over to hug him when I noticed the cast on his leg. "Phil," I gasped. "What happened to you?"

"I had an accident, Ronnie," he said. "I nearly killed myself in the car." I looked at Phil, standing there with his cane and bandages, and I suddenly realized how fragile he was.

I walked him over to the living room couch and put my arms around his neck. "Oh, Phil," I told him. "I'm so sorry. I'll never leave you again. Never."

That night I stayed with Phil at the Navarro Hotel, which is where he always stayed now that he no longer had an apartment in New York. I took the longest bubble bath of my life that night. As I shaved my legs and washed my hair and made myself beautiful, I thought of how nice it was to be clean again. The last three weeks never happened, I decided; they were nothing but a bad dream. When I unpacked my travel bag, I found one of the half-empty gin bottles that had helped get me through my ordeal. That was one souvenir I didn't need to keep. I threw it under the bed and hoped the maid would take it away in the morning.

I wanted to see my mom one more time before I left, so I had Phil stop at her house the next morning on our way out to the airport. "I'll just be a minute," I told Phil, and he waited in the car with George Brand.

Mom was in the kitchen scrambling some eggs when I walked in. "I just came back to say good-bye," I announced. She looked up, but she didn't seem very surprised to see me.

"Umm-hmm," she said. "I just hope that man plans to marry you."

"Oh, he does, Mom," I told her. "I'm sure of it."

"Well. All right," she said, softly. "You all grown now, I guess you know what you want." She didn't say anything else, so I just stood there watching as she picked up a fork and stirred the eggs that were cooking in the skillet. I'd seen her do that a thousand times since I was a little girl, but for some reason, this time it made me cry.

"Oh, Mom," I said, trying to hold back the tears. But I couldn't stop them from coming, so I just let loose. I reached over and hugged her, wiping my runny nose on her shoulder, hoping she wouldn't notice, but knowing she wouldn't care if she did. "I love you, Mom."

She held on to me for a long time before she said, "Okay, Ronnie. You go on now. Phil's not going to wait forever down there." Then she turned and went back to her eggs.

"G'bye, Mom," I said. And then I closed the door.

12

In the Dark

$\mathcal{T}$he one thing I never understood about Phil is how a man who loved California as much as he did could be so afraid of the sun. He hated it. He liked to keep his house dark and gloomy, and you couldn't get any light in there no matter what you did. If you opened a window, one of his servants would come by five minutes later and close it. Phil had his help very well trained.

I got along with most of the people who worked in the mansion. But George Johnson, the cook, was my favorite. He was a big, sweet black man. One of his eyes was crooked, so he always looked at you with his head tilted over to one side. Phil kept George jumping in that kitchen, but he was never too busy for a kind word or a story. And he had some tales you wouldn't believe.

George Johnson had once been Humphrey Bogart's personal cook, and he loved telling stories about old Hollywood almost as much as I loved hearing them. I'd sit there drinking my morning coffee while George told me all about Lauren Bacall and Dick Powell, and a lot of other people I knew only from the late, late show.

Phil didn't drink coffee, so he'd usually be upstairs during all this. But one morning George was in the middle of a story about Humphrey Bogart when I caught Phil eavesdropping on us. "Phil," I said after I saw him standing in the hall with his ear to the door. "What are you doing out there?"

"Just listening," he said. I could tell he was in some kind of mood, but he didn't say anything else. He just walked into the kitchen for breakfast. I didn't understand how upset he really was until the next morning, when George refused to tell me any new stories.

"I got no more stories, Miss Veronica," he told me. It was obvious that Phil had forbidden him from talking to me so much. But I couldn't figure out why Phil even cared.

"What's wrong, George?" I asked. "I love your stories."

He didn't say a word until he walked over to the sink and turned both faucets on full blast so no one would hear him. Then he leaned over and whispered, "Some people don't like other people to hear stories that have too much happiness in them."

I nodded my head as George walked back to the sink to turn the faucets off. He may have had one bad eye, but sometimes I think George Johnson could see things better than anyone in that house.

George actually did play lookout for me from time to time. Phil hated to see me spend money on clothes, but every so often I'd sneak out with my credit cards and buy myself a new blouse or some nice underwear. Then George would help me sneak the stuff in through the servants' entrance. We had a whole system of signals worked out.

George would stand watch at the kitchen window whenever I drove up with packages. If Phil was around, George would close the curtains and I'd stay in the car and hide the packages under the seat. But if it was all clear, he'd pull the shade up and I'd make a run for it.

As much as Phil hated to spend money on clothes, he loved it when I found a bargain. I once picked up a great double-breasted woman's pants suit for $16.95 on sale at Orbach's. It was very sixties, with a frilly Edwardian collar, and I modeled it for Phil as soon as I got home. He loved it, especially when I told him the price.

"Wow," he said. "You've got to go back and get one for me."

"But, Phil," I explained. "You can't wear this. It's a woman's suit."

"For sixteen ninety-five, I'll take my chances," he said. "Go back to Orbach's and get another one. On me, everyone'll think it cost five hundred bucks."

I did go back to Orbach's, and I bought a second suit for Phil that was just like mine. And at the end of the year we sent out a Christmas card with our picture on it. George Brand posed as Santa Claus, and Phil and I stood on either side of him wearing matching Edwardian suits—the same suits I picked up at Orbach's for $16.95 each!

I didn't question Phil when he first started building the walls that would keep me a prisoner in his house—I didn't even realize he was doing it until it was too late. That's why I didn't think too much about it when Phil installed an intercom between our bedroom and his study. I knew that was his way of trying to keep an eye on me, but I didn't think it was any big thing. I figured Phil's possessiveness was just his way of letting me know that he loved me, so I let him play his little games.

Unfortunately, once you give up a little bit of your independence to someone, it's hard to draw the line later. I learned that lesson the first time I failed to answer when Phil buzzed me. I was running water in my bathroom, and I couldn't hear the intercom from in there. I was already soaking in the tub when Phil burst in shouting.

"Why didn't you answer the intercom?"

"I didn't hear it, Phil," I told him. "The water was on."

"Oh," he said, as he finally noticed that I was naked and up to my shoulders in a bubble bath. "Okay," he muttered, and walked back to his study. A few days later the workmen came and installed an intercom box in every room of the mansion, including the bathrooms.

By the beginning of 1968, Phil almost never left the house anymore. And the more reclusive he became, the more reclusive I became. Most of Phil's friends were in the music business, but now that we weren't making records anymore, we didn't even see them. The only girlfriend I had was a lady named Bobbie Golson, who was married to a jazz musician named Benny Golson. I always liked hanging around with

Bobbie because she had a little daughter I used to play with all the time.

The only other woman I ever saw was Phil's secretary, Gloria Dimino. After Phil stopped going into his office on Sunset Boulevard, Gloria became his only real contact with the outside world. She'd drive up from the office every afternoon with messages, contracts, or checks for him to sign. I'd never been to his office, but I was always curious about what went on down there. One day Gloria offered to sneak me in for a little peek, and what I saw made my eyes bug out.

Gloria and I were driving back from a little shopping trip when we drove past Phil Spector Productions at 9130 Sunset. I happened to mention that I'd never been inside, and Gloria was shocked. "Why on earth not?" she asked. "Phil shouldn't have anything to hide from you."

"Yeah, but you know Phil," I answered. "He likes his privacy."

Then Gloria got a real mischievous look in her eye, and she pulled into a parking spot. "Well, if you want to take a look now," she said, swinging her key ring in front of my nose, "let's go."

It was already after six o'clock, but she still walked into the offices first, just to make sure no one was around. Then she came to the front door and waved me through. "C'mon," she giggled. "The coast is clear."

Then Gloria went into her office to do some work and left me to wander around on my own. I walked past the reception area and flipped on the light in Phil's private office. One look at the place and I knew instantly why Phil had never let me in there. I gazed around his office in absolute amazement. Every square inch of wall in that room was completely plastered with *pictures of me!*

There were tiny little black-and-white snapshots and big, poster-sized blowups that stretched from floor to ceiling. There were shots of me sleeping, shots of me laughing, even shots of me eating. I saw pictures of me alone, pictures of me with the Ronettes, and a few that had me and Phil together. I was really flattered, of course. But I couldn't help thinking how sad it all seemed. It was like some kind of bizarre shrine.

I stood there looking at the girl in those pictures, and it seemed like they were taken a lifetime ago. What ever happened to that happy, energetic little girl who spent all her time singing and having fun? I sure wasn't her. It was like she had died, and standing in her place was me—a rich, bored, Beverly Hills housewife. And I wasn't even that, legally.

It was all so depressing that I finally just started sobbing. I cried so loud that Gloria came running in to see what was wrong. But one look at me standing there in front of these pictures from all my past lives, and Gloria didn't have to ask. She just plumped down on a chair, and I climbed over and sat on her lap like a little kid. Then I cried like a baby for about a half hour. It felt great.

When Gloria finally dropped me off at the mansion that night, I walked into the hallway—dark, as always—and felt so lonely I almost started crying all over again. Phil didn't meet me at the door, but I knew he was home, because I could hear the sound of opera music echoing down from behind the locked door of his study. It was Wagner's "Ride of the Valkyries," which he loved to play. I heard that spooky "Da-da-da-DA-DA," and it made perfect background music as I walked up those creaky stairs to our bedroom. Something told me I wouldn't get to sleep for a long time. And I was right.

I crumbled two Sominex into a glass of Coca-Cola, but even that didn't work fast enough. I closed my eyes to hurry the sleep along, but every time I did that I'd see those pictures of me singing and having fun, and I'd be wide awake again. Then I'd look up and see Lenny Bruce staring down at me, and I'd start to cry all over again.

After about an hour Phil turned off the music and came to bed. He'd already taken off his toupee, so it was dark when he climbed in next to me and started rubbing my shoulders. I was in no mood to have sex, so I stiffened my body and refused to give in. That confused the hell out of him, and he tossed himself back on his side of the bed in exaggerated frustration.

We lay there for a good two or three minutes before I got up the nerve to speak. I had a feeling it was now or never for me, so I just spoke right up. "Phil," I said. "I want to go back to New York."

"What for?" he said, getting annoyed. "I thought we scheduled your trip home for next month."

"I'm not talking about a visit. I mean to stay. I miss my family." I spoke with such determination that I think I surprised him. I must have caught him off guard, because he didn't once try to interrupt me.

"I love you, Phil," I continued. "You know I do. But I can't keep on going like this. I'm a family girl. I love people and kids and noise. But everything's always so quiet here, sometimes I get so lonely I feel like I'm gonna crack up. I need that noise, Phil. I need to be part of a family."

Phil was quiet after that, and I didn't push him. He finally just turned over, and a few minutes later I could tell that he'd fallen asleep. But even that didn't bother me. I had gotten the last word with Phil Spector, and that didn't happen very often.

The next day was hell. Phil got up and went straight into that damn study. I was sure he was really pissed off at me this time, and I lost my nerve completely. I just knew Phil would want nothing else to do with me, and that put me into a real panic. I started worrying that he might call my bluff and ship me back to my family. And what would I do then? By this time, I hadn't recorded or released a record in almost two years. I had no career left. All I had was Phil. And the thought of losing him only made me want to hold on to him more than anything else in the world.

I sat down at the top of the stairs and waited for him to come out of the study. I was ready to apologize and promise that I would never ever leave him if only he'd take me back. Finally, after what seemed like hours, Phil opened his door and saw me sitting there like a little puppy by the stairs. "What time is it in New York?" he asked.

I knew it was about two in the afternoon, three hours earlier than it was in New York. "Around five, why?"

"You think your mother's home?"

"I guess. Why?"

He walked toward the kitchen. "Let's give her a call. I want to invite her out here for the wedding."

"Whose wedding?" I asked like I didn't know what he was talking about. But my heart was pounding so loud in my chest that I'll bet George heard it in the kitchen. It's funny how quickly your feelings can change. A day before—hell, *five minutes* before—I had just about given up all hope. But that was before I heard Phil say five words that would change my entire life.

"Our wedding. Yours and mine."

13

Honeymoon

Phil had finally come around, and I was ecstatic. I was convinced that everything would be different once we became a real family, and I had a whole fantasy worked out about how great our new life was going to be. First off, I'd be a star again. Phil would be so inspired by married life that he'd climb right out of his rut and write half a dozen new songs for me, and every one would be an even bigger hit than "Be My Baby."

Once we got back on top, we'd be the king and queen of rock and roll, and our life would be one never-ending party. Elvis and the Beatles and all the stars from the late, late show would drop by the mansion just to be around us. And Phil would never be jealous when John Lennon or Mick Jagger walked in, because he would know that I was his wife now, pledged only to him forever and ever.

And even after the guests all went home, our mansion would still ring out with the laughter of our little children—two girls and a boy. Maybe more. In my fantasy marriage, I'd have the greatest little family to love me and play with me and keep me from ever getting lonely again. That was my fantasy.

The reality wasn't quite so good. It never is, of course. After the honeymoon ends, most married people discover they have to settle for less than their dreams. But I didn't even have to wait for the honeymoon to end. Things were already getting weird for me a week *before* the wedding.

Phil and I planned to get married in a small ceremony in Beverly Hills on April 14, 1968. But ten days before that date, Martin Luther King was shot in Memphis, and that was the last anyone saw of Phil until a few days before the wedding.

Phil always had this great love of black people. He always used black singers on his records, and he loved any kind of music that was black, from blues and jazz to gospel. Sometimes I think he wished he was black.

When Phil heard that Dr. King had been shot, he took it worse than anybody I know. He went straight into his study and locked the door behind him. And he stayed in there, locked away with a record of Martin Luther King's speeches, which he played over and over as loud as he could. For days on end Martin Luther King blasted away behind that door. I heard "I have a dream" so much I thought I was losing my mind.

After a few days of this, I started to wonder how long Phil could carry on. But as strange as Phil's moods could get, they usually floated away as quickly as they came. So I waited it out. And sure enough, three days before the wedding, Phil walked out of his study as calm as could be.

My mother finally arrived the day before the wedding. There was a little one-bedroom guest apartment downstairs in the mansion, and I'd spent the last few days before Mom arrived decorating it for her. I talked to her on the phone every week, but I hadn't seen her since the day I left New York with Phil, and I missed her a lot. When she finally showed up, I almost knocked her off her feet. "Mom," I cried out. "I'm so glad to see you!"

And I was. Having my mom around brought me back to happier times. I'd always had a strong bond with her, but I don't think I ever realized how strong until the week of my wedding. And after she got settled into her little apartment downstairs, I came right out and told her so. "Mom," I said, "sometimes I miss you so much I don't even understand it."

"That's only natural, Ronnie," she replied. "No matter how growned you get, you don't never outgrow your mother."

"What about after I'm married?"

"Your husband, he can love you, too," she explained. "But not more than your family. Family love is forever love. I'm always gonna stay by you, I can promise that." In the years to come, there were days when I would wonder if that was a blessing or a curse. But Mom kept that promise, right up to this day.

After our little talk, I tried to give Mom a hug. But she's never been too big on physical affection, so she pulled away after a few seconds. "Okay, now, Ronnie," she said, smiling. "I know you're happy, but you ain't got to break me in two."

Phil and I spent the rest of the day before my wedding taking care of all the paperwork downtown at the Beverly Hills City Hall. When we finished all that, he took me out for a big dinner at Chasen's. The food looked great, but I was so excited I didn't even touch my plate. I'd had butterflies in my stomach all day, but now, for some reason, they were turning into the worst stomachache I'd ever had.

Phil got pretty concerned, naturally. "There's nothing wrong, is there?"

"Oh, no," I explained. "I'm just so nervous. I think I have a little stomachache, that's all."

Poor Phil looked brokenhearted. "You're not having second thoughts about tomorrow?" I could see that he was as much of a wreck as I was, so I gave him a big kiss.

"No second thoughts," I reassured him. "I just can't quite believe it's really happening."

"Yeah," he said, looking a little surprised himself. "Me, either."

Then he did the most romantic thing. He reached under the table like a shy teenager and grabbed my hand. It was such a sweet thing to do, I almost forgot my stomach cramps. I sat there like that for a long time, clutching my aching stomach with one hand, and holding his hand with the other. And all the while I was dreaming about how great my life was going to be as Mrs. Phil Spector.

We got married the next day, but the ceremony was nothing special. At about four o'clock that afternoon Max pulled the car around to drive us down to the city hall for the ceremony. Max was another one of Phil's drivers—when Phil played a drug pusher in *Easy Rider* about a year later, that was Max driving the Rolls. Phil joked around with Max a lot, so much that I was never really sure whether they were kidding or not. And my wedding day was no exception.

"So, who's going to be the best man?" Max asked as we climbed into the back of the Rolls.

"I dunno," Phil answered. "Why don't you do it?"

"Naw," he said. "I've got to keep my eye on the car. Maybe George Johnson?"

"No," Phil said, thinking. "I already gave him the day off. What about your brother, Serge? What's he doing today?"

"I'm not sure," Max replied. "Want me to swing by his house on the way to the wedding?"

My mother and I couldn't believe it. Phil and his chauffeur were picking the best man for our wedding the way kids choose up sides for a stickball game. My mother was speechless—she just sat there looking at Phil like he was from another planet. Finally, he broke down and started laughing.

"Gotcha, Mrs. Bennett," Phil said. "We really had you going, didn't we?"

"You sure did," she admitted. "But tell me, who *is* going to be best man at this wedding?"

"Oh, Serge is," Phil said. "That wasn't a joke. We were only kidding when we said we were going to drop in and surprise him. He's actually known about this since . . ." Phil turned to Max. "When was it we told him?"

Max could barely keep from giggling as he steered the Rolls out into traffic. "Yesterday."

"Yesterday," Phil repeated to Mom. Then he and Max both started cracking up. I finally broke down and started laughing, too, but my mother never did see the humor. She just shook her head and looked out the window as we drove into Hollywood to pick up my chauffeur's brother and his wife, Terry, who together would be the best man and matron of honor at my wedding.

I hardly remember the ceremony itself. It was held in an office in the Beverly Hills City Hall, which Phil had somehow convinced them to open up for us on a Sunday. A justice of the peace married us, but I don't remember much else about it except that when we were supposed to say "I do," we did, and after that we really were man and wife.

We celebrated our wedding night at a Mahalia Jackson concert. Guess whose idea that was? Phil bought tickets for the entire wedding party, and he was in heaven the whole time. I couldn't stand it. I'm not saying I have anything against Mahalia Jackson, it's just that there are a lot of other things I would rather have been doing on my wedding night than sitting at a gospel show with my mother, our chauffeur, and his family. But I decided not to make a big deal out of it, especially since Phil seemed to be having such a good time.

But something mysterious happened to Phil's high spirits as soon as we left the show. We were walking out to the parking lot when I noticed how quiet he'd become, like there was something weighing heavy on his mind.

When we got to the Rolls, Phil asked me if I would take my mom home without him. "I'm going to have Serge drive me over to my mother's house." I felt like I'd just been stung by a bee. Here it was my wedding night, and my husband was on his way to his *mother's* house.

"Oh, Phil," I asked him. "Why's it so important for you to go over there tonight?"

"Because," he confessed, "I still haven't told her I got married."

I knew how badly Phil's mother wanted to keep him tied to her, but as of four-thirty that afternoon we were a married couple, and there was nothing she could do about it now. "Hurry home, husband dear," I told him. Then he went off in Serge's car with Max, and I got behind the driver's seat of the Rolls and drove back to the mansion with my mother.

All the way home I kept repeating over and over, "I'm Mrs. Ronnie Spector." As we wound through Beverly Hills, I glanced over and saw my mom smiling, and I knew she was as proud as I was. Then I swung the Rolls onto La Collina Drive and up to the house that now belonged to Mr. and Mrs. Phil Spector.

When we got in the house, I kissed my mother good night and went up to my bedroom to get ready for my wedding night. I was usually pretty modest in bed. I'd always put my shirt and underpants back on after Phil and I had sex. It was a habit I picked up when we were little and our mother made us wear underwear to bed in case one of the uncles peeked in to check on us late at night.

But there would be no underpants and a T-shirt tonight. For

my wedding night, I put on a sheer nightgown that I'd bought especially for this occasion. Very sexy. I was so anxious to see Phil's reaction, I didn't think I could wait. But I did anyway.

It was over two hours before Phil came back from his mother's house, slamming the door behind him. By this time I'd been with Phil so long that I could tell his exact mood just by how hard he slammed the door when he came in. And judging by the sound of this one, I got a feeling we weren't going to be having sex that night.

I was right. When he walked into our room, I could tell that the last thing he was interested in was my body. He was a completely different person than the man I had sat with at the concert three hours earlier.

"You *bitch!*" he shouted. I couldn't believe how mad he looked, worse than I'd ever seen him. He was raving so loud that the veins in his neck were bulging blue.

"I know your game, Veronica," he shouted. "You just want my money. That is it, isn't it?"

I was so scared that I got up and ran out of the bedroom and into the hallway. If Phil was going to kill me, I wanted him to do it where there might be witnesses. "What's wrong, Phil? What did your mother tell you?"

"The truth," he panted. "That this whole marriage is about one thing—my money!" He was so mad he could hardly catch his breath now. Scared as I was, I couldn't help staring at this one vein that kept bulging out of his forehead. "Everyone told me to have a prenuptial agreement drawn up—but I didn't! And do you know why?"

"No, Phil, why?" I was completely lost. I had no idea what a prenuptial agreement even was.

"Because I'm a romantic!" he cried. By now he was pacing up and down the hallway, running out of steam. He finally plopped down in one of the antique French armchairs that no one ever sat in. "A hopeless fucking romantic!"

After that last outburst he just slumped over like he was dead. I was hugging the opposite wall like a girl in one of those vampire movies. Then I saw my mother standing at the other end of the hall with her arms crossed on her chest, nodding her head like a stern schoolteacher.

I gasped and ran over to her. When Phil caught sight of my mother, his head popped up like a squirrel's and he jumped up from his chair and ran into his study, slamming the door behind him, of course. Mom just shook her head and looked over to me. "We better go downstairs. I think that boy's on dope."

I disagreed with my mom on that point, and after we ran into her guest apartment and locked the door behind us, I told her so. "I'd know if Phil was on dope," I said. "Wouldn't I?"

"Not if he's taking cocaine. When someone uses that stuff, you can't see it or smell it." I was amazed at how much my mother knew about these substances, and I wanted to ask her more. But my lesson in drug abuse got cut short a few seconds later when Phil came down and started banging on her door.

"Open up, Mrs. Bennett!" he called out.

"Not until you start acting like a grown man, Phil," she answered.

"To hell with you!" he shouted. And he was gone.

Mom and I moved over to the couch, and that's when I suddenly realized that I was still wearing nothing but my see-through nightgown. I was embarrassed to have my mother see me that way, so I crossed my arms to cover my breasts. We stayed on the couch for a few minutes while I tried to catch my breath. But just as I started to relax, we heard the jangling of keys outside the door.

"Keys!" I shrieked. "Phil's got keys!"

Thank God he had to try a few of them before he found the right ones, because that gave us time to lock ourselves in the bathroom. But even in there, we could still hear Phil outside the front door, cursing every time he tried another wrong key. He must've finally found the right one, because a few seconds later we heard him shouting through the bathroom door from inside the apartment.

"Cut the shit, Mrs. Bennett—you've got my wife in there. And I have a right to see her."

"She was my daughter before she was your wife," Mom yelled back. "So you ain't got no rights."

He didn't say anything else. Instead, he started pounding on the door in a steady rhythm.

Wham. Wham. Wham.

I guess he thought it would wear us down, but it didn't. My mother just sat calmly on the toilet seat while I lay shaking on the floor, scared to death of what might happen if that door ever opened.

Phil had stopped yelling, but it wasn't the shouting that had scared me. I'd heard him shout like that a thousand times. But I'd never seen him looking quite so mad, with saliva dripping down the side of his mouth and his eyes bulging out like a wild coyote's. He looked like someone you'd see in a movie about insane people. And it was scaring the shit out of me.

I was just glad there was a carpet in that bathroom, because I had a feeling we were going to be spending the night. And I was right. My mother and I had been lying on that pale blue carpet for over an hour when Phil finally wore himself out and went to bed. After that, we got kind of drowsy ourselves. I was just drifting off to sleep when I heard my mother sigh, "Ronnie, Ronnie, Ronnie. What did you marry?"

I moved in close to her and started to cry. "Isn't this something?" I sniffed. "Here it is my wedding night, and I'm spending it curled up on the bathroom floor with my mother."

Saying it out loud like that made it seem more ridiculous than scary, and I couldn't keep myself from laughing. When Mom heard me cracking up, she couldn't keep a straight face, either. So we lay there all night, giggling on the bathroom floor until sleep finally came and carried us away to morning.

14

Inflatable Man

The morning after my wedding night, I woke up to the sound of a pile driver in the front yard. It was like coming back from a bad dream. I was lying on my mother's bathroom floor, my back felt like a pretzel, and I couldn't even remember why I was there. That's when I heard the construction crew banging away outside the window. I looked around for my mother, but she was already up.

The clanging outside was getting louder and louder, so I walked over to the window and peeked through the curtains. That's when I saw about a half dozen men putting up these big ten-foot poles all around the edges of the yard. I couldn't figure out what they were doing—I was so groggy I thought maybe they were putting up basketball hoops.

Then I glanced over to their truck, were I saw six other guys unrolling about a hundred yards of barbed wire and chain link. They were obviously building some kind of fence, but I didn't know why.

I was still trying to figure it out when I noticed that some of the guys had caught sight of me standing in the window, still wearing my skimpy negligee from the night before. I jumped back and closed the curtain. Then I grabbed my mother's robe and headed upstairs to my bedroom, praying that Phil wouldn't be in there.

I didn't have to worry—no one was in the room. But there were a dozen red roses on my pillow. I picked up the card and read an apology written in Phil's scratchy handwriting.

Forever yours,
Okay?—Phil

I sat down on the edge of the bed and breathed a sigh of relief. "Thank God, the nightmare's over." I guess I should have still been mad, but I wasn't.

By the time I got down to the kitchen, George Johnson was already fixing breakfast for Phil and my mom. Phil got up and pulled my chair out for me, like I was his little queen. It was crazy. Here he was acting like a perfect gentleman, when only a few hours earlier he had been raving like a maniac. But what's even crazier is how willing I was to forgive and forget.

The truth is, I didn't hold it against Phil when he went nuts like that. And I still don't. I knew that he only flipped out because of his insecurities, and I figured he hated himself enough without me adding to his troubles. If I could remain his loving and patient wife, I thought, Phil would eventually come around to being a kind and loving husband. At least that was my fantasy. And I was determined to make it come true. I was going to have my Ozzie and Harriet life, even if I had to go through hell to get it.

I had high hopes for my marriage, but I soon discovered that life as a millionaire's wife wasn't all that different from just being shacked up with a millionaire. At least not if that millionaire was Phil Spector.

After the wedding, Phil seemed no more eager to get back to the studio than before. But by that time it almost didn't matter—I'd been away from recording for so long that my confidence was almost completely drained away. I'd always been a little insecure that I didn't have a gospel-trained voice like Patti LaBelle, but after my own husband turned his back on me, I began to wonder if I was ever any good to begin with. Finally, I just grew to accept that I was all washed up.

"Forget about singing," I told myself. "Your voice is not happening. That's done with. Just try to be a good wife. That's your life now."

The trouble was, I didn't know how to be a good wife when there was nothing wifely for me to do. I'd get up in the morning and there'd be a maid there to do up the beds. Then I'd go downstairs and find another maid vacuuming my rugs. There was even a guy who came in twice a week to do the dusting.

I wasn't even welcome in my own kitchen. I found that out the hard way, after I snuck down there late one night to fix myself an egg salad sandwich. George couldn't find his measuring cup the next day, and I caught hell for it. No matter how much I denied touching that measuring cup, Phil wouldn't let up.

"It doesn't matter!" he shouted. "You were in the kitchen, and you shouldn't have been there. I pay George good money to cook for us, so stay the hell out of there and let him do his job."

I looked over at George, hoping he might come to my defense. But he kept right on chopping onions. After Phil left, he looked up and said, "This isn't my argument, Miss Veronica. You know that."

My only household duty was to get up in the morning and discuss with George what Phil and I wanted for dinner. After that, I'd go out to the pool and watch Phil do his laps. I never learned how to swim, so I'd just splash around in the shallow end. Then I'd go back into the house and watch other people do my housework. I felt so bored and useless that after a while I'd just go into the TV room and watch old Bette Davis movies. And those didn't exactly cheer me up.

Bette always seemed to be crying about something. Or getting drunk. After I saw a few of these films, I started to notice that whenever Bette Davis or Joan Crawford got depressed, they always went to the bar and got a drink. After a while I started doing the same thing.

Phil had a liquor cabinet in his downstairs game room. It was hidden away in the wall behind the fireplace, but I discovered it by accident one night while he was out at the pool hall. I was poking around the game room, bored as usual, when I saw this little button hidden away in the back of a thick wooden pillar.

Naturally, I pushed it. Out of nowhere this antique bar swung down like something out of an old mystery movie. And suddenly I'm standing there looking at a half dozen bottles of vodka, scotch, and rye whiskey.

I poured myself a full glass of scotch in a big beaker. No one ever taught me how to drink, so I just treated alcohol like it was soda pop. Of course, it was a lot harder going down than pop, and it didn't taste as good. In fact, I hated the taste of liquor. But I knew that if I drank enough of it I would begin to feel a little light-headed, so I'd hold my nose and down it went.

After I discovered Phil's magic bar, I'd sneak down there and make myself a drink whenever he left me alone at night. Then I'd take it back up to the TV room and sit there, my drink in one hand and a cigarette in the other, just like Bette Davis. If the movie was sad—and they always seemed sad to me, even the comedies—I'd run into the bathroom and cry. Pretty soon I'd pass out and go to sleep. And that was always the best thing about alcohol, that it made me sleep.

Of all the things that seemed to go wrong during that first year of marriage, I think the thing that depressed me worst of all was that I couldn't get pregnant. And I wanted kids more than anything. My fantasy of marriage had always been to have kids, a loving husband, and a great career. After six months of marriage to Phil, I would have been willing to settle for just the kids. But I couldn't even have that. No matter what we did, I just couldn't get pregnant. And we tried everything.

We kept a thermometer near the bed and tried to have sex when my body was at just the right temperature to make a baby. We had sex in all different positions, and at all different times of the day. I even had artificial insemination. I'd take Phil's sperm to the doctor's office and have it injected. But that didn't work either.

I went to ten different doctors. I saw specialists in England and America and Europe, too. And every one said the same thing: "Your body's fine. Just relax and let nature take its course." But when nature didn't take its course, I blamed myself completely. And once I decided it was all my fault, I started putting myself down worse than ever. I couldn't make it as a singer, I was a flop as a wife, and now I find out I'm a failure at being a woman, too! It wasn't long before I began to seriously wonder if maybe I wasn't just a bad person all around.

It never even occurred to me that the problem might have been with Phil. Of course, he never considered going in for an examination himself. The most he ever did was go into the bathroom and jerk off into a jar so I could take it to the doctor for artificial insemination. But none of the doctors ever suggested that it might be a low sperm count on Phil's part. "Just relax," they told me. "You'll have your baby." But I convinced myself they were lying.

The worst part about not being able to have kids was that this was the one area where Phil and I agreed completely. He wanted children as badly as I did. That was all we talked about. I guess we both wanted to start building a family because our careers just weren't happening.

Our lovemaking got a little strained under the pressure to get results, but we kept at it. Up until then we'd always had a pretty good sex life. He sometimes wore a hat to bed because of his hangup about being bald, but other than that, I had no complaints. Even so, good sex or bad, we still couldn't make any babies.

Phil still spent a lot of time alone in his study. There, or downstairs playing pool in his game room. Phil's pool craze began around the time he went into retirement in 1966, but after we got married it turned into a real obsession. He actually started paying big-time pool hustlers like Minnesota Fats and Willie Moscone to come over to the house and play with him. And whenever those big shots came over for one of Phil's all-night tournaments, I'd have to go downstairs so he could show me off.

"This is my wife, Veronica," he'd announce. And then there would be the pictures. "Hey, Fats," Phil would say. "You want to take a picture with my wife? Come on, Veronica, stand over there with Fats." From the way they looked at me, it was obvious that most of these guys thought I was pretty hot stuff. Phil noticed this, too, so he always made sure to pack me up and send me back upstairs as soon as the cameras stopped clicking.

Then he'd follow me upstairs to give me a good-night kiss before he went down to be with his pool friends. I'd just have time to get snuggled up in bed when he'd come walking in with a tray of grilled cheese sandwiches in one hand and my favorite doll in the other. Then he'd set the tray on my bedside table and place the doll gently in my arms. "Good night, darling," he'd say, stroking my cheek with the back of his fingers. "I'll see you in the morning." He'd put on a Tony Bennett or Frank Sinatra record and turn off the lights. Then he'd be gone. Even when he was abandoning me to play pool with a bunch of fat guys, Phil still made me feel like I was the only girl in the world.

The fact is, for Phil I *was* the only girl in the world. And he never let me forget it. I thought he'd be less jealous after we got married, but he actually got worse. I came down to the swimming pool in a bikini once, and Phil practically fell off the diving board.

"Are you crazy?" he asked. "Get back in the house before somebody sees you."

"Oh, Phil," I said, trying not to take him too seriously. "Who's gonna see me in my own yard?"

"The *manservants*," he whispered, as if I was an idiot for not realizing it sooner. So back I went to change my suit.

I never could get used to the life of a recluse. I grew up in New York, where you could always run out to the corner store in rain or sleet or snow. But there are no corner stores in Beverly Hills. Where I lived, you were lucky if you could find a corner. The only time I got out was when Phil let George Brand or one of the other servants drive me over to my friend Bobbie Golson's house, and even then he would have them wait outside in the car so they could bring me back after an hour. I was starting to feel like a prisoner in my own house, and it was beginning to get to me.

Phil must have sensed I was going a little nuts under the strain, because he finally surprised me with a car of my own for my twenty-fifth birthday in 1968. It was a Camaro, orange and white, and I was blown away when I first saw it in the driveway, all wrapped in a huge white ribbon.

A brand-new car! All shiny and new. And it was mine, all mine. And there certainly wasn't any doubt about that, because

Phil had it monogrammed in about twenty-three places. No matter where you looked—on the doors, on the top of the trunk, even on the glove compartment—you couldn't miss the initials *V.S.* for Veronica Spector.

Looking back, it's interesting that he chose those particular initials. Veronica was Phil's name for me. He never called me Ronnie anymore. It was like he saw me as two different people—Ronnie, the happy, sexy rock and roller that I was before the marriage; and Veronica, the obedient Beverly Hills wife that he wanted now.

After Phil went into his early retirement, my rock and roll past became a painful reminder of the accomplishments he could no longer live up to. So he erased Ronnie from his mind. And now, in her place, he was trying to create Veronica, a loyal and quiet wife who would be perfectly happy to waste away with him in the dark corners of his musty old mansion. He may not even have been completely aware of it himself, but Phil was trying to brainwash me every single day of our marriage.

And he was a born expert at mind control. His giving me a monogrammed car is a perfect example. He knew that the only time I would ever really be alone was when I was driving, so he made sure that the car I drove was loaded with little initials that sent a message loud and clear: "You may be alone in your car, but you're not free. You're 'V.S.' now—Mrs. Veronica Spector—and don't you forget it. Little Ronnie Bennett is dead."

It might seem farfetched that anyone would put that much energy into controlling someone else's life, but that was Phil. You've got to remember, the man was a genius. And he had nothing better to do with his life after he retired from rock and roll. So turning me into the perfect wife became his major project, just as making me into a number-one singer had been his goal five years earlier.

Monogramming my car was just the beginning. That was nothing compared to my custom-made inflatable Phil. I got him the same night Phil gave me the car. In fact, I was still gushing over my new Camaro when Phil walked back and popped open the trunk. "There's more," he said. "Wait'll you see this." And in all the years I knew Phil, I don't think I was ever quite as amazed as when he reached into the trunk of my brand-new car and pulled out that life-sized inflatable plastic mannequin.

"What do you think?" he asked, holding it in the air like a giant trophy. I didn't know what to say. The thing was as big as he was, and it was dressed in a pair of his best pants and a freshly ironed shirt. In fact, the thing looked exactly like Phil in every way, except that its knees were bent in a permanent sitting position.

"Well," I said. "It's you, right?" He nodded his head.

"C'mon," he said. "Is it perfect or what?"

"Yeah. It's . . . really . . ." I paused, wracking my brain for the right word. "Perfect. But, Phil. What is it supposed to do?"

"I'll show you," he said. I watched in utter amazement as he walked to the passenger door, opened it, and carefully placed the inflatable Phil in the bucket seat. Then he fastened a seat belt across the guy's lap, straightened its shirt collar, and adjusted the cloth hat that sat on top of the thing's pink plastic head. "There," he said, stepping back. "Oh, wait," he added. "Almost forgot the finishing touch."

Then he ran back over to the inflatable man, pulled out a cigarette, and fitted it into the thing's mouth. Finally, he slammed the door and stood back. "Tah-*daah!*" he said, turning to me with a crooked little smile. "What do you think?"

"It's great, Phil," I said, and I wasn't lying. Sitting there like that, this plastic guy really did look almost real. "But I still don't get it," I said. "Why do I want it to look like there's somebody in the car with me when there isn't?"

"Don't you get it?" he asked in a tone of voice that made me feel like I must've missed something. "It's for when you're driving alone." I still looked completely confused, so he spelled it out for me. "Now nobody will fuck with you when you're driving alone."

So that was it. Phil had actually gone to the trouble of making a dummy of himself to watch over me when he wasn't around. I was wondering if he'd gone insane as I watched him make a few last-minute adjustments in the tilt of the guy's hat. He really was proud of his little masterpiece.

"Phil," I said, giving him a great big kiss. "Sometimes you really are too much."

*　　*　　*

Inflatable man or not, I loved having my own car. With my Camaro, I had complete freedom to drive myself anywhere I pleased. Now all I needed was somewhere to go.

I drove over to my friend Bobbie Golson's house, but that was about it. She was the one girlfriend I had, and I didn't really have any other place to go. I suppose I could've snuck off to the movies or gone out to eat or something. But going to public places alone was something I'd never done, even before I met Phil. As a kid I never went anywhere without my mother or an aunt around to keep an eye on me. And after I left home I always had Phil around, so I never did get into the habit of going off exploring on my own.

My idea of a big adventure was to get behind the wheel of my Camaro and drive around Beverly Hills. And I did that a lot. I'd cruise up and down the tree-lined streets, looking at the houses and wondering where all the people were. Beverly Hills always seemed like a ghost town, because I never saw anybody walking down the street. Sometimes it was so deserted out there that I'd come home feeling even more lonely than when I left.

One time I did run into Cher. I was waiting for a traffic light on Sunset Boulevard with my plastic Phil at my side when I glanced into the limo next to me and saw her. She didn't notice it was me until I honked my horn, but then she was all smiles. "Ronnie!" she screamed. "Pull over!"

We parked our cars at the curb and jumped into each other's arms. I hadn't seen her since she and Sonny left Phil to make their own hit records, and they'd become huge stars in that time.

"I'm so proud of you, Cher," I told her. "Whenever I hear you on the radio I always brag about how you got your start as one of my background singers."

"Oh, God," she said. "I miss those days! Ronnie, can you believe that was only about three years ago?"

"Sometimes it seems like a whole other lifetime."

We traded small talk for a few minutes, and before long we got around to Phil. "How *are* things with you guys?" she wanted to know.

"Oh. You know. Phil's still as crazy as ever," I said. "Crazier, maybe. But I'm still in love with him. So what can I do?"

Cher laughed out loud. "I know what you mean. You just described me and Sonny."

I knew I couldn't stay out too long without Phil getting frantic, and Cher had to get back to Sonny, too. But it was so much fun seeing her again that we sat there talking for more than half an hour. We must've made quite a sight—a pair of twenty-five-year-old rock and roll queens reminiscing on a curb in Beverly Hills.

We finally stood up, exchanged phone numbers, and promised to call each other. But even then I knew it would never happen. Phil made it next to impossible for me to make calls from the house. And if Cher tried to call me, I knew she'd never get through. No one ever did.

So we both got back into our cars and got ready to drive our separate ways. But just before the light changed, Cher turned to look at me one last time. Then she rolled her window down. "Hey, Ronnie!" she yelled. "You take care of yourself, okay?"

There was something in the way she said it that struck me, and all the way home, I couldn't get those words out of my head. "You take care of yourself," she'd said, almost like she was giving me a warning. It turned out to be good advice, maybe the best advice anyone could've given me. Too bad I wasn't ready to take it. Yet.

Except for my drives, about the only other time I left the house was when I'd take a little walk around the grounds. And after Phil turned the yard over to his dogs, I couldn't even do that anymore.

Phil's dog phase started out when he got Grishka, this big Russian wolfhound—you know those dogs with the big, long noses? This was a gigantic thing, and I was scared to death of it. But Phil loved that dog so much he even made poor George Johnson cook dinner for it every night. And this dog didn't eat Alpo—Grishka ate steak.

Of course, whenever Phil liked one of something, it was just a matter of time before he got more of them. And so, a few months after he got Grishka, he brought home these two giant borzois. Then he got a couple of German shepherds, too. Pretty soon our yard looked like a kennel, with five dogs barking and running around at all hours of the day and night.

The only reason Phil even kept these crazy dogs at all was to build up his image. He wanted everyone to see him as this eccentric genius, so whenever a reporter came to interview him at the mansion, he made sure Grishka and the two giant borzois were sitting on the living room sofa. The reporter would take a look at these three skinny dogs and think Phil was a little nuts, and he'd put that in his article. And Phil loved it. He figured everyone already thought he was nuts, so he was damn well going to act the part. The problem was that he got caught up in his own craziness, and after a while even Phil couldn't tell where the act ended and real life began.

Phil wanted to be like Orson Wells in *Citizen Kane*. That was his favorite movie, and he used to show it over and over and over again. There's not that much to do in California after you've planned out what you're having for dinner, so Phil used to set up a projector and we'd watch movies at home. And most of the time the movie was *Citizen Kane*, which is all about a rich man and a girl who wants to sing but doesn't have what it takes.

Watching that film didn't do a whole lot for my self-confidence. I mean, the guy in the movie was so in love with this girl that he buys her coaches and mansions, and he even builds her an opera house of her very own. But after all that, he still can't make her a good singer. Phil would play this film for me night after night, so naturally I began to wonder if he wasn't trying to tell me something.

I started to feel like Susan Alexander, the girl in that movie. When I saw her sitting around her mansion with nothing to do but put together jigsaw puzzles, it gave me a chill. I would cry for that poor girl every time I saw that movie. But Phil never shed a tear. Not until they burned up Rosebud, and—I'm sorry—that was only a damn sled. Looking back, it's not hard to see that Phil based his whole life on that crazy film. Charles Foster Kane turned his Xanadu into a walled fortress, and that's just what Phil did to our house.

Phil had the mansion surrounded with ten-foot electrified gates, and he had his wild German shepherds running around the yard to guard the place. But the more walls he built, the more walls he needed. He finally put up so many bars and gates on the doors and windows that our house started to look like a maximum security prison, which is about what it felt like inside.

And as hard as it was to get in there, it was even harder to get out. The doors were always locked, and I had to get George Brand or George Johnson to open them whenever I wanted to go anywhere. And they weren't allowed to open a door until they checked with Phil. Then, if Phil didn't think I had a good enough reason to leave, he'd yell at me until finally I'd just go back to my room. He made it so hard to get out of that house that after a while I just stopped trying. I once asked Phil why he had to have so many bars up around our house. "Why does anyone build a gate?" he said. "To keep people out."

Or to keep them in.

During the day I could usually get out into the yard through the servants' door in the kitchen. But after the help went home, the doors would be locked and the electric gates would be turned on. When that last servant went home, you were in for the night.

On nights when Phil didn't want to watch a movie, he'd go lock himself in his study. Once he closed that door, I'd sneak downstairs and pour myself a beaker of scotch. Then I'd smuggle it up to the TV room, where I'd drink along with Bette Davis on the late, late show. I never worried about Phil catching me when I was in there—he never came into the TV room unless "Mission: Impossible" was on.

I'd go on one of these little drinking sprees about once every three or four weeks. I figured I was taking such a small amount of liquor that Phil would never even miss it. But I was wrong. I was in the kitchen with George Johnson one afternoon when Phil stormed in carrying a half-empty bottle of scotch.

"George," he shouted, slamming the bottle down on the counter. I recognized that bottle in an instant. "Looks like your pal Bill found my liquor cabinet." Bill was a down-on-his-luck guy who came in twice a week to do the dusting. Phil knew the guy had a drinking problem, but he'd hired him anyway because he was a friend of George's.

"I don't think Bill would drink your liquor," George said. "But if you want me to tell him not to come anymore, I will."

I felt terrible. George's friend was about to lose his job because of me, and I couldn't let that happen. Besides, I knew it was just a matter of time before Phil found out about my drinking anyway, so I just blurted out the truth. "Bill didn't drink that stuff," I told him. "I did."

Phil had been raging mad just a minute before, but he was so shocked by what he'd just heard that he stood there dumbstruck for a few seconds. I have to admit I got a kick out of shutting him up like that. It was so much fun that I almost didn't care what happened next.

And as it turned out, nothing happened. I think Phil was so surprised that he didn't even know where to start. So he didn't say anything. He just went down to the game room the next morning and stuck a big gray padlock on the cabinet.

But you can't stop someone from drinking by locking up the liquor—that just forces them to be more clever. And I was. I came up with a plan that would get me out of the house long enough to buy my own liquor, which I would then smuggle in and hide in my private bathroom. Every few weeks I'd set this plan in motion when I'd make up a craving for something we didn't have in the house, like hard peaches.

"Peaches?" Phil would say. "Don't we have peaches in the kitchen?"

"Not hard ones," I'd tell him. "The ones we have are too ripe. I want fresh, hard peaches."

Then, after I convinced him that we didn't have the peaches—or New York steaks, or apricot juice, or whatever else I said I craved—Phil would go ahead and let me drive down the hill to Carl's Market at Santa Monica and Doheny to pick some up. Once I got there, I'd stand at the magazine rack for a half hour or so reading all the magazines that Phil wouldn't let me have in the house. Then I'd go into the liquor department and try to pick out a bottle of alcohol.

I knew so little about liquor that I bought grape Manischewitz because I remembered seeing it on the table at Phil's mother's house. It was the worst stuff you could possibly drink, but I picked it out because you didn't need a corkscrew to open the bottle, which was an important detail for someone who did a lot of her drinking in the bathroom at 1:00 A.M.

When I got home, I'd take the bottle of Manischewitz into my private bathroom and hide it in the toilet tank. Then, whenever I got depressed, I'd go in there and reach into that icy water and pull out that bottle of syrupy wine. It tasted awful, but at least it was cold.

15

Seizure

When I hear some of the stories that go around about my marriage to Phil, I'm amazed. Everybody assumes he must have beat me all the time to keep me there at the mansion with him. But he never laid a hand on me. Physical abuse was not his style. Psychological torture was his specialty—name-calling, shouting, cursing, those kinds of things. And I'll tell you, there were times when he shouted so much that I almost wished he would just go ahead and hit me.

The one time I did get hurt, it was from trying to get away from him. It was the day before he was supposed to leave on a business trip to Philadelphia, and I had made plans to visit my family in New York while he was gone. Phil usually let me go to New York for a week or so every couple of months, but for some reason he didn't want me leaving town while he was away. I was standing at the top of our staircase when he explained his reasoning. "You've got to stay here and watch over things while I'm gone," he said. "I'll let you go to New York after I get back."

And that was the end of the discussion. Or so he thought. But I needed a break from California too desperately to let it drop that easily. "Why can't George watch things while I'm gone?" I asked. But the thing about Phil was, he could only talk about something reasonably for so long, and after that you had to be careful. When he started turning purple, I knew we'd gone past that point.

"Why must you always *defy me?*" he shouted. "Do you have some secret desire to hurt me?" By this time he was shouting right in my face. I got scared and took a step backwards. But I didn't have a very strong foothold, and I lost my balance and went tumbling back down the stairs.

I watched my hand reach out to grab the railing, and I saw it miss the wood by that much. Then I saw the carpet on the first landing getting closer and closer until I smacked right down onto it. When I got up I was stinging all over, and my ankle felt like there was a knife sticking out of it.

"No, no, no!" Phil shouted, running down the steps. "Don't walk on it. Something might be broken."

"I don't think so," I told him. I felt so stupid about falling down my own staircase that I just wanted to forget about the whole thing. But Phil insisted we go straight to the doctor's office.

The doctor agreed that it was probably just a minor sprain. But then a funny thing happened. He walked into the next room to have a little talk with Phil, and about two minutes later he came back in and announced that he was going to put my whole leg in a cast. "Just to be certain," he said.

Phil went to Philadelphia the next day, but before he left he called a private medical service and hired a nurse to watch over me while he was gone. With all the servants we had running around that place, I didn't see why we needed a nurse, too. "Can't George take care of me?" I asked.

"You're not thinking, Veronica," he said. "What would George Johnson do in case of a medical emergency?" I had to admit he had a point. And besides, I'd seen a movie where Bette Davis played an invalid, so I had the idea it might actually be fun having a twenty-four-hour nurse waiting on me hand and foot.

Far from it. She was a nightmare. This woman put me in a wheelchair and stared over my shoulder day and night. She was worse than Phil. And every couple hours she'd bring me these little red pills and a glass of water.

"What are these for?" I asked her the first time she handed them to me.

"They'll help with the pain." she said. "Now open up."

I took them, but all they did was make me sleepy. I was dying to know what they were, so one day while she was in the shower, I limped into her room and took a peek into her medical bag. The thing was filled with pills. There were red ones and blue ones and yellow ones, too. It looked like she had a rainbow in that case. When I heard her getting out of the shower, I grabbed a handful of the pills on impulse and stuck them in my robe pocket before I hopped back to my wheelchair. She never mentioned the missing pills, and after a few hours I forgot all about them myself.

The best thing about having Phil out of town was that I could finally have friends come over to the house. Or *a* friend, I should say, since I only had one in those days, Bobbie Golson. Like most people who ever knew me, Bobbie didn't care much for Phil, and she knew he felt the same way about her. So naturally she was surprised when I called to invite her up to the house for lunch. "Phil's letting you have company at the mansion?" she asked. When I explained that he was out of town that week, she laughed. "Oh. Well, I knew something strange had to be going on."

I loved the idea of being a hostess, and I really got into the role. I put on my frilly white lace robe, and, wheeling around on my wheelchair, I gave Bobbie a complete tour of the mansion. No one was ever supposed to go upstairs, but I took her up there, anyway. I think she was the only person other than the servants who ever saw our twin bathrooms. After the tour, we sat out by the pool, where George brought us lunch.

When Bobbie asked about my broken leg, I told her the whole ridiculous story of how the doctor put the huge cast on my leg, and how Phil hired a nurse to watch over me while he was out of town. I wasn't even halfway through the story when I noticed that Bobbie had a real serious look on her face as she listened to me. And the more I said, the more serious she got. When I told her how the nurse was giving me pills, she stopped me dead.

"What kind of pills?"

"Red ones, mostly. Sometimes green." Then I remembered that I still had a few of the pills in the pocket of my robe. I reached in and pulled out a small handful. "Like these."

I held the pills out to Bobbie, but she wouldn't touch them. She just stared at them, shaking her head back and forth. "You want to be careful with this stuff, Ronnie." Then she leaned back in her pool chair. "My God. I had no idea things had gotten this bad."

"What do you mean?"

"With Phil." She looked around to make sure no one was listening. "You don't see it? The full leg cast, the wheelchair, that nurse? Phil's worked this whole thing out so that you'll remain a prisoner in his house even though he's three thousand miles away."

I thought about how Phil took the doctor aside just before the guy decided to put the cast on. And I wondered if it was just a coincidence that I had this nosy nurse standing over my shoulder all the time. It would be just like Phil to plan something like this out. But I couldn't be sure, so I decided to give him the benefit of the doubt. "Phil just wanted to be sure I was under proper medical care," I explained. "He gets worried—"

"Ronnie, what's wrong with you?" Bobbie said. "That lady walking around in there is nothing more than a twenty-four-hour-a-day jailer."

"So? What if she is?" I said. "What am I supposed to do about it?"

"Let me get you to someone who can help."

"No," I told her. In my heart I knew that Bobbie was right, of course. But I still felt that it was a matter between Phil and me. "I can handle this myself," I said. "I can. I know it."

Bobbie wasn't so sure, so she just sat there frowning and shaking her head. "Yeah, Phil's got his problems," I continued. "But he wasn't always this way. This is just a stage—"

Then she cut me off. "How many years are you willing to waste waiting for him to come out of this *stage*?"

"As many years as it takes," I told her. "I *love* Phil. He's my husband. Nobody cares about him the way I do. Don't you understand? He'd be lost without me." I tried to sound firm, but my voice was cracking and my eyes were filling up with tears. "*I'm* the only thing he's got." Then Bobbie reached over the glass table and touched my hand. "And *he's* the only thing I've got."

She held my hand while I sat there, sobbing like a baby. I felt sorry for Phil, but I felt even sorrier for myself. A few minutes later, the nurse walked out to see what was going on.

"Now, now," she said. "We can't have my prize patient getting upset on a beautiful day like this, can we?" Then she opened her palm and held out a red pill. "Here, take this. It'll calm you down."

That was more than Bobbie could take. "Look," she said, staring the nurse straight in the face. "If you don't leave Ronnie alone this minute, I'm going to stick *you* in that wheelchair and make *you* swallow that pill. And if you're not careful, I might decide to take your ass over to that pool and throw you right in." The nurse looked at Bobbie like she was insane. And then she left us alone to finish our lunch.

After Bobbie went home, I couldn't stop thinking about all the stuff she said. Maybe she was right. Maybe that nurse was nothing more than my hired keeper. But if she was, I sure wasn't going to play along and make her job any easier.

George Brand was out of town with Phil, so that night I asked George Johnson to bring my car around. "I'm going for a ride," I announced. "Alone."

George nodded his head and walked out to get the car, but the nurse didn't give up. "I'm not sure about this, dear," she said. "Will you be okay with just your crutches?"

"Sure," I told her. "I don't need them to drive the car anyway. I'll be fine."

She made a sour face, but there really wasn't anything she could do. George came and wheeled me out to the car, and we tossed the crutches into the backseat. "Free at last," I sang as I steered the car out the front gate. "Free at last. Thank God Almighty, I'm free at last."

Of course, I had no idea where I was going, so I just drove. I went up Doheny to Sunset, and then down Sunset to La Cienega, where I went past all the big restaurants that were filled with happy people. I finally ended up on Santa Monica Boulevard, which is where I saw Vinnie Poncia. Vinnie was one of my old songwriters—he'd written "(The Best Part of) Breaking Up" with Phil and Pete Andreoli. He was walking on the sidewalk, so I honked my horn and pulled over to say hello.

Vinnie and his wife were staying at the Tropicana, which was a motel right nearby. So when he invited me to join them for a drink, I said, "What the hell?" and hobbled up on my crutches. I was there maybe half an hour, just long enough to have a couple drinks and make some small talk. Then I said bye-bye and limped back out to my car.

I'd only had a couple drinks, but all of a sudden I felt really dizzy. I didn't know that you weren't supposed to mix pills and alcohol, but when those drinks hit the three days' worth of pills I'd been taking, it was just too much. By the time I got down to the street, I could barely stand up. I finally just dropped the crutches and lay down on the sidewalk. It was scary. I wasn't just drunk—I'd been smashed often enough to know that this was something different. That's when I started to panic.

Then, slowly, my body started shaking. All of a sudden I felt like I was losing control of my arms. They just started jerking around on their own, and I couldn't do a thing to stop them. A few seconds later my entire body doubled up and began twisting itself in painful contortions that I had no control over. Finally, my eyes rolled way back into my head and I passed out right there on Santa Monica Boulevard.

I had just had my first seizure.

I don't know how long I was out, but when I woke up I saw my pocketbook lying on the sidewalk, and my makeup was scattered everywhere. I knew I was on the ground, but I had no idea how I got there. No one even saw me, because in California there aren't a whole lot of people walking around at night. I finally grabbed my crutches and pulled myself to my feet, but I stayed completely disoriented for at least fifteen minutes. And it was another half hour before I finally figured out where I was.

I got back in the car and drove home. The experience had scared the shit out of me, but I decided not to tell anyone about it. Phil was still out of town. And what he didn't know couldn't hurt me.

16

Unnatural Childbirth

*A*fter all the shit that happened in 1968, the New
Year had to be an improvement. And it was. In
January Phil announced that we were going back
into the studio to make my first new record in almost three
years.

I couldn't believe it. One morning he's swimming around the
pool, doing his laps, just like every other day. The next minute,
he's drying himself off with a big, flowered towel, saying, "I
think I'm going down to the studio today, do you want to
come?"

"Phil," I asked, "is this a joke?"

"Veronica," he sighed. "Why would I joke about a thing like
that?" He knew he was torturing me with this casual attitude,
but I think he was afraid of making too big a deal out of going back to work, just in case he flopped again. But I didn't
care. I always knew Phil had it in him to come back—making
records is a disease that we both had, and there just isn't any
cure. You just have to keep going back and trying to make
more hits. And that's what Phil and I were going to do. I was
sure of it.

Phil even had a brand-new song for me, "You Came, You
Saw, You Conquered," which he wrote with Toni Wine and
Irwin Levine. I thought it was going to be just like old times in
the studio. But Philles Records had been out of business since

1966, and a lot of things change in three years—especially in the music business.

For one thing, we recorded in a brand-new studio. Phil had a deal to release his new stuff through Herb Alpert's A&M label, so we showed up for work in this fantastic state-of-the-art studio that Herb had at A&M. Phil was used to working with the antique stuff they had at Gold Star, and I think he felt a little intimidated around all these space age recorders and microphones. Unfortunately, instead of admitting he was out of his class, he tried to make up for his ignorance by acting more tyrannical than ever. Especially to me.

On our first day there I walked around and said hello to all the musicians and engineers, like I'd always done at Gold Star. But Phil didn't like that, and he let me know it. "Veronica, where do you think you're going?" he shouted over the studio speakers. "Don't walk away from the microphone, goddamn it! We're trying to get levels here."

When he didn't have me stuck to one spot on the studio floor, Phil kept me locked up with him in the control booth. I'd hoped that Phil would have more respect for me now that we were married, but it was just the opposite. Things got so bad that I actually started to miss the way he behaved at Gold Star. At least there I could hide out in the ladies' room.

I think Phil missed Gold Star, too. In those days everyone put up with his shit. But these guys at A&M didn't depend on Phil for their jobs, so they treated him like the nut that he was. They even had a picture of him that they threw darts at. I was walking through the employees' lounge with Phil one day when I saw it. I was sure he was going to have a fit, but Phil just walked up to it with a big smile on his face.

"Aren't you going to make them take it down?" I asked.

"Not in a million years," he answered. "That dart board is a bigger honor than a Grammy."

"Why?"

"People only throw darts at someone they feel threatened by," he explained. "The guys who put that up know that I've already accomplished more in my career than they could ever hope to do. And they can't face that, so they throw darts at me. Go count the holes. I'll bet I've had more darts thrown at my face than any producer in the history of records."

I finished my vocals after a couple of days and Phil sent me home. But the way he'd been acting, I was glad to be out of there. That was the last I heard about my comeback, and it was the last I heard of "You Came, You Saw, You Conquered." The record actually did come out in March of 1969, but it flopped so badly that Phil might as well have left it on the shelf with all my other unreleased songs.

The strange thing is, I wasn't even disappointed when it bombed. By now my confidence was so low that I just accepted that record's failure as further proof that I wasn't a singer anymore. Looking back, I have to wonder if that wasn't what Phil wanted all along. Why would he write me a song called "You Came, You Saw, You Conquered" unless he was trying to send me a message? He came, he saw—and with that song—I was finally conquered.

Once I'd finally given up my dream of ever singing again, I had nowhere to go but down. I'd sit in the TV room all day with my soap operas and Manischewitz. And that's when I started to wonder what I was really living for anyway. My career was a joke, my family only wanted to see me when I had money for them, and my married life was a living nightmare. I was miserable, but I didn't even have the nerve to kill myself—I was too much of a coward for that. Instead, I'd drink my purple wine and watch "All My Children" until I fell asleep. Then I'd hope I wouldn't have to wake up again, ever.

I know now that I could've saved myself a lot of heartache if I'd just faced up to my problems and looked for the answers. But that wasn't my style. Avoiding things was my family heritage. All my life I'd been taught that if you turn your back on bad things, they'll go away eventually—whether it was junkies in my grandma's yard or my father sleeping off a bottle of gin on the front stoop. It was the way my mother dealt with all her problems, and the way Phil did, too.

I was only twenty-five years old, but I'd already ignored so many things in myself that I wasn't even sure who I was anymore. I desperately needed to find an identity—and quick—or Phil and Manischewitz and Bette Davis were going to drive me completely nuts. They came pretty damn close as it was.

The identity I finally chose for myself was a natural—I would be a mother. I'd always loved kids, and I desperately wanted a family. I knew I'd make a great mom; all I needed was a kid. And I found him, believe it or not, watching television.

I was watching this documentary about unwanted babies on TV when the host held up this tiny baby boy. He was only a few days old, with smooth brown skin, and the waviest black hair I'd ever seen on a baby. He was a half-breed, like me, and he was beautiful.

"Oh my God," I said to myself. "He's adorable." He even looked like what I'd always imagined our child would look like. I took it as a sign from God. I was going to be a mother, and I couldn't wait.

And I didn't wait, either. I called and found out where the adoption agency was, and I drove down there that afternoon without even consulting Phil. The place was all the way down-town, and Phil had my car that day, so I had to take his big white Rolls on the Hollywood Freeway. And that scared the shit out of me. I was so nervous I weaved in and out of my lane the whole way. And after all that, when I got to the agency, the baby's adoption counselor told me I couldn't even see him.

She introduced herself as Miss Tracy, and she was very nice. But she said there were rules she had to follow. "What do you mean?" I asked. "What rules?"

"We usually show the children by appointment only," she explained. "And it's customary to have both prospective parents present during the preliminary interview."

I was so crushed that I actually started crying. "You don't understand. My husband wasn't home when the TV show came on, but I couldn't wait. I had to see that little baby. And I drove all the way down here. On the freeway. By myself."

I wasn't kidding, but for some reason Miss Tracy thought that was funny, so she finally dropped her guard. "All right, Mrs. Spector," she said, smiling. "For a lady who took on the Hollywood Freeway all by herself, I suppose we can bend the rules a little bit."

She went into another room, and when she came out she was carrying the baby. He was a tiny little thing, with a perfect little nose and long, curly eyelashes. Miss Tracy told me he was born on March 23, 1969—and this was April—so he was only a few weeks old.

I was stroking one of his little eyebrows when he looked up at me. Then I started crying. He was just a baby, but already he was all alone in the world. I felt so sorry for him that I wanted to take him home that day. But Miss Tracy wouldn't let me.

"We've got to arrange an interview first," she said. "And I'll need to visit you and your husband at home."

"And then how long before I can get the baby?" I asked. In my mind he already was mine. He had to be.

"It takes a little time," she said. "But if everything works out, you might have him by this time next month."

"Okay, then," I said. "But you won't show him to anyone else before then, will you? Because I know everything's going to work out. It has to. I really want this baby. He even looks like me."

Then Miss Tracy took the baby in her arms and smiled. "If it's meant to be, it will be. Just go home and stop worrying." I was already out the door when she called out to me. "And talk to your husband!"

I did. And Phil was just as excited as I was about adopting a baby. I think we both felt that having kids would bring us closer together, so we went crazy waiting to hear if we'd been approved for adoption. We even picked out a name for him—Donté—just as if he was our own natural baby.

In those days it was a lot harder to adopt than it is today. They really checked you out back then. Even so, we found out it was easier to get a kid if you were rich. Miss Tracy came over to the house, took one look at our mansion, and told us we were going to get the baby.

I was so happy. That month of waiting for the paperwork to go through before we actually got Donté home was the longest four weeks of my life. I felt like a kid waiting to open her toys on Christmas Eve. And I knew I was getting the greatest present of all.

Even though Donté was adopted, Phil wanted to raise him just like he was our natural child. I didn't see anything wrong with that, but—like everything else in his life—Phil took that philosophy to a ridiculous extreme. In his fantasy world, Donté *was* our natural child. And Phil was going to do everything he could to convince the rest of the world that it was true, including me.

I was setting up Donté's nursery one day when Phil walked in and handed me a little yellow card. "What's this?" I asked.

"Donté's birth announcement," he told me.

I looked at the card. On one side was a drawing of a baby, and underneath it were the words PRESENTING THE SMASH-HIT PRODUCTION OF DONTÉ PHILLIP SPECTOR. I smiled at Phil's joke, treating the baby like he was one of our hit records. I thought it was cute. But I stopped smiling when I read the little scenario Phil had printed on the other side of the card:

ACT ONE:
Scene:
Hospital . . . March 23, 1969
Action:
Little baby boy born prematurely . . . Mother fine . . .
Baby's outcome ambiguous.
Parents go home nervous . . .
Baby remains in hospital.

ACT TWO:
Scene:
Four weeks later in hospital.
Action:
Baby doing fine . . . Named Donté Phillip. Parents thrilled
but still reluctant to admit success of it.
Can't believe it!

ACT THREE:
Scene:
Ten weeks later.
Action:
Baby going home with mom and pop.
Baby's weight 11 pounds. Parents believe it!
Ordeal Over . . . Happy Ending.

The above is a Veronica and Phil Spector Production

I hadn't even finished reading it before Phil asked me, "What do you think?"

"I don't know," I said, watching every word. "It makes it sound like I had Donté myself."

"That's what I want people to think. And if we want to raise Donté as our own baby, that's how we have to think of him, too."

"But, Phil," I protested, "everyone's going to know I wasn't pregnant."

"If I say you were pregnant, who's going to say any different?"

He had a point. People saw so little of me that everyone did assume I'd been pregnant for the previous eight months, just because Phil said so. He was manic about making people think this was his baby. He even had me stick a pillow under my shirt when his secretary Gloria came over to the house.

The day we finally went to pick up Donté was probably the only truly happy day of our entire marriage. When we walked out of the adoption agency with our brand-new baby in his blanket, we were just like any other happily married couple. It was our dream come true—at last we had a family of our own.

We spent the rest of that afternoon feeding and fussing over Donté, just like any other normal parents. I loved it. For a few hours I was sure that things really were starting to change between Phil and me now that we had our little family. But that fantasy lasted about one day before Phil went back to his usual tricks.

I was playing with Donté in the nursery when George Johnson brought this older lady in. She was carrying a big bag filled with diapers and baby toys. "This must be Donté," she said. "And you must be the new mommy?"

"Yeah," I said. "And who are you?"

"I'm Mrs. Taylor," she said. "Didn't your husband tell you? He hired me to watch the baby." And this lady wasn't kidding. She checked Donté's diapers and had already started changing his sheets before she finished her sentence. I was amazed. This lady walks in out of nowhere, and in three minutes she's already outdoing me with my own child.

I couldn't believe that Phil would hire a governess without talking to me first. But when I walked out to the pool to confront him about it, he acted like it was no big deal. "You don't know the first thing about raising a kid, Veronica," he said. "I hired Mrs. Taylor because she's a trained expert. Don't you want the best for Donté?"

"Of course I do," I agreed. "But a mother's love is the best thing you can give to a kid."

"So love him. That doesn't mean you have to change his diapers, too."

"What if I want to change his diapers?" I argued. But Phil wouldn't budge. We were rich and we were going to have a governess and that was that.

"Besides," he pointed out, "who's supposed to take care of the baby while we're in the studio?"

Phil knew he had me. I wasn't about to argue against anything that might get my career back. So I accepted it, and from then on we had a live-in governess for Donté. Of course, whenever I asked Phil *when* we were going back into the studio, I never got a decent answer. "When are we going to record?" I'd ask, and he'd tell me not to bother him.

"Get out of here, Veronica," he'd say. "I've got some calls to make." And that was when he was in a good mood. If I dared to ask him about my career when he was in a bad mood, he'd go on for three days. "You self-centered bitch!" he'd yell. "I've other things on my mind besides your fucking career."

Who was going to ask this guy a question like that again? Not me. I finally gave up and dropped all discussion of my career. It was becoming obvious that baby or no baby, Phil was Phil, and that wasn't going to change with fatherhood.

After we got Donté, my mom came to stay with us all the time. She loved staying in the little guest apartment we kept for her downstairs, and I loved having her around. I think Phil liked having her around, too, because he could talk to her. And he could also ask her to do little favors for him, like the time he sent her to Watts to buy him an Afro wig.

The Afro hairstyle was a big thing during the late sixties, so Phil decided he had to have an Afro wig. He thought it was the perfect hairstyle for a toupee, because you couldn't see the net under all that hair. I also suspect he liked the idea of wearing a black man's haircut. I swear, sometimes Phil thought he *was* black.

So he spent all kinds of money having these white wigmakers design him Afro wigs, but they always looked ridiculous. That's when he finally got desperate enough to send my mother and me into Watts to find him an Afro wig that looked right.

My mom and I drove around to all the black hair salons in Watts looking for an Afro wig, size extra-small. When we finally found a place that had them, we bought three and brought them home. Of course, you couldn't just hand Phil a box and say, "Here's your new hairpiece." So we left the boxes sitting on the kitchen table. We knew that Phil would take it from there.

Phil was always very particular about his wigs. He would sit in front of his dressing room mirror for days trying to get his toupee to look real. We hardly ever went out, but on those rare nights when he did take me out to eat, he'd be up there for hours before we finally left. And if Phil couldn't get his wig on right, we didn't go out. His hair was a large part of our marriage.

But Phil loved his Afro wig. I guess it made him feel like he had soul or something, because after he got it, he wanted us all to go back down to Watts to hear some real gospel music at the Reverend James Cleveland's church. I wanted no part of it. I never liked straight gospel music because I could never understand what they were singing.

Of course, Phil had his heart set on it. So we all piled into the back of his limousine—me, my mother, and Phil. He also brought along a pair of bodyguards. Afro wig or no Afro wig, Phil wasn't taking any chances going down to Watts. He even brought one of his pistols, which he tucked into his jacket pocket.

My mother just shook her head. "Phil!" she said. "Why you want to bring a gun into a church?"

"This?" he said, patting his gun like he was in the Old West. "This is my peacemaker. I brought it along in case there's any trouble." Thank God he at least had the sense to have the bodyguards wait in the car when we went into the church.

We found seats in the back just as Reverend James Cleveland's choir started singing. They were wailing and moaning and singing out in that way that gospel people do, and Phil was moaning and wailing right along with them. He was rolling his shoulders and shaking his arms, and pretty soon he was sweating and shouting out "Amen" like he was at a Baptist revival meeting. It was funny, really. Here I was, this black girl, bored out of her mind at a gospel concert, sitting with a Jewish man in an Afro who looked like he was about to speak in tongues.

After the singing, Phil kept on shouting "Amen" all through Reverend Cleveland's sermon. When the Reverend held out the collection plate, Phil jumped to his feet with a hundred-dollar bill in his hand. "Oh, no!" my mom gasped under her breath. But it was already too late to stop him.

We bit our lips and watched Phil jog all the way up the aisle of that crowded black church, an Afro wig on his head and a hundred-dollar bill in his hand. When I saw the handle of his .38 bobbing up and down in his jacket pocket, I actually started praying. "Please, God," I whispered. "Don't let it fall out."

After the service, people were still staring at Phil as we worked our way through the crowd to the limousine that was waiting at the curb. My mother and I were embarrassed for him, but Phil actually looked proud as he smiled and wiped the sweat from his forehead.

"I guess I showed them I'm not just *any* white guy," he bragged.

"That you did, Phil," my mother agreed. "That you surely did."

17

Out of Control

M uch as he hated to go out, Phil always made it a point to celebrate my birthday. No matter how long we'd been locked away in the mansion, whenever August 10 rolled around, we always went out for a night on the town. In 1969, Phil flew me to Las Vegas to see Elvis Presley for my twenty-sixth birthday.

Elvis was still in good shape then. He was making a comeback after doing shitty movies for about ten years, so he really cared about his stage act. I thought it was a great show, and I wanted to tell him so. But when Elvis invited us backstage afterward, Phil hardly let me near the guy. There were about twenty or thirty people packed into Elvis's dressing room when we got up there, so Phil left me stranded in the hallway with his bodyguard while he pushed his way through the crowd to see Elvis.

I was standing there, trying to peek through a crack in the dressing room door, when this beautiful young girl pops out and nearly smashes the door in my face. I didn't recognize her at first, but when I saw she was the only girl there wearing even more mascara than I was, I knew she had to be Priscilla Presley.

"Oh, hi," she said, talking like we were old friends. "What are you doing out here? Come on in, Elvis is dying to meet you."

She grabbed my hand and led me through the crowd. I could tell she was shy, but Priscilla didn't seem to have any trouble talking to me. "You know," she said, "I have to tell you. I've always loved the way you look. You really are pretty."

"Oh, thank you," I said. I was really touched. I don't know why she was so sweet to me, but I've never forgotten it.

Priscilla dragged me right up past Phil to Elvis, who seemed even more shy than she was. "I'm pleased to meet you," he said, and that was about all I heard before Phil grabbed my arm and started dragging me away. I guess Elvis had looked at me a second or two longer than Phil thought was proper. Or maybe he couldn't stand the competition. Whatever the reason, Phil got me out of there quick.

"Why don't you and George go back to the hotel room and wait for me?" he asked after we got back out to the hallway. Then he pulled out a big roll of hundred-dollar bills and handed five of them to George Brand. "Here, George," he said. "Take her through the casino and let her play anything she wants. It's her birthday."

But what girl wants to celebrate her twenty-sixth birthday playing craps with her bodyguard? I said to hell with the casino and told George to drop me off at my room. I sat there for two hours waiting for Phil, and it was hell. I did everything I could to pass the time—I took a bath, I watched TV, I even took the beds apart and made them up again. But I was so depressed that everything I did only reminded me of how lonely I was.

I finally got sick of waiting for Phil and called room service. The bellboy brought up six Pepsi Colas and a bottle of vodka. I handed him one of the hundred-dollar bills and told him to keep the change. Then I locked the door. If I had to spend my birthday alone in my room, I was sure as hell going to have a celebration.

Phil finally tiptoed in at about 5:00 A.M., only to find me passed out in front of the TV. By this time, he knew I liked to drink when I got depressed, but I don't think he'd ever actually seen me drunk before. Not like this. And it scared him.

He called George Brand to our room, and the two of them started pouring coffee into me. They hoped to sober me up enough for the morning flight back to L.A., but I was in no shape to fly. They practically had to carry me onto the plane, which embarrassed the shit out of Phil. I was still so fucked-up, all I could think was, "It serves Phil right for leaving me alone on my birthday."

As freaked out as Phil got about my drinking, he never did much to help me in those days. He thought he could manage my alcohol problem by tightening his control over me, even though that suffocating control was one of the things that made me drink in the first place. But he refused to see that. He figured that if he turned his back on my alcoholism, it would go away. I practically had to kill myself in the Camaro before he—or I—understood how serious my problem really was.

I was driving back from Bobbie Golson's house the night I had my accident. Phil sometimes let me go over to Bobbie's after dinner, as long as I promised to come back within an hour. George Brand usually had to drive me—after Phil found out about my drinking, he hated to let me go anywhere alone—but George was busy that night, so I drove over there on my own. Just me and my inflatable man.

I was in one of my typical depressions that night, so the first thing I did when I got to Bobbie's was pour myself a drink. And then a second one. And a third. I often had a couple of drinks with Bobbie, but I was really getting carried away this time, and she knew it.

"Ronnie," she asked, "what are you trying to do to yourself? That's just what he wants."

"How do you know what Phil wants?" I snapped. I was already drunk and running out of patience. The last thing I needed was a lecture.

"I don't know what Phil wants," Bobbie continued. "But you do. You know that he wants to control you, mind and body. But he can't. He can lock your body away for the rest of your life, but he'll never take control of your mind—unless *you* give it to him. And every time you drink like this, you lose a little more control and you let Phil get just a little bit closer."

Bobbie was trying to talk sense, but it was too late for that. I couldn't deal with the truth, so I turned on her.

"Why doesn't everyone just mind their own damn business and leave me and Phil the hell alone?" I demanded. "You don't love Phil. You don't even know him. That man can move mountains. And he would, too, if everyone would just let him be."

Then I grabbed my keys and stomped out to my car. Bobbie
didn't try to stop me. In the mood I was in, she knew it was best
to leave me on my own.

I revved the Camaro up in her driveway and tore out onto
the road. I barely remember what led up to the accident, but I
can recall every detail of the inside of that car just before it
happened. I can still feel the braided leather strip that covered
the steering wheel, and I can picture the long black dashboard
with the glove compartment that had my initials stamped on it
in silver letters. And I don't think I'll ever forget the unlit
cigarette that was dangling from the plastic lips of my inflatable
man when I looked up and saw the tree about to come crashing
through my windshield.

I turned the wheel sharp to the left, and the whole car felt
like it was floating. That's all I remember until I woke up in a
strange house with three hippies and Phil Spector standing
over me with a pot of hot coffee. I knew I must be alive then,
because that sure wasn't my idea of heaven.

"Phil?" I asked.

"Veronica! Are you okay?"

"What happened, Phil? Where am I?"

"Drink this," he said, holding up a cup of coffee. It was hot.
Too hot, and it burned my lips.

"Ouch!" I squealed. "Who are these guys?"

"Wow!" one of the hippies said. "I told you she wouldn't
remember."

"Amnesia!" the second hippie said. "Far out."

Then the third hippie explained how they'd found me stag-
gering around my wrecked car in a daze. It happened right
outside of their house, so they took me in. They found Phil's
business card in my pocket after I passed out, so they called
him.

"You're a very lucky girl, Veronica," Phil added. I expected
him to be mad, but if he was, he didn't let it show while we were
with the hippies. "You'll see what I mean when you get a look
at your car."

After all the coffee and hippies, Phil walked me out to see the
wreck. I couldn't believe my eyes. The whole front end of the
Camaro was hanging right over the side of a cliff. The car was

balanced so close to the edge that the slightest touch could have sent it crashing straight down about a hundred feet. I peeked over the cliff, then jumped back and caught my breath.

"That's how close you came to killing yourself," Phil said, shaking his head back and forth. Then we walked back to his Rolls, and George Brand drove us home.

After the accident, Phil decided I had to see a psychiatrist about my drinking. I didn't like the idea at first—I thought it was Phil's way of telling me I was crazy. But I went anyway. If I was going nuts, at least I wanted to hear it from an expert.

The psychiatrist was an older guy with an office way in the back of this medical building on Sunset. I was supposed to go in there once a week to talk about my drinking, but I ended up telling him about everything that was bothering me. About how miserable I felt living my life for someone else, and how much I missed performing, and how nothing seemed to give me joy in my marriage anymore. Not even sex.

"Do you still have sex?" he asked.

"Yeah," I said. "But it's not fun anymore. Some mornings I'll climb on top of Phil when we wake up, just to get it over with. I figure that if he starts the morning that way, he might not yell and scream so much the rest of the day."

"Does it work?"

"No. He still yells."

Then I would talk, and he would listen patiently. It was great. I never got the feeling that he was looking down on me like everyone else seemed to do. I wish I could've kept seeing him. But around the third week of sessions, he made the mistake of suggesting that maybe Phil needed help, too. And that was the beginning of the end.

"Maybe you could get Phil to attend a group therapy session," he said. I agreed to check with Phil, but I had a pretty good idea what he'd say.

And I was right. Phil went through the roof at the slightest hint that he might need psychiatric help. "Group therapy? Come on, Veronica. What would I need group therapy for?" he shouted. "Do I look like the one with the problem here?"

After that, Phil refused to pay for any more sessions with "the

quack," as he called him. But my problems didn't go away just
because I stopped seeing my psychiatrist. If anything, they were
getting worse.

I'd had such high hopes after we got Donté, but by the end of
1969 I knew that nothing was going to change. Being a father
hadn't magically changed Phil into Prince Charming. And being
a mom didn't change me overnight, either—I wasn't any happier
just because I suddenly had a baby to share my misery.

At least I didn't have to worry about hiding my drinking
from Phil anymore. And once my problem was out in the open,
I got a lot bolder. When I'd want a drink, I'd walk right down
to Phil's liquor cabinet and force the padlock open with a screwdriver. When he found the lock broken, he'd replace it with a
bigger one. Then I'd find a bigger screwdriver.

Of course, whenever Phil came up to my room and found me
drunk, he would still yell and shout and curse me out. But I
discovered that getting drunk had a wonderful side effect—it
made Phil seem a lot less scary to me. Once I learned that little
secret, drinking became my main defense against him. And that
completely freaked him out. He felt like he was losing control
over me, and he couldn't stand that.

Once, after I'd been drunk for three days straight, Phil got so
frustrated he finally called my mom in New York. "You've got
to get out here, Mrs. Bennett," he told her. "Veronica won't eat.
She won't sleep. She won't do anything!"

The day my mother finally showed up, I was a complete
mess. I'd been drinking all morning when Phil found me passed
out in the TV room. But then, instead of leaving me there, he
pulled me to my feet and dragged me downstairs.

"Your mother's coming up the driveway," he told me. "Come
on, let's meet her at the door."

I was too groggy to make sense out of what he was saying, but
I did understand that my mother was nearby, and that made
me feel a little better. She was just coming up the walk when
Phil propped me up against the inside of the door. "Answer it,"
he said.

"Don't push me," I said.

"Well, go ahead," he ordered. "Open the door. I want your
mom to see exactly what you've been putting me through."

I pulled the door open a crack, and I felt relieved when the first sliver of sunlight sliced its way through the darkness of the front hall. Then my mom pushed the door open the rest of the way, and I got a full blast of sunlight felt like a slap in the face. My knees got all rubbery, and suddenly I felt like I just *had* to lie down. I started to fall backwards, but Phil grabbed me behind the shoulders and held me up. I tried to focus my eyes in front of me, but I could just barely make out my mom's silhouette against the background of white-hot sun.

"Mommy?" I squeaked. Then Phil let go of my shoulders and I lunged forward toward my mom. I reached for her, but I guess I missed, because I lost my balance and slid right down to the floor. I was almost unconscious, but I remember feeling my mother's arms as she cradled me in her lap. "Phil," she said, "what in the world's been happening around here?"

Phil didn't have an answer, so he just walked away in disgust. "I'm sorry, Mrs. Bennett," he muttered. "But I don't know what to do with her anymore. Maybe you can get through to her."

When I woke up the next morning I was still in the mansion, but I was in my mother's bed. And she had a big glass of orange juice waiting for me when my eyes opened.

"Drink this," she said.

My mouth felt like a big brown sponge, and I drank it all in one long gulp. It wasn't until I set the glass down that I heard the shouting outside the window. It sounded like Phil. "Sit down!" he was yelling. "Sit down!"

"What's going on out there?" I asked.

"Oh," Mom said, walking over to the window. "Phil's out there trying to train one of his dogs. Been at it all morning. I don't know why he don't just give up."

She pulled the curtain open just wide enough so I could see. Phil was standing by the pool, dressed in these terrible little red shorts that he'd been wearing since high school. He was waving a stick in the air like a circus lion tamer, but this poor German shepherd just lay there shaking at his feet. And Phil kept staring this poor animal down the whole time.

I'll never forget the look in his eyes. Phil stared at that dog with a cold, killer gaze that said, "I *will* control you." I couldn't believe the man I loved was capable of such a cruel stare. Then, suddenly it dawned on me that I was seeing Phil in a true light for the first time in years. The sad part is, I should've recognized it sooner. He'd stared at me that exact same way at least a hundred times before. I stood at the window watching Phil for the longest time. When I'd finished, I turned calmly to my mother and said, "I hate him."

Up to then I'd felt disappointment toward Phil. And fear, and anger—but never hate. It was an odd feeling. The only thing that had kept me going for all these years of slow torture was the fact that I loved Phil without question. And now, suddenly, I didn't even have that anymore.

"You look like you seen a ghost," my mother said.

I wish I had. It wouldn't have been as scary. "Mom," I confessed, "I don't know how much longer I can stay here like this."

"I know what you mean, Ronnie," she said. "Married life ain't never easy."

I thought that was a funny thing to say, but I wasn't exactly in a laughing mood. My mother handed me another glass of orange juice, and I drank it down as quickly as the first one.

18

Not My Key

In January 1970, the Beatles asked Phil to come to London to help them produce their *Let It Be* album. It was great to see Phil going back to work, and I sure didn't mind that the job would take him out of the country. We needed a break from each other.

Phil didn't want to keep flying back and forth from London to the West Coast while he was working for the Beatles, so he got us a New York apartment in the Mayflower at Seventy-second and Central Park West. He fixed the place up for Donté and me, and it was a big change from life at the mansion. Just being in New York made a world of difference. Donté was just starting to walk, and I loved being able to take him out to Central Park just like any other mom. That time I spent in New York was the happiest period in my marriage. I hardly ever got depressed, and I didn't even think about drinking the whole time we lived there.

It was a good time for Phil, too. He really got along with the Beatles, especially George and John. They liked what he did with the *Let It Be* album so much that they asked him to produce their first solo records. One project led to the next, and Phil ended up staying in London for the next year.

Working with the Beatles at Apple Records really seemed to bring Phil's confidence back. He seemed excited about his work for the first time since he shut down his label. Every few weeks he'd fly back with tapes of the songs he'd been working on with John and George, and it was always great stuff. We had a big piano in our apartment at the Mayflower, and Phil loved to sit down and have me sing these songs when he got home. "Try this one," he'd say. Then he'd play "The Long and Winding Road" and I'd sing my heart out.

It was just before Thanksgiving when Phil brought home George's "My Sweet Lord." He played it through for me on the piano so I could get the melody, then he had me sing it. "Wow," he said. "That's the way it should sound!" Then he'd play it again and again. I must've sung that song twenty-five times. Every time I finished, Phil would smile and say, "Once more?" Then I'd do it again.

Working on songs that way can be hard work, but I didn't mind. Phil hadn't rehearsed me like this since before we were married, and I was thrilled. I had no idea what it was all leading up to, but I knew he must have something up his sleeve when he asked me what I thought of George's song.

"I love it," I told him.

"Is it the kind of thing you'd like to do?"

"Are you kidding?" I said. "I'd kill for a song like that. Why?"

"Oh, no reason," he said, closing the piano cover. "I was just curious."

I knew there was more to it than that. Phil wasn't warming me up by the piano every night for nothing. But if he was planning to record me, he wasn't in any hurry to tell me about it. Phil was teasing me to the point of torture, and he knew it. I could've killed him!

He didn't mention another word about it before he went back to London. But then, three days later, I got a call at 6:15 in the morning. I knew who it was before I even picked it up.

"Do you think you can get your mother to fly out here with you after the first of the year?" he asked.

"To London?"

"Yeah," Phil answered. "Somebody's got to take care of Donté while you're in the studio. Think you can work it out?"

"What!" I screamed. "I'll be there if I have to strap the baby on my back like an Indian."

I was stunned. I hung up the phone, sat up in bed, and tried to figure out whether or not I was awake. When the phone rang a second time, I nearly jumped off the mattress. "Hello?"

"Hi, Ronnie?" the voice at the other end said. "This is Pete Bennett from Apple. I'm sorry to ring so early, but I wanted to be the first to congratulate you."

"Thanks, Pete," I said. "But what did I do?"

"Phil didn't tell you, then?" he said. "You've just been signed to Apple Records."

Then it was true! After all these years, George and John hadn't forgotten me. I was so excited that I had to tell someone. But nobody I knew was awake yet, so I ran into the baby's room and picked up Donté.

"Hey, baby boy . . . guess what?" I said. "Your mommy's got a label!" The poor kid was still scratching his sleepy eyes when I picked him up and started dancing him around the room. "It's true! It's true! Mommy's on Apple. We're going to England to make records with Daddy!"

When my mother and I flew to London with Donté in March 1971, I still had no idea what songs Phil was going to have me record. We went straight from Heathrow to the Inn on the Park Hotel, where Phil had reserved a luxury suite for all of us. We had practically a whole floor, and this place was ritzy. Our bed was the size of two normal king-sized beds, with two or three goose-down comforters piled on top of it. Mom and I couldn't find Phil anywhere when we got to the hotel, and it was two hours before we realized he'd been in the bed the whole time. The blankets were so thick we hadn't even seen him!

The day after I arrived, Phil took me to EMI's Abbey Road Studios to start rehearsals for my record. Pete Bennett met us there, and that was when I found out I'd be recording under the name *Ronnie Spector*. Later on I discovered that Phil had wanted to use the name Veronica, which I would've hated, because that was his name for me. But John Lennon and George Harrison had convinced him that *Ronnie Spector* was a better stage name. And I agree. I always liked being called Ronnie, and the Spector part made sense because it reminded people that my roots were with Phil and his wall of sound. I kept the name Ronnie Spector even after my divorce. It's funny to think that if it hadn't been for two of the Beatles, I wouldn't have the name I've got today.

Pete Bennett wanted to give me a tour of the whole studio, but Phil was anxious to get started right away, so he dragged me off to this gigantic old recording studio they had reserved for us. When we walked in, I thought we must have been early, because the only one there was this long-haired guy who was picking out chords on a piano at the far end of the room. He had his back to us, so I asked Phil if he was one of the engineers.

"Engineer?" Phil whispered. "No. That's the guy who wrote the song we're about to record." Then the man stopped playing and turned around. I practically fell over when I saw who it was.

"George Harrison!"

"H'lo, Ronnie," he said, grinning. "S'good to see you again. You look great."

"So do you," I said, taking a seat next to him on the piano bench. It was a great reunion while it lasted, but after we'd exchanged about three sentences, Phil began clearing his throat, which was his way of letting us know it was time to get to work. George laughed a little and said, "I guess you want to hear the song."

"Sure," I said. "Great!"

"It's called 'Try Some, Buy Some,'" he said, handing me a lead sheet. "The words are all written down, in case you can't make them out when I sing them."

I was so excited I could hardly breathe. Imagine sitting down with one of the Beatles to learn the song he'd just written for you. I was sure that this would be the ultimate moment of my entire career. I finally understood why Phil hadn't told me sooner—he knew I wouldn't have been able to sleep for a month.

Then George started playing. He banged out the slow melody on the piano and sang along in a high-pitched chant. The first verse didn't exactly grab me. It was written in the voice of a guy who kept talking about how he wanted to try some and buy some. Exactly what it was he was trying to try and buy wasn't exactly clear. Religion? Drugs? Sex? I was mystified. And the more George sang, the more confused I got.

By the time he got to the second verse, I was completely lost.

He had one line in there where I was supposed to say that I'd seen gray skies and met "Big Fry." And I had absolutely no idea who or what he was talking about. All I knew for sure was that this was not "something in the way she moves."

I looked over at Phil, half expecting him to crack up any second over this practical joke. But he didn't. In fact, he was more into the song than George was.

"What'd you think?" George asked when he finished. I was quiet for a few seconds before I responded.

"Wow," I told him. "You sure took a different approach with that one." What else was I going to say? I thought it was terrible. When he started playing it again, I stopped him in the middle of the second verse. "George," I told him, "I don't think I can do this song. I don't understand a single word of it."

He didn't seem too upset. He just picked his hands up off the keys and shrugged his shoulders. "That's okay. I don't either."

"Well, then," I teased, "why are you giving it to me? Why don't you sing it?" I was only joking, but a couple of years later George did do a version of "Try Some, Buy Some" on one of his own albums.

After I learned the song, Phil got the engineers in there and we started recording my lead vocal. But as soon as I heard the background track that Phil had done with the musicians, I knew we were in trouble. It wasn't even in my key.

"This is too high for me," I said.

"I don't think so," Phil replied over the intercom speaker. "Just reach a little. I know you can hit these notes." But I couldn't, and George finally had to cut some of the lyrics, because I couldn't hit those notes on some of his original words. I kept at it until we got a complete take, but the song never did feel right.

After we finished, I sat on a folding chair and listened to the playback with George and Phil. I was hoping for a miracle, but when I heard my voice fighting that droning melody all the way through the song, I knew my first impression was right. The record stunk.

George just sat there with his elbows on the piano and his head resting in his hands. I don't think he moved a muscle during the entire playback. Phil, on the other hand, couldn't stop moving. He paced back and forth in the studio, with his head cocked up toward the speakers. When the song ended, no one said a word. I knew I had to say something, and that it had to be diplomatic. "Guys," I said, "I'm still not sure that's my kind of song."

Neither of them said anything, so I tried again. "What if we redid it?" I said. "Maybe I could put a little more vibrato in there?"

"Forget the vibrato," Phil said, rolling his eyes. "Vibrato is sixties," he said. "Nobody wants to hear that anymore. This is nineteen seventy-one."

He sounded so sure of himself, I had to wonder if maybe he did have a point. I hadn't made a record—or even listened to music—in years, so maybe I *was* a little out of touch. I knew *I* didn't like the record, so I figured the only thing to do was let Phil go with his instincts.

The flip side was an even weirder song called "Tandoori Chicken," which we recorded a few nights later. John Lennon dropped by for that session, which surprised everyone, including Phil. John knew Phil and I were recording with George at Abbey Road that night, so he just marched in at around nine o'clock with a whole gang of people and announced to Phil, "We're here to make a record with Ronnie Ronette."

Phil tried to laugh it off, but I could tell he wasn't pleased at the thought of having *another* Beatle standing around looking over his shoulder. Especially John. Phil tensed up the minute John walked in, and his eyes started darting around the room. I was glad to see John, but the last thing I needed was for Phil to throw one of his tantrums, so I stayed glued to his side the rest of the night.

It turned into more of a party than a recording session. Phil sent out for tandoori chicken from the Indian place across the road, and then somebody pulled out a few joints. Before long the marijuana smoke got so thick you couldn't help but get high just sitting there. After we'd eaten the Indian food, John stood up and shouted to no one in particular, "When are we going to start the record?"

"Right now!" Phil answered. "We're going to do a song called 'Tandoori Chicken,' " he said. Then he sat me down in front of a mike and he wrote it on the spot. It wasn't even a song, really, just me singing the words "tandoori chicken" over and over. We didn't have an ending, so I sang, "and a great big bottle of wine," for a finish, because somebody had been passing a big jug of red wine around the studio. And that was the B-side to my first—and only—single for Apple Records.

I had my doubts about the record, but I didn't really give up on it until Phil brought the test pressing back to our hotel suite. "Well, c'mon, Phil," my mother said. "Let's hear it."

"Oh, no, Mrs. Bennett," he told her. "Not yet. It still needs a little work." Ever since "Be My Baby," Phil had always brought a test pressing of my latest record home to play for my mom. It was like a ritual with them. But he refused to even put "Try Some, Buy Some" on the turntable! That's when I knew that even Phil thought the record stunk.

If I had any dreams of going back to Apple for another session, they were crushed when Phil handed my mother and me plane tickets home. Mom's ticket was from London to JFK, but when I looked at mine I got quite a shock. "Phil," I said, "there's something wrong. This ticket says London to Los Angeles."

"So?" he said.

"I thought I'd be going back to our place in New York."

"Oh. Uh, no," he replied, without even looking at me. "I'm just about finished up here, so I'm going to have the New York place closed up."

I dropped back onto the bed, dreading what I knew Phil was about to say. "It's time to go back home," he announced. "And our home is in California."

My big comeback on Apple Records turned out to be nothing but a joke. There was no way radio guys were going to play "Try Some, Buy Some," and Phil knew it. I was the girl who sang "Walking in the Rain"—who wanted to hear me sing about meeting Big Fry? Who the hell was Big Fry? I didn't know, and neither did anybody else. It drove me crazy. My husband produced "My Sweet Lord" for George Harrison and "Instant Karma" for John Lennon, but when it came time to record me, what did he pick? A song about Indian chicken. So it was back to California, and life as Mrs. Veronica Spector, wife of Phil.

*   *   *

You know how you can return to a place and feel like you never left? That's how it was for me in the mansion. On my first day back, I was sitting on my bed, working on a paint-by-numbers picture of *The Blue Boy*, when Phil walked in.

"Let's go downstairs, Veronica," he announced. "I'm going to run a movie." It was barely eleven in the morning and he expected me to go down and sit with him for two hours in a dark room watching a movie.

"What movie, Phil?" I don't even know why I bothered to ask. I knew the answer already.

"*Citizen Kane*. C'mon."

That's when I snapped. I tried to drop my paintbrush in the glass of water and follow him downstairs like a good little wife, but I just couldn't move. Something had come over me. Before I knew it, I was saying the one word that I never dared utter around Phil.

"No!"

He froze dead in his tracks. "No?" he said, spinning around. "No . . . what?"

"No movie." I couldn't believe I was talking like this. I felt like a ventriloquist's dummy, whose words were coming from somewhere else. "No, I don't want to see *Citizen Kane*. Not now. Not ever again."

"Why?" he gasped. "Why not?"

"Because I hate it, Phil. Okay? I hate *Citizen Kane*!"

"You hate it?" Poor Phil. He actually seemed hurt. He continued talking, but he looked dazed. "How could anyone hate *Citizen Kane*?"

His confusion didn't last long. It was only a few seconds before his lips curled into a snarl and his eyes starting glowing with a wild animal look that most people only see in monster movies.

"I don't like what's come over you," he said. "I know you've been drinking. But I have news for you, little girl. I won't take this kind of shit. Not in *my house*. Not from *my wife*."

"Then maybe you should let *your wife* out of *your house* every once in a while."

"You can leave here when you've learned how to act like a

responsible grown-up!" Phil shouted. "And at the rate you're going, that might never happen." Then he slammed the door to our bedroom and tried to lock it from the outside. I didn't care. I felt great. I'm not sure what made me speak up that day—I suppose I just couldn't face going back to life in that musty old house after the freedom of living in New York again.

Phil was still trying to get the door bolted when I realized that there was another way out. How could he have forgotten that the bathroom opened out into another bedroom? It didn't matter. I ran through that bedroom and out to the hallway, where Phil was still fumbling around with the keys.

He almost jumped when he saw me, but I was halfway down the stairs by then. He ran to the top of the staircase and shouted after me, "Go ahead! Try to leave! See how far you get."

A couple of the downstairs maids peeked out from behind doorways to see what all the yelling was about, but nobody tried to stop me. I had no idea where I was going, but I knew I had to go. And there was only one door that I knew would be open—the servants' entrance in the kitchen. I pushed my way through the swinging doors and saw George Johnson calmly slicing tomatoes on his cutting board.

"Hi, George!" I yelled out as I ran past him.

"Hello, Miss Veronica," he answered. And then I disappeared out the back door to freedom.

19

Field Trips

I was still wearing my slippers when I left the house, but I kicked them off as soon as I got outside the front gate. Then I walked along barefoot down La Collina Drive. For some reason, I couldn't stop crying. I'm not sure if they were tears of joy or sadness. Maybe they were just tears of relief. Whatever they were, there was no stopping them as I trudged on down the hill to Sunset.

I finally got to the edge of Beverly Hills where it turns into West Hollywood, near the Hamburger Hamlet. I had nowhere special to go, so I just kept walking. Before long I came to one of those little two-story apartment buildings, the kind you see all over L.A., with a swimming pool in the courtyard. There was a plump, middle-aged lady standing out in front with a garden hose in one hand and a cigarette in the other.

"Hey, little girl," she shouted. "You better put some shoes on. There's glass all around here."

I looked at her and tried to smile, but my face was so streaked with mascara that it was obvious I'd just been crying.

"Well, now, you just stop that," she said, walking over to me. "What's wrong with you anyway, walking around barefoot out here? You want some tea?"

I nodded my head.

"Good. You come on in and I'll make you a cup. Then you can tell me what's so damn terrible that you're out here bawling like that."

After I sat down at her kitchen table, she told me her name was Phyllis, and that she managed that little apartment complex. I don't think she knew what to make of me, sitting there in my white jeans and cowboy shirt tied at the waist, with my hair in those Chinese bangs. But even if she didn't know who I was, she could see that I was a lost person, so she was nice to me anyway.

I sat there for an hour or two, drinking her tea and talking. Mainly just small talk, because she never did ask who I was or where I came from. She seemed like such a nice, motherly type that I nearly dropped my teacup when she pulled out a pack of Zig-Zag papers and started rolling a joint. And she knew what she was doing—that joint was perfect.

She lit it up and offered it to me. I'd been curious about marijuana ever since I first heard that the Beatles smoked it, but this was the first time I'd ever really tried it myself. And I liked it. I liked the groove it put me in, and I loved the way it helped me relax. Having a cup of tea and a joint with Phyllis seemed like the ultimate high.

We were still sitting there a few minutes later when a couple of gay guys who lived in her building dropped in to say hello. "Guess what?" one of the guys announced. "We got tickets to see Diana Ross in concert."

"Oh, that's great, boys," Phyllis said. Then she introduced me. "This is my friend Veronica."

"Hi, Veronica," the second guy said. They seemed like nice guys, but they were so wrapped up in Diana Ross that they barely even looked at me.

"They're big fans," Phyllis explained. And they certainly were. Before they left, they did their imitation of Diana Ross singing "Ain't No Mountain High Enough," and they were pretty good. They had the hand movements down and everything. But the whole thing was painful to me.

I mean, here *I* was—one of the Ronettes—sitting right there in front of them, but I was just a nobody. I felt like saying, "Hey, don't give me that Supremes shit. I was a Ronette! And we had a little something going, too."

But I didn't say it. Because I wasn't a Ronette anymore. Sitting there in my bare feet at a strange lady's kitchen table, I realized that maybe these two guys were right. I was a nobody.

"Phyllis," I asked, "do you have anything to drink?"

*   *   *

It was past seven o'clock that night when I made it back home. I'd gotten pretty drunk at Phyllis's house, so she offered to take me back up the hill in her car. I still hadn't told her anything about myself, so she was shocked when she saw where I lived. "Are you sure this is *your* house?" she said. I just laughed, said good-bye, and stumbled into the kitchen through the servants' door.

I heard Phil playing pool downstairs when I walked in, so I tiptoed up the back stairs to our bedroom. I dreaded having to face him again, especially in the condition I was in. He was wild enough when I ran out that morning, but there was no telling what he'd do if he saw me now. My only hope was to get upstairs and try to pass out on the bed before he saw me.

I took my clothes off and laid my head on the pillow and waited for sleep to come take me away. But it never did, not that night.

As soon as my arms started trembling, I knew I was going into a seizure, but it was already too late to do anything about it. I tried to cry out for help, but my tongue felt like it was stuck deep in my throat. I tried to pull myself out of bed, but my legs just buckled under and sent me tumbling to the floor. And that's where I lay, helpless, until my head clouded over and I lost consciousness.

I woke up in a hospital. I looked around my bed and saw a big oil painting of a seashore hanging on the wall, like one you might see in a Holiday Inn. There was a couch next to the bed, and a coffee table stacked with magazines. It didn't look like any hospital I'd ever been in before.

Nobody said anything when I got up and wandered around the halls. I finally found a door that opened out onto a big lawn. I looked through the glass and saw a bunch of ladies sitting around on sun chairs watching another bunch of ladies play volleyball. I walked out and started a conversation with one of the chair ladies.

"Hi," I said. "This might sound like a stupid question, but can you tell me where I am?"

She laughed and said, "Sure. I didn't know where I was for the first six weeks I was here. You're at Saint Francis Hospital."

"Hospital?" I gasped. "It looks more like a country club."

"You could call it that," the lady said, lighting a cigarette. "A country club for rich ladies who need a quiet place to dry out."

"Wow!" I said. "My husband put me in a sanitarium."

I met with one of the doctors that afternoon, and he explained that the program was voluntary. "You can leave any time you want," he said. "But if you want to give your system a chance to clean itself out, I'd suggest you stay at least ten days."

"Are you kidding?" I told him. "I'd like to stay here a year. I love this place."

And I did. It was heaven in the sanitarium. There were people to talk to, and there was always a volleyball game or something else to do. They let you read as many magazines and newspapers as you wanted, and you could even play records. That's where I first heard Carole King's *Tapestry* album. Compared to where I lived, that institution was a vacation playground.

Which is how I started thinking of the place. I was out in ten days, but after a few weeks at home, I couldn't wait to go back. Going into rehab became my habit, something to break the boredom, like cigarettes. When things got bad at home, I'd get raging drunk, pass out, and then spend ten days in rehab.

I made friends with some of the other ladies I saw there every month, and it got to be fun. We'd go on field trips and do all kinds of things that Phil would never let me do. One day a whole group of us went to see a taping of "The Carol Burnett Show." I sat there in the audience at CBS Television City with my group of mentally depressed people, and it was great.

Of course, Phil didn't think it was so great. Saint Francis was expensive, and he hated paying the bills for my monthly visits. So when I got home, I'd have to listen to him complain. "I'm going broke so my wife can spend half her life lounging around a hospital? This isn't a home, it's a halfway house."

When he talked that way, I actually felt sorry for him. I knew that deep down Phil wanted a normal married life as much as I did, but he could tell that I'd lost all hope in our marriage— and that scared him more than anything else. He couldn't stand to think that I might leave him, so he started cooking up all these desperate schemes to keep me with him. Like adopting more kids.

I guess he figured that if we had more kids, we'd somehow be more of a family. So in December 1971, Phil gave me the strangest Christmas present a woman ever got—twins.

Phil was already grinning when he pulled up to the hospital gate to pick me up after one of my monthly visits. "You look like you're in a great mood," I told him.

"I've got a little surprise for you," he hinted.

"What?" I asked. But he wouldn't tell me. Then I noticed that George Brand was taking a detour from our usual route home. "Where are we going, Phil?"

"To a playground," he said. And then he clammed up.

Even after we got to this playground, Phil didn't say a word. He just got out of the car and started walking toward a fence that surrounded the swing sets. "Phil," I asked, "what the hell are we doing here?"

"See those two kids?" he said, pointing to a pair of six-year-old boys playing on the swings. "Their names are Gary and Louis. They're twins and they're up for adoption. I wanted you to check them out before they saw us. That way they won't get hurt if we decide not to take them."

I thought they were adorable, and I told him so. But that's all I said. The last thing I wanted to do was bring two more kids into that house. But I didn't say anything then, because I figured there would be plenty of time to think about it. I was wrong—there wasn't any time at all.

When we got home, I was shocked to find that the adoption people were already there waiting for us—with the twins! Phil must've had George Brand take us home the long way, because by the time we drove up, Gary and Louis were already chasing each other around the fountain in front of the house.

"Merry Christmas!" Phil said.

My jaw dropped. "Phil, you didn't already adopt these kids?"

"I set everything up while you were in the hospital. Surprised?"

"Oh, yeah," I said. "I'm surprised." But *surprised* was too mild a word for how I felt. *Stunned* was more like it.

The worst part about Phil adopting twins was that I knew it

was just another one of his schemes to keep me at home. He thought that if having one kid didn't keep me chained to the house, maybe having three of them would. So he went out and found two older kids to go with the hand-picked baby we already had at home. *Presto! Instant family.* The whole thing was orchestrated like one of his recording sessions—except that you can't build a family the way you put a band together. I'm still not sure if Phil understood that.

I'd only been married three years and already I had three kids, five dogs, and twenty-three rooms. And I didn't know what to do with any of them. It was too much, too soon, too fast. Everything was getting crazy, and I was running out of places to hide.

Thank God I found Alcoholics Anonymous. The time I spent at AA meetings gave me the only sanity I had in the last year of my marriage. Actually, my going there was Phil's idea. He saw that my visits to Saint Francis weren't doing me any good, so he just said, "Why don't you try AA?"

I didn't argue. I was all for anything that got me out of the house for a couple of hours every day. And that's all AA was at first—a perfect excuse to get away from Phil's yelling and screaming. When things got too hot at home, I'd just say, "I don't have time for this, Phil. I've got a meeting." And then I'd walk out. And he couldn't say no to that.

But the more I went to those meetings, the more I learned about my problem. I found out that I'm what's called a periodic alcoholic. That means that I drink during periods of high stress, which was pretty much all the time at my house.

This all happened in early 1972, which was about the same time I first realized that Phil had been hiding a drinking problem himself. I was sitting in the back of the Rolls with Donté one morning, waiting for Phil to come down so we could go to the doctor for the baby's shots. Phil finally dragged himself into the backseat, but he didn't look too good. It was ten o'clock in the morning, but he looked like he hadn't slept in days.

Before George even started the car, he slid the chauffeur's window open and handed Phil a can of Shasta Cola. "What a way to start the day," I joked. But Phil didn't laugh. He put that soda to his mouth and sucked the whole thing down in one long gulp. When he took the can down, I couldn't help but notice his teeth were bright green. When he caught me staring at them, he wiped his mouth with one of his ruffled sleeves and threw the can right out the window.

"Phil," I said. "What's in that can that makes your teeth all green?" He tried to play dumb, but his breath gave him away. He couldn't cover up the sickly sweet smell, and it sure wasn't Shasta Cola.

My mother finally discovered Phil's little secret a few days later when she was poking around the downstairs game room. "Look at this," she whispered, holding out a half-empty bottle of crème de menthe. "I found it hidden under the stairs. Now I know why Phil's teeth is always so green."

I went to AA meetings almost every day during the spring of 1972. I couldn't get enough of them—it was nice just to be around people who were drinking coffee and talking. At first I was too shy to stand up in front of the group and testify like a lot of people did, so I sat on a folding chair in the back of the room and listened to other alcoholics talk about their struggles to stay sober. After a while I noticed that they all told pretty much the same story with slightly different details. It seemed like every one of them had started drinking because they thought it might give them a way to escape their lives.

"I know you feel trapped," my AA sponsor told me. Her name was Verda, and she was this great old lady who looked a lot like Bette Davis. We'd go out for coffee after the meetings, and she'd tell me how there were lots of other ways to get out of the house besides getting drunk. "And as soon as you *stop* drinking, you'll find them."

I told her how I drank hoping that Phil would get so disgusted that he'd finally just leave me alone. "That's not going to work," she told me. "You can't wait for somebody to throw you out. If you're going to leave that house, you're going to have to walk out on your own two feet."

And that's exactly what I did.

20

Barefoot and Broke

I left Phil for good on June 12, 1972.

The whole thing started the night before, when Phil locked me out after I came home a little late from an AA meeting. When I got home at ten o'clock, I found every door to the mansion locked tight. "Oh, shit," I said to myself. "Phil's playing games."

I didn't want to deal with him, so I snuck around and tapped on my mother's bedroom window. "Mom," I whispered. "Let me in."

She opened her window a crack and whispered through the security bars. "Go round to the kitchen door. I'll meet you there."

When I got to the servants' entrance, I found Mom waiting. "C'mon," she told me. "I'm keeping you with me tonight. Phil's acting so crazy, I don't want him seeing you."

We tiptoed down the dark hallway to her door. But just when we thought we had it made, we heard a voice booming down from the top of the stairs that stopped us dead. It was Phil. "Must have been a mighty interesting night down at the AA, huh, Veronica?"

My mom tried to pull me into her apartment, but I stood my ground. Phil was standing half in shadow beside one of the big pillars in the hallway, and for some reason I wanted to get a good look at him. I could smell his crème de menthe breath all the way down the hall.

"I mean something really fascinating must have been going on to make you completely ignore your family, right?"

I took a deep breath and stood there, waiting for him to finish. Then he stepped out into the light and swayed toward me. I started to say something, but he cut me off. He obviously wasn't through torturing me yet. "Do you have a boyfriend down there or what?"

By now he was leaning right in my face. The smell was so sickening I wanted to vomit. But I didn't budge. "Phil," I said, "why do you always have to hurt me?"

He didn't say anything. He just stood there glaring at me with his arms crossed on his chest. "I've never done anything to hurt you," I continued. "But you always do your best to insult me. Well, I can't take it anymore." It took all the strength I had, but I was determined to tell him the truth. "And if this doesn't stop right now, I'm going to have to go away."

He'd been relatively calm up until that moment, but when I mentioned leaving, he went absolutely nuts. When I saw that wild look come over his face, I instinctively tried to back into my mom's doorway for protection, but he lunged at me and pulled me down to the floor. I wrenched my legs free and started kicking him, but he just reached out and grabbed my foot. Then he pulled my shoe right off.

"You're leaving, huh?" he gasped, tucking the shoe inside his belt. "Let's see how far you get now." This was nothing new; Phil always hid my shoes when we fought—it was one of his ways of making sure I didn't walk out. "Don't even dream about divorcing me!" he shouted. "You'd never even make it through the trial. I'd destroy you after five minutes on the witness stand." He was holding me down on the floor and yelling so loud I couldn't stop shaking. My mother had been standing back until now, but this was too much for her. She jumped right onto Phil's back and started whacking him all over his shoulders and head with her fists.

"You let my daughter up," she screamed, "or I'll kill you myself!"

All of a sudden she was screaming. Then he was screaming. Then I was screaming. And everyone was punching and hitting everyone else. In all the scuffling, Mom finally managed to shove me in through her doorway. Then she blocked the doorway and dared Phil to cross. "I'll tear that wig right off your skinny little head, I swear I will."

He didn't try to get past. But he didn't back down either.

"Who do you think you're dealing with?" he said, trying to catch his breath. "If that bitch tries to walk out on me, I'll have her killed the minute she steps outside the gates. And I can do it, too."

"Go to bed, Phil," my mother said, getting her wits back. "You're acting crazy." But he'd already worked up too much steam to back down now.

"I'm completely prepared for that day," he raved. "I've already got her coffin. It's solid gold. And it's got a glass top, so I can keep my eye on her after she's dead."

"I'm going to bed, Phil," my mother said. Then she slipped through the door and bolted it tight behind her.

"Don't you believe me?" he shouted from the hallway. "Well, come on out. You, too, Veronica. I'll show it to you. It's right downstairs. Come on."

But we weren't about to go anywhere. I was already curled up in a ball on Mom's bed when she came in and found me crying hysterically. "All right, now," she demanded. "Stop it, Ronnie." But I couldn't. My mother must've realized I was close to having convulsions just then, because she leaned back and slapped me right across the face, just like you see them do in the movies.

It shocked the shit out of me, but I think it scared Mom even worse. As soon as I stopped crying, she sat back on the bed. "Ronnie, we got to get you loose from Phil," she sighed. "You been here so long, you beginning to act crazy yourself."

My mother was right. I was convinced that if I stayed in that house another day, I would leave in a straitjacket. That, or a solid gold coffin with a glass top. That's when I made up my mind, and I spoke the words out loud so I couldn't go back on them in the morning. "I don't care what happens tomorrow— this is the last night I'll ever spend in this house."

Once I'd made up my mind, I lay back on my mother's bed and had my first good night of sleep since I'd moved into that place. As things turned out, it would also be the last restful night I'd spend for a long, long time.

*   *   *

The next morning, Mom and I woke up early and started planning my escape. I'd already got the name of a good divorce lawyer from someone I'd met at an AA meeting—all I had to do now was get out of the house and get to him. And that wouldn't be easy. After last night, Phil would be watching me like a hawk.

"I'll tell Phil I'm taking you for a walk," Mom said. "That'll get you out the door. But you gonna have to leave everything behind. Your pocketbook, your credit cards—"

"Mom," I interrupted. "What about Donté?"

"Don't worry about Donté. He'll be all right with the nanny until we can have the lawyer get him back for us. But first we got to get you out of here."

"All right, Mom," I told her. "Let me just say good-bye to the baby. Then we can go."

"Well," my mother said, "okay. But hurry up."

The first thing I saw when I walked into the nursery was the nanny, who was sitting next to Donté's crib reading a book. "Shh . . ." she whispered. "He's asleep."

I looked down at my baby. He was only two years old, but his feet already stretched almost all the way to the bottom of his little crib. I leaned down and gave him a kiss on his head. Then I noticed that the nanny was smiling. "He really is a good baby," I said. "Isn't he?"

"One of the best I've had," she answered. I felt a tear creeping down my cheek, but I left the room before the nanny saw it.

Mom was waiting for me when I got down the stairs. "It's open," she said, pointing to the front door.

"I can't leave yet," I told her. "Phil still has my shoe, and I'm afraid to go back upstairs to get another pair."

"Then you gotta go barefoot," she said. "That's better anyway. He'll never suspect you're not coming back if he's still holding on to your shoes."

"Okay," I said. And then we walked out the front door of that dark house into sunlight. It was a June morning, but the air felt as bright and cool as an autumn night in New York. We walked down to the driveway, where I could feel tiny stones cutting little marks into the bottom of my feet. But I didn't care, I would've walked on broken Pepsi bottles to get out of that place.

Once we'd made it past the fountain, we were almost sure we could make it to the gate. If only Phil would stay away from his window for the next two minutes—I would have my freedom. I glanced back at the house. No sign of him. Good. Nothing can stop me now. Nothing.

Except . . . the sight of Phil standing ten yards in front of us on the driveway.

"Mrs. Bennett?" he asked. "Are you and Veronica going somewhere?"

He'd been standing in the yard the whole time—just a few feet away—talking to one of the gardeners. Damn!

My mother stepped in between us. I knew she would do all the talking, so I wandered away and pretended to look off into the fountain.

"I'm gonna take a little walk around the property," she said. "And Ronnie's coming with me."

"Oh?" Phil said, suspicious as ever.

"Yes," she continued, without missing a beat. "After what she's been through, I think the best thing you could do is let this girl get some sunshine."

Phil still looked distrustful, but then he glanced at my feet and figured that I wasn't going to wander very far with no shoes. He turned to walk back up the driveway, and we breathed a sigh of relief and started back toward the gate. But when he got about halfway to the house, Phil stopped. "Mrs. Bennett," he said, and we froze in our tracks.

"Yeah, Phil?" she said.

"Don't let Veronica step on anything sharp."

"Don't worry," she shouted, without even turning back to look at him. "You know I always watch out for Ronnie." And then we kept right on walking, side by side, until we were on the other side of those ten-foot metal gates.

"Let's walk a little faster," I whispered. Before long we were practically jogging, and we didn't slow down until we got all the way to the Sunset Strip.

I couldn't believe we'd actually made it out. But it was true. After all those years of hospitals, phony pregnancies, and inflatable men, I was out of that house forever. I was so relieved that I just started laughing out loud, right there on Sunset Boulevard.

It had finally hit me, how funny life can be. I'd just spent more than five years living like a millionaire in a twenty-three-room mansion, and I felt helpless the whole time. Now, here I was standing at the corner of Sunset and Doheny, barefoot and without a penny to my name, and I'd never felt stronger in my life.

Somehow, my mother found us a cab, and we made it over to the law offices of Stein and Jaffe on Wilshire Boulevard. Jay Stein was my lawyer, and he was a great guy in every way. The first thing he said when he saw me was, "You look like you could use some rest."

He booked my mother and me into a room at the Beverly Crest Hotel in Beverly Hills. "Don't worry," he told us. "Phil's paying for everything."

A few days later Jay served Phil with divorce papers, and then he went over to the mansion to pick up my things. I needed fresh clothes pretty badly by then. I'd been living in the same jeans and red shirt for three days already.

But when Jay got back to the hotel, all he had was one tiny overnight bag. "That's it?" I asked. "That's all you got?"

"According to Phil," he replied, "this is all the clothing you had in his house."

I opened the little bag and nearly cried. All Phil sent over were three shirts and a pair of pants. He didn't say a word about all my stage outfits, my jewelry, my makeup, or any of the other clothes I'd bought over the years.

"Phil's trying to keep all my stuff!" I told Jay. "He can't do that, can he?"

"Unless you can legally prove that you have additional property in that house," he explained, "there's almost nothing we can do."

Then I reached around in the overnight bag and found a couple things I'd missed at first glance, including a pair of woman's panties I'd never seen before, and an enormous women's bra that obviously wasn't mine. "Phil's idea of a joke?" Jay asked.

"I suppose so," I answered.

Jay just stared at the underwear and shook his head. "Why do I get the feeling that Phil's not going to be a very good sport about this divorce?"

I wasn't really surprised. After being married to this guy for nearly four years, I knew what kind of childish behavior he was capable of. But after we got to court, I found out that being married to Phil Spector was a picnic compared to getting divorced from him.

Phil was forbidden from seeing me outside of court, but that didn't stop him from calling my room at the Beverly Crest Hotel at all hours of the day or night. I accepted a phone call from Phil once, but that was enough to teach me never to do it again.

As soon as I got on the line he tried to sweet-talk me, telling me how he'd changed his ways. When that approach failed, he started making threats. "If you go through with this divorce," he told me, "I'll pay someone to take care of you. And I know guys who would be glad to do it—"

I slammed the phone down, shuddering.

When Phil wasn't calling me, he was sending people over to the hotel to bug me. One time George Brand showed up at my door with this guy I'd never met. My mother wasn't there, but George had been Phil's bodyguard forever, so I let him and his friend in. I thought the other guy must've been a lawyer, because he handed me a contract as soon as he walked in.

"What's this?" I asked. Then I looked at it. It was a paper giving Phil complete custody of the twins. "I can't sign this until my lawyer sees it."

George's friend never said a word. He just walked over to the telephone, dialed a number, and handed me the receiver. "It's your husband," he explained.

"What's going on, Phil?" I asked.

Then Phil started raving on about how this guy with George wasn't a lawyer at all, but a trained hit man. "And he's been paid to blow your brains out if you don't sign that paper right now."

I told Phil he didn't need a hit man to make me sign away the twins. I loved Gary and Louis, but I never wanted responsibility for them in the first place. I guess that was all George and this guy needed to hear, because they left without even having me sign the paper.

The divorce itself was a nightmare. Jay Stein filed the papers in June 1972, and for the rest of that summer I must've spent about half my life in the cafeteria of the Santa Monica Civic Courthouse. It just dragged on forever. And since Phil didn't want the divorce in the first place, he was always coming up with new stunts to slow things down. When the court ordered him to pay me $1,300 a month in support payments, he had the first month's payment sent over to Jay's office in nickels.

As many times as the judge told Phil to stay away from me outside the courtroom, he'd always make a complete fool out of himself as soon as the court let out. He'd follow me and my lawyer down the courthouse steps, shouting the worst obscenities at my mother and me. But he'd save his most vicious curses for my lawyer.

"Leech!" Phil would shout. "Why don't you motherfuckers mind your own business and leave us alone?"

"Just ignore him," Jay would say, staring straight ahead. "Let's just walk calmly to the car."

But as soon as we'd get into Jay's car, Phil would climb behind the wheel of his Rolls-Royce and tailgate us all the way back to the hotel, honking his horn the whole time. Then he'd stick his head out the window and scream, "Okay, Veronica. Go ahead, divorce me! Time will tell who's right and who's wrong!"

Phil was bad enough when he was in a spiteful mood, but he was even more pitiful when he was feeling sorry for himself. We walked past Phil on the courthouse steps one afternoon and he didn't say a word. He just stood there looking like a sad-eyed dog that had been kicked once too often.

We had already climbed into the car and started the motor when we heard this long, loud moan coming from behind us, like some kind of human fire siren. We looked back and saw that it was Phil, crying out on the courthouse steps.

"Veronica!" he was shouting. "Don't do this to me!"

"Drive away, Jay," my mother said, taking control. "Let's just get out of here."

But Phil didn't give up. He turned and stomped down the

courthouse steps like a *Night of the Living Dead* zombie, crying out, "Veronica! Don't leave me! Veronica!"

Jay was halfway down the street when my mother glanced back and saw Phil was standing at the curb, hollering like a sick coyote. "Veronica! Come back to me! Veronica!"

"My God," she muttered. "Do you *see* that?"

But I didn't even look. My days of watching Phil make a fool of himself were over. I kept my eyes glued to the road ahead and never looked back.

Phil had always told me I'd never be able to make it through a divorce without going nuts. After about three months of that hell, I was beginning to see what he meant. My mother and I spent almost every afternoon in that miserable courthouse. And when we weren't in court, we'd end up sitting around the coffee shop at the Beverly Crest, surrounded by a bunch of depressing old ladies who ate nothing but cantaloupe and cottage cheese.

I couldn't have gone through it without Mom. And she knew how much it meant to me to have her there. That's why it practically killed me when she announced she was going back to New York.

"You're not my only daughter, Ronnie," she said. And then she packed her bags and left. Estelle had just had a baby girl with Joey Dong, and Mom was anxious to see her first grand-daughter. But I needed her, too, and in my mind, Mom was deserting me when I needed her most of all.

Phil must have had a radar that could sense when I was at my weakest, because he called me up exactly two hours after Mom's plane left, and I was already a complete wreck by then. The switchboard wasn't supposed to put his calls through, but some-times they made a mistake.

As soon as I heard Phil's voice on the line, my first impulse was to hang up. Phil knew this, so the first thing he said was, "Don't hang up! It's about Donté." That got me hooked.

"What's wrong?" I gasped.

"I don't know. He just got finished crying himself to sleep for the third night in a row. I'm getting worried."

"Why?" I asked. "Phil! Is anything wrong?"

"I don't know. He keeps asking for Mommy. And when I tell

him she's gone, he just cries until he goes to sleep." Then Phil got a little sarcastic. "I don't know. Does that *sound* like something's wrong?"

I was tortured by the thought of Donté crying himself to sleep, and Phil knew that. "Put him on the phone," I demanded. "I want to talk to my baby."

"No!" Phil replied. "He doesn't need a *phone call*. What Donté needs is a full-time mother. When you get your ass back here, *that's* when he'll stop crying."

It was killing me, but I knew that if I went back to Phil now, I'd never get Donté away from him. "I'm sorry, Phil," I said. "But I can't go back to that house. Ever."

"Fine," Phil snapped. "Next time I hear Donté crying, I'll be sure to tell him how you feel."

"I've got to go now, Phil."

Then I slammed the phone down. It made me angry just to think about the games Phil was already playing with Donté's head, and it made me sick to think that there was nothing I could do about it. I knew that leaving Donté behind was the only choice I had—I never could have made my escape if I'd tried to take him with me. I told myself that I was doing the best thing I could under the circumstances, but that didn't make me feel like any less of a failure as a mother.

What a night! First my mom walks away from me. Then all of a sudden I've got to deal with how I walked away from my own kid. I felt like my whole insides were coming apart. The only way I got through it was by promising myself that if I ever did get legal custody of my kid, I'd never let him out of my sight. But getting custody would take time. And I wanted my baby there with me that night.

Suddenly, I had to have a cigarette. The smoking habit I picked up at the Brooklyn Fox had only gotten worse during my divorce. I hadn't gone twenty minutes in the past three months without a Marlboro between my fingers. I lit one and took a long drag. Then I lay back on the bed and tried to force myself to sleep. But every time I closed my eyes, all I could see were Donté's eyes crying out for me from his crib.

It was useless—there was only one way I'd get to sleep that night. I dialed room service and started looking through my purse for a dollar to tip the kid who brought the bottle up.

*M*ademoiselle magazine sure gave me a different look for this fashion layout in 1965. (Courtesy *Mademoiselle*)

*W*e may look happy here, but when this magazine came out at the end of 1966, things were going so badly for the group that we'd already decided to go our separate ways. (Courtesy Kevin C. Dilworth)

Posing for a picture just after I became Mrs. Phil Spector. I thought marrying Phil would solve all my problems, but the real nightmare had just begun.

Our bodyguard, George Brand, played Santa for our 1968 Christmas card. Phil and I wore matching suits that I got on sale at Orbach's for $16.95 each. "On me," Phil bragged, "everyone'll think it cost five hundred bucks."

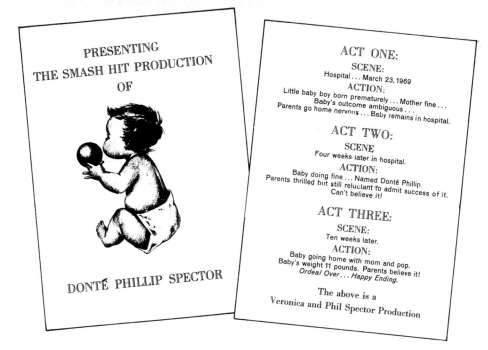

PRESENTING
THE SMASH HIT PRODUCTION
OF

DONTÉ PHILLIP SPECTOR

ACT ONE:
SCENE:
Hospital . . . March 23, 1969
ACTION:
Little baby boy born prematurely . . . Mother fine . . .
Baby's outcome ambiguous . . .
Parents go home nervous . . . Baby remains in hospital.

ACT TWO:
SCENE
Four weeks later in hospital.
ACTION:
Baby doing fine . . . Named Donté Phillip.
Parents thrilled but still reluctant to admit success of it.
Can't believe it!

ACT THREE:
SCENE:
Ten weeks later.
ACTION:
Baby going home with mom and pop.
Baby's weight 11 pounds. Parents believe it!
Ordeal Over . . . Happy Ending.

The above is a
Veronica and Phil Spector Production

*W*hen we adopted my first son, Phil sent out this birth announcement so everyone would think Donté was our natural baby. He even had me stick a pillow under my shirt to make it look like I really was pregnant. (Courtesy Keith Beach)

*D*onté was a half-breed, like me, and he was beautiful. I took it as a sign from God that he looked exactly like our baby would have if Phil and I could've had one.

A family snapshot taken a few years after my divorce from Phil. That's Donté standing with Gary and Louis, the twin brothers that Phil adopted as a surprise for me when I got out of the sanitarium.

*T*he sleeve of "Try Some, Buy Some," the song George Harrison wrote for me in 1971. John Lennon showed up to help us do the B-side, but the record was a big flop anyway. (Courtesy Jay Lammy)

A promotional postcard for my 1975 comeback single, "You'd Be Good for Me." Like almost everything else I'd recorded since the sixties, the record's release was practically a secret between me and the label. (Courtesy Kevin C. Dilworth)

*B*ackstage with Bruce Springsteen and a fan after a show near Cleveland, February 1977. Billy Joel had just given me "Say Goodbye to Hollywood," and Bruce let me use his E Street Band to record it. (Photo by Janet Macoska)

*W*ith Stevie Van Zandt, backstage in 1977. Stevie did a great job producing me, but he and Springsteen nearly drove me crazy with questions about their hero, Phil Spector. (Photo by Janet Macoska)

*M*y publicity picture from the early eighties, right after I recorded my first solo album, *Siren*.

A family photo of my second—and last!—marriage, to Jonathan Greenfield. That's Jon with me on the far right. His mom and dad are standing in the center, and my aunt Helen is the one on the far left. That's my mom standing in front, with my little second cousin, Dawn.

$\mathcal{E}$ddie Money called me at home one day to ask if I wanted to make a record. Six weeks later we had a top-ten hit! Here we are after the American Music Awards in 1987. (Photo by Dave Elkouby; courtesy Star World)

$\mathcal{I}$ love being a mom, but I'd go nuts if I didn't get back up onstage every few months. Here I am at Madison Square Garden, still rocking at age forty-six, November 1989. (Photo by Richard Bonenfant)

*B*ackstage with Jonathan and Bo Diddley at Madison Square Garden, 1989. (Photo by Richard Bonenfant)

*A*t home in Connecticut, a normal wifc and mom at last! Jon's carrying Austin, and that's Jason in my arms. After so many years of hell, having those boys was the miracle that finally turned my life around for good. (Photo © 1990 Maddy Miller)

After I finished off a fifth of vodka, I drifted off faster than I expected. I didn't even bother to put my cigarette out before I went to sleep—or so the fire inspectors said after I nearly burned the hotel down. All I remember is waking up at the UCLA Medical Center in the morning with Jay Stein standing over me.

"What happened?" I asked in a hoarse voice.

"You breathed in a lot of smoke last night," he explained. "But the doctor says you're fine, otherwise." Then he told me how I'd fallen asleep with my cigarette still burning and ended up setting my own bed on fire. "I've already talked to your mother," he said. "She asked me to put you on the first plane to New York. And that's what I'm going to do."

I was so happy I nearly floated right off the bed. "You mean I don't have to go down to the courthouse anymore?"

"Not for the time being," Jay said. "We can handle things here for a few months. But right now, I think you could use a little break in your routine."

"A break?" I said. Then I broke out laughing. "Jay, you just said the magic words."

21

Up for Grabs

My lawyer had arranged for me to live at the Navarro Hotel during the divorce, and I loved it there. I'd been lonely for so long that I was thrilled just to be able to walk outside my door and find myself in a crowd. I had a yearning for people that wouldn't go away. I'd go out of my way to bump into them on the street, just so I could remind myself that they were real. I wanted to walk with them and talk with them and eat with them. But most of all, I wanted desperately to get back on the stage and perform for them.

The trouble was, I'd been out of circulation for so long that I didn't know a soul in the business anymore. I was completely out of touch. In my last five years with Phil, I'd barely listened to a radio. So I decided that was where I'd start, by flipping on the radio.

And who do you suppose was the first voice I heard? It was Murray the K, who was still doing the afternoon show, except that now he was on WNBC. I just laughed. He wasn't calling himself the fifth Beatle anymore, but he was still making corny jokes and playing records. I listened to him for a few minutes, and then I grabbed the phone. I dialed WNBC, and when the operator answered, I asked to be connected to Murray.

"Who should I say is calling?" she asked.

"Tell Murray it's one of his dancing girls."

There was a short pause before Murray picked up on the other end. He nearly freaked when he heard it was me. "Ronnie! Boy, are you a sound for sore ears!" he said. "Hey, honey, let me put you on the air."

"Okay," I said. "Why not?"

He was so excited, it was really sweet. We stayed on the air for maybe ten minutes, talking about the shows we did at the Brooklyn Fox and all the fun we had doing his show. It seemed like such a long time ago, but I remembered so many pictures vividly. That was the first time I'd ever really looked back at what the Ronettes had done, and by the end of the call I felt very proud.

"Gee, Ronnie, that was just like the old days," Murray said after he took us off the air. "I had one of my guys record it. You don't mind if I play it again a little later, do you?"

"Not at all," I laughed. "I could use the publicity."

I was only kidding, but as it turned out, that ten-minute call to Murray the K was the best publicity I could've hoped for. He played it about ten times over the next few days, and every time it went on, the WNBC switchboard lit up with calls. And a few days after that, *my* phone started ringing.

Dave Zaan was the first to call. Dave had been a booking agent for the Ronettes in the sixties, and now he was with Banner Talent, which was an agency that booked a lot of acts on the oldies circuit in the early seventies. The first thing he asked me when I got on the line was, "Are you ready to go back on-stage?"

"Are you kidding?" I said. "I'm dying to get back up there. Just name the time and place."

"Well," he said, "nothing's definite yet, but *Rock* magazine's sponsoring a rock and roll revival at the Brooklyn Academy of Music in January. And I know you'd be perfect."

"I'm there!"

"Great," he said. "I assume you'll contact the other two Ronettes?"

I almost dropped the phone. "The other two Ronettes?"

"Of course. What's Ronnie without her Ronettes?"

"Yeah," I said. "I guess you've got a point." Then I told him not to worry, that I'd get the other girls together in no time. But

I knew I was in trouble before I even hung up the phone. It was already after Thanksgiving, which meant I had maybe six weeks to reform a group that hadn't performed together in almost six years.

But the worst part was that I'd seen Estelle recently, and I knew she was in no shape to do a show. She'd put on about thirty pounds since the Ronettes split up, and I wasn't sure she could even handle the moves anymore. Boy, was I right about that.

I invited her up to my room at the Navarro for a rehearsal. I figured that if I could teach her a few new steps, maybe she could fake her way through a show. But it was a disaster. I put on a record and tried to get her started, but it was hopeless. She had completely lost her coordination. It was bizarre. I'd move one way, but instead of following, she'd do a sidestep in the opposite direction. I thought she must have been putting me on, so I called her on it.

"Hold it a minute, Estelle," I said. "Are you joking or what?"

She didn't answer, but I saw a look of such shock and pain come over her face that I felt terrible. Estelle *was* trying her best, but it just wasn't good enough. And now I had shamed her. But there was nothing I could do about it. As hard as it was for me to imagine—my sister just wasn't a Ronette anymore.

I had a whole different set of problems with Nedra. We couldn't even reach her at first, because she was spending most of her time at a hospital in Ithaca, New York, where her mother had just undergone minor surgery. Finally my mom and I decided to go to Ithaca ourselves and bring Nedra back, even if we had to drag her. Then, as if things weren't already bad enough, it was snowing so hard the day we left that the airports were closed. We ended up taking a Trailways bus all the way to Ithaca in a blizzard.

Mom and I finally tracked Nedra down in the hospital cafeteria. "Nedra!" I screamed. "They want us back!"

"Who wants who back?" she asked.

"The Brooklyn Academy of Music," I told her. "We've got a show there in January. But we've got to get back to New York to start rehearsals right away."

"This *is* the Ronettes you're talking about?"

"Of course, who else?" I asked.

"Well, let me set you straight on something, Ronnie," she said. "I have children now. I am a Christian. My husband's a minister."

"Scott?" I couldn't hide my surprise.

"Yes, *Scott*," she answered, a little indignant.

"Well, that's great," I told her. "But what does that have to do with the Ronettes?"

"Well," she said, suddenly sounding very self-righteous. "You can walk up on that stage and shake your rear for the Brooklyn Academy of Music or anybody else, for all I care. But I won't. I prefer to use my vocal gifts to spread the word of our Lord, Jesus Christ."

"Okay," I said, stunned.

"But thanks for asking me, anyway," she added.

"No, Nedra," I said, getting up from the table. *"Thank you."* Then I left the hospital, got on the bus, and cried in my mother's lap until we got back on the highway.

When we got to New York, I decided that my only hope was to find two new Ronettes. I remembered how Phil replaced me when I couldn't go on that Beatles tour, so I figured I'd do the same thing, only in reverse. As long as my voice was out front, I figured, no one would pay any attention to who was standing behind me.

The Banner Agency put me in touch with all the black acting schools and theaters in town, and I must've looked at every light-skinned black singer or dancer in New York before I found Chip Fields and Diane Linton. They were perfect—two skinny, light-skinned girls who could move well. As soon as I put those two together, I called my aunt Maddie and told her to start making three new Ronettes outfits.

But just having three dresses that matched wasn't enough. I knew that our audience had very definite ideas about how a Ronette should look, and I was determined that these new girls would live up to that image. So I helped Chip and Diane pick out makeup, and I found them two long black wigs to wear. Then, before we went out onstage, I even put their eye makeup on for them, because they never used enough mascara when they did it themselves.

I'll never forget the look on their faces the night of our first show. We were backstage at a theater in New Haven, Connecticut, for a preview performance when Chip and Diane first saw themselves in a full-length mirror—all decked out in their gigantic wigs and wearing about two pounds of mascara. They were absolutely startled.

"Oh, my God!" Chip gasped. "I look Chinese!"

The New Haven show was supposed to be a dry run to get us ready for our big show at the Brooklyn Academy the following week. But I was so nervous, it might as well have been Carnegie Hall. When the emcee introduced us, I went kind of limp for a second and wondered what I was going to do if they hated us. But I knew there was no point worrying, so I bounced out with the girls and laid right into our first number, "Baby I Love You."

We were only supposed to do three songs for our little section of the revue, but after we finished our finale, "Be My Baby," I didn't think the audience was ever going to let us off that stage. Poor Chip and Diane stood there with frozen grins on their faces, but by that time I was in no hurry to get off, so I drank it up. Then, finally, I led the way, and we walked off the stage like three skinny queens. It was a night to remember.

After Dave Zaan saw that first show, he got on the phone and lined up bookings for us in small clubs and oldies revues straight through the spring. I was thrilled to have all that work fall in our laps, but I also knew that going on tour took a lot of organization, a lot more than my mother and I could ever handle by ourselves.

The first thing we had to do was put together a small band to tour with us. And the first step to getting a band together was finding a bandleader. As it turned out, the guy who led the band on my first few comeback shows was a young guitarist named Billy Vera, who's still making great records today. Billy was good, and he was also a cute guy. He reminded me a little of Phil—he had the same dimple when he smiled, and the same receding hairline. I have to admit I had a crush on him, and I got the feeling he liked me, too. So, after we'd done a couple shows together, I walked right up to him and said, "Billy, everybody says you're the best bandleader around. I'm going back to work, and I need somebody good. Can you do it?"

He said, "Sure." And that was it.

Billy hired a band for us, and then we started rehearsing a lineup of songs that I felt comfortable doing on tour. In those early days, I wasn't yet confident enough to do any new material, so I stuck pretty much to stuff I'd done with the Ronettes. In fact, people who saw my act in 1973 heard almost the entire *Presenting the Fabulous Ronettes* album, which included all of our Philles hits, along with "What'd I Say?" and a couple of others.

Billy Vera and I hit it off right from the start. He was a great bandleader, and a nice guy, too. After we'd worked together for a few weeks, we started hanging around together offstage, too. We spent a lot of time playing records and eating at my mother's apartment. He even stayed overnight there with me a few times. But I wasn't ready for a real romance yet. Not as long as I was still drinking.

I'd stopped going to AA meetings after I got back to New York. I figured my career was back on track—so who needed AA? You know the answer to that one.

When I was with Phil, I thought I only had a drinking problem when I was depressed. But once I got back on the road, I discovered that I had to have a few drinks whenever things got tense. And things are always so tense on the road that I spent a whole lot of time drunk out of my mind. I'd have a few vodka and Cokes to calm me down before a show. I always thought I could handle it, but there were times when I went completely out of control.

One night we were playing a nightclub that Billy lined up for us in Boston. Like a lot of the little clubs we played, this was a very scary place. I don't know if the guys who ran the club were mobsters or just liked to act like they were, but every one of them wore an expensive suit and never seemed to have anything better to do than stand around making me nervous. And that nervousness was always good for at least three drinks. By the time I got onstage, I could barely stand up.

I made it through the first number, but the audience knew I was bombed and they let me know they didn't like it very much. Nobody yelled obscenities or anything, but nobody clapped either, which is really just as bad. Then Billy started the intro to "Walking in the Rain." But instead of singing on my downbeat,

I walked right to the edge of the stage and started giving the audience a hard time.

"Hey! I don't hear you guys," I slurred. "S'everyone asleep or what?" The room was completely silent. "Well," I tried again, "maybe I can get you going. Who wants a kiss?"

A guy in the front row popped out of his seat and raised his hand. Billy kept right on playing the song, and Chip and Diane kept right on dancing—but you could tell they were expecting the worst. And they got it. I leaned forward to give the guy in the front row his little peck on the cheek, and that was the end of the show for me. I lost my balance and fell right off the stage.

Boom. Straight to the floor.

The next thing I knew, one of these mob guys had picked me up and dragged me off to a tiny office behind the kitchen. He sat me up on a little desk and yelled, "Sober up. Now!" Then he left the room. All of a sudden I couldn't keep my head up, and I passed out right on this guy's desk.

When I woke up I was back in the motel with Billy. He was pouring coffee into me and acting very pissed. "Ronnie, you could've been killed back there. Those gangsters wanted to break both of your legs! And they probably would've, too, if they hadn't known me."

That incident scared me, but not enough to make me stop drinking. I couldn't—I was an alcoholic. Billy tried to help me. When he saw me with a drink before a show, he'd walk over and say, "What's in the glass, Ronnie?"

"Coca-Cola," I'd always answer, never bothering to mention the two shots of vodka that I usually had the bartender mix in. I never admitted I was drinking, because that would have meant admitting I was an alcoholic. And that was something I couldn't face.

After a few months, Billy Vera got tired of looking after me, and he just gave up. We'd just done a gig in Florida, and he walked into my hotel room with an envelope full of cash. "Here's your share of the money we made," he said. "Everyone else has been paid. I'm out of here." I was shocked when Billy just walked out on me like that. But, looking back, I can see that he really had no choice. He couldn't stand by and continue to watch me hurt myself, but there was nothing he could do to stop my drinking, and he knew it. So he left.

*   *   *

Alice Cooper called me in October of 1973 and asked me to sing on his *Muscle of Love* album. Why he thought of using *me*, I'll never know, because he also invited Liza Minnelli to show up on the same day. I think it was more of a publicity stunt than anything else, because he had photographers and reporters all over the studio.

The press posed the three of us together at the microphone, but I don't think Liza was too happy about having to share the spotlight with me. I was so happy for all the attention that I let loose with a few "ooohs" and "ahhhs," and the reporters got a kick out of that and started applauding. And that really got Liza steamed up. She couldn't figure out why this girl with the weird voice was getting all the laughs, so she just stood there snuffing out cigarettes and glaring at me while I put on my little show for the photographers.

She was going out with Edward Albert, Jr., at the time, and he came over to the studio that day. The instant he walked in, Liza grabbed him and spun him around so that his back was toward me the whole time. I guess she was being protective of her man. I still don't know exactly what was going on with her.

I continued to make live appearances all through 1973 and '74, but my recording career was going nowhere. All the major labels looked down on me as an oldies artist, and no one was interested in what I could do now. I finally signed a two-year deal with Buddah Records, mainly because they were the only ones who asked. They put me together with a producer named Stan Vincent, and we did two singles—an awful song called "Lover Lover," and a remake of "I Wish I Never Saw the Sunshine," which I originally recorded with Phil in 1966, though he never put it out. I should have left well enough alone, because the remake was just terrible. Stan Vincent was a great guy, but he was no Phil Spector, and both of the singles I did with him were dismal flops.

In November of 1973, my mother and I took a break from touring to go back for the final round of my divorce trial in California. I dreaded going back to court. When I thought of how badly Phil had behaved in the courtroom, I could only hope that after all this time he might've mellowed out a little. I should've known better.

Things turned into a circus the minute he walked into the courtroom. He came in surrounded by a whole entourage of Oriental girls, which was supposed to make me jealous, I suppose. One of the girls was May Pang, who was John Lennon's girlfriend in those days. Phil was producing an album for John, who actually wandered into the courtroom a few minutes later.

John walked in just in time to see Phil make a complete fool of himself. My soon-to-be ex-husband wasn't in court three seconds before he started shouting, "You bitch! You thieving bitch!" It was pathetic. The judge held him in contempt and called a recess, but Phil wouldn't shut up until the bailiff physically dragged him out of the courtroom. John just watched the whole thing and shook his head. Then he glanced over to me and mouthed the words, "Good luck." He got up and left after that, obviously disgusted by the whole thing.

I was finally granted my divorce from Phil Spector in February of 1974. The judge gave me a small community property settlement plus alimony payments for five years. But as far as I was concerned, Phil came out the real winner—*he* got custody of Donté.

"How could they have given my baby to that crazy man?" I asked my mother. I'd already given up the twins and that wasn't so hard—I'd only lived with them for about six months. But how could I give up Donté? It made no sense—I was only thirty years old, and I had so much love to give him.

I decided to go right back to work—it was either that or sit around depressed for six months. I called Dave Zaan, who said he could book me on an oldies tour that was leaving in three days. "You'll be touring in the South for the rest of the winter. Can you do it?"

"Yeah," I told him. "Maybe I can get some sunshine."

The tour turned out to be good therapy. I did shows every night and didn't have time to think about how lousy my personal life was going. About three days into the tour I even found a new boyfriend. We'd just finished a show in Memphis when Jerry Summers, who was one of the Dovells, walked up to me dragging this shy little guy in his early twenties behind him. "Ronnie, this is our guitarist," Jerry said. "He's in love with you, but he's too shy to say so. His name is Stevie Van Zandt."

It was the same Stevie Van Zandt who would later play guitar for Bruce Springsteen's E Street Band, but back then he was a kid. Stevie finally got up the nerve to ask me out, and we went to see *The Exorcist* before our show the next day. We ended up having a little romance—nothing too serious, just some good times on the road. When the tour ended, Stevie took me for a little weekend trip to Puerto Rico. I was pretty much finished with the relationship by that time, but I didn't know how to tell him. So I didn't. Instead, I got drunk and stayed that way the whole weekend. When we got back to New York he didn't call me again, which was fine with me. Crazy as it sounds, that was the way I ended all my relationships with men in those days.

Guys had a tendency to fall for me right away, but I was so bad at saying no that I ended up going out on a lot of dates that I wasn't too sure about. Trouble is, if I didn't like a guy when I was out with him, I would never come out and say so. Instead, I'd just get so drunk he wouldn't want me anyway. Then he'd leave. It got me through a lot of bad dates, but you don't start too many relationships that way.

In March 1974, rock and roll promoter Richard Nader offered the new Ronettes a chance to play Madison Square Garden. Richard was staging one of his rock and roll revival shows there on the fifteenth, and Dick Clark was hosting, so it was like old home week. I did the show with Chip Fields and a new Ronette named Denise Edwards, and it was probably the biggest crowd we ever played. Twenty-three thousand people showed up that night, and we had them in the aisles before we were through. They were standing on their chairs, lighting matches in the air, the whole bit.

That was a great night, but I think the most memorable show I did in those days actually came a few months later, in May 1974, when I played the Continental Baths with Chip and Denise. The Baths was a small club in midtown that catered to a mostly gay audience—which was perfect for us. The gay crowd had always been right there for the Ronettes from the earliest days. And they were certainly there that night. Before that show was over, we'd worked that crowd into a frenzy.

The Baths was one place where I knew I could really let loose, so that night I wore a sheer gold jumpsuit that left nothing to the imagination, and the guys loved it. The club had Murray the K there as our emcee, and he brought along his usual supply of bad jokes, which actually went over pretty good with the crowd at the Baths.

"I noticed Patti LaBelle's in the house tonight," he announced before he introduced us. "Last time I saw you, Patti, it was at the Brooklyn Fox. You were having a big fight with Shirley of the Shirelles. Now you're here and she's not. Guess that means you won."

Then he brought us out and the place went up for grabs. We did all of my Ronettes classics, and some newer stuff, too. My version of Stevie Wonder's "Superstition" put the crowd over the top, and by the time we got to our encore, they were ready for anything. I started singing "Love Train," and one guy got so excited he jumped up and joined me onstage.

He didn't have a shirt on and he was wearing the tightest leather pants I'd ever seen, with a thick belt that he left hanging unbuckled around his waist. I started dancing with him, and then I couldn't resist having a little fun. I reached down, pulled off his belt, and started whipping him playfully across the legs. That cracked the whole place up completely. Then I held the belt above my head and turned to face the audience. "All right!" I cried out. "Who's next?"

All hell broke loose, of course. Seven or ten guys fell all over each other to get onstage, while the rest of the crowd laughed and egged them on. Then one of the guys actually grabbed my mike and started singing, so I just shrugged my shoulders and walked down to the front row to watch him. The whole room was in convulsions by the time I finally got things back under control. But I have to say it was one of the best shows I've ever done.

In all those years I spent locked away with Phil, I never really lost touch with my love of that stage. When I stood out there in front of the crowd, I'd soar so high that nothing else mattered. The only trouble with flying that high is that it can be a long way down.

I never did get used to the idea of being a part-time mom. The terms of my divorce gave me visitation rights to see Donté for about four hours a day, for four days every other month. And even then, I had to fly all the way out to California and see him in a hotel room just to do that. I hated traveling back to Phil's turf, but I did it. I still had such terrible associations with California that I'd puke my guts out every time I got on that jet for the West Coast.

Once I got to L.A., I'd go straight to the hotel and wait for my son to arrive. It was ridiculous. Phil always sent Donté over in a big limousine. He was five years old and he would climb out of this Rolls-Royce like some midget prince. And even then Phil would send a governess along with him, which I put up with only until I discovered that one of these nannies carried a gun.

She was a tough old lady who always made me nervous anyway. I'd be sitting on the floor of my suite eating hamburgers with Donté, and I'd look up and catch her staring at us. She was more like a cop than a nanny. I knew something wasn't right, so I never let her out of my sight. At one point she opened her purse to get a cigarette, and I glanced over and noticed that she had an automatic pistol tucked in between her compact and change purse.

My lawyer told me she was probably a private investigator whom Phil had hired to watch over Donté, which really made me mad. He finally got Phil to call her off, and I saw my son without his "nanny" from then on. But even without a detective staring at you, four hours a day is hardly enough time to get to know your son. It seemed like I barely had a chance to buy him a hamburger and a toy before the limousine would be there to whisk him away again. After the fourth day, I'd give Donté a kiss good-bye and I'd be back on the plane to New York.

It was a pretty sorry way to be a mom. Sometimes I wondered if I wouldn't have been better off forgetting about the whole thing. But I still loved my Donté. He was the only kid I'd have until I finally grew up myself. And that was still a long way off.

After our successes at Madison Square Garden and the Baths, I continued doing concerts with the girls through the rest of 1974. But nothing ever matched the excitement of those shows. We spent most of our time marching in and out of oldies revues, and that got pretty depressing after a while. I was barely thirty years old, and everywhere I went people were calling me an oldie but goodie! A girl could get a complex from stuff like that.

It drove me crazy—and it sure didn't help my drinking problem any. I used to stand backstage at these rock and roll revivals and cringe when the emcee announced us as oldies singers. I'd be standing off in the dark somewhere in the wings and raise my Dixie Cup of vodka and Coke in a silent toast. "Here's to little Ronnie Spector," I'd whisper to myself. "An oldie. But a goodie!" I'd say it as a joke, but I can tell you there was nothing funny about it.

Whether it was for good or bad, my oldies career finally came to an end during the holiday season of 1974. That was the year Dick Clark signed the Ronettes to take part in a rock and roll revival show he was staging at the Flamingo Hotel. And I'll never forget my nightmare in Las Vegas.

It was great to be working with Dick Clark again—his shows were always professionally run, and this was no exception. I rehearsed my numbers with Chip and Denise onstage in the late afternoon, and we were dynamite. Dick and everyone on his staff were predicting that Vegas would be the start of a whole new career for the Ronettes.

And when I finally saw our name up in lights outside the casino, I began to think so, too. They do everything about ten times bigger than life in Vegas. So naturally, the marquee outside the hotel was about a hundred feet tall, with the names of all the groups in the show spelled out in letters twelve feet high. I'd never seen "The Ronettes" spelled out that big, and I loved it.

Dick gave us a dinner break between the afternoon rehearsal and our first evening show, so I took the elevator back up to my room to rest up. I was so high from the excitement that I didn't think anything could bring me down. Then the phone rang.

"It's me," the voice said. He didn't bother identifying himself. He didn't need to.

"Phil?" I hadn't spoke to him in so long that I actually thought he might be calling to wish me well on the show.

"Veronica," he said. "What in God's name makes you think *you're* ready to play Vegas?"

I should have known Phil would be up to his same old tricks. "Okay," I said. "Is that all you called for?"

"No," he said. "I just wanted to give you fair warning that tonight could be the last time you appear onstage in Las Vegas. Or anywhere else."

He was talking so calmly, for a minute I actually thought that he was saying something sensible, and that *I* was the one confused. "What *are* you talking about?"

"I always said I'd kill you if you left me," he explained. "And tonight I'm making good on that promise. In two hours you will be assassinated onstage at the Flamingo Hotel."

"I'm calling the cops, Phil," I told him. "If you even try to set foot in the Flamingo, I'll have you arrested." I tried to stand up to him, but he just laughed in my ear. It was a sound that went right down my spine.

"You don't think *I'd* be stupid enough to pull the trigger?" he said. "That's what I pay hit men for. And I've hired six of them for this job. Three black and three white. You might spot one, but you'll never be able to get them all. They'll be at your show tonight, and I've offered a million-dollar bonus to the one who shoots the bullet that does the job."

I dropped the phone like it was a dried fish and ran out of the room. I figured the whole thing was just one of Phil's dumb stunts, but it still scared the hell out of me. One thing I knew about Phil is that you couldn't second-guess him. What if today was the day the guy finally did crack up?

I decided to find Dick Clark, and get his advice. But by the time I got down to the showroom, he was already gone. I walked through the casino with my hands shaking so bad I knew I had to get something to calm me down before I rattled myself to pieces. So I walked into the bar for one quick drink. But in those days they were never quick. And it was never just one.

I grabbed my nose and sucked down a vodka and tonic, then I set my hands down on the bar. They were still shivering. "One more," I told the bartender. I felt so much better after the second drink that I was sure a third would do the trick. Five vodka and tonics later, my problem was solved. I no longer had to figure out whether to go through with the show or not. Dick Clark would make that decision for me.

He tried to look the other way when I stumbled into the backstage area that night. But Dick couldn't ignore the fact that I was too drunk to make it through even one verse of "Walking in the Rain" at the final dress rehearsal. "Ronnie," he said, steering me over to a quiet corner backstage. "You're in no shape to go on tonight. I'm sending you up to your room."

Dick Clark and I go way back—I did my first national TV appearance on his show. So when I saw that glint of disappointment in his eyes, that hurt almost as much as being fired.

"I'm sorry, Dick," I slurred. "I just didn't want the hit men to get me." I was trying to give him an explanation, but it was useless. He had no idea what I was talking about, and he had better things to do than listen.

It was already noon when I crawled into a cab the next day with Chip and Denise. I told the driver to take us to the airport. The girls didn't say a word, which was actually a great relief for me, considering the circumstances. I told them how sorry I was, but there didn't seem to be much else to say after that.

As the taxi pulled out of the driveway, I turned to take one last look at the giant marquee. The Flamingo already had a couple of workers up there changing the sign. As we drove off down the strip, I couldn't take my eyes off of it. I watched the guys pull the letters of our name down, one by one, until all I could see was "ETTES." Then we turned a corner. Chip and Denise never even looked up.

I didn't know it then, but when I got out of bed on New Year's morning of 1975, I was facing what would be one of the worst years of my entire life. I had no friends, no family of my own, and my career was one big zilch. Buddah Records had dropped my recording contract after my two singles flopped, so I didn't even have a label anymore. And after my binge at the Flamingo Hotel, I couldn't even look forward to doing revival shows, since that little incident pretty much killed the Ronettes as an oldies act. Looking back, I think that might have been the only bright spot in the whole mess.

I went out and found a little apartment on York Avenue, on the East Side. And then I basically retired for a year. I don't remember doing much of anything except sitting around the house and drinking. Sometimes I'd go to see my family, but that usually only made me want to drink even more.

If I went to Mom's house, I'd pray that none of my aunts or uncles would be there, because I knew how they liked to ride me about my drinking. "Oh, you're a natural alcoholic, just like your father was," somebody would always say. I couldn't take a drink without hearing it.

Things finally got so bad that my entire day's routine revolved around drinking. I'd get up in the morning, brush my teeth, and have a beer. And then at night I'd drink until I fell asleep. I was killing myself a little more each day. But I didn't care. I wanted to die. If I was so much like my dad, I figured I might as well see if I couldn't beat him to the grave.

My mother finally saw how bad I was getting and took me down to the rehab program at Metropolitan Hospital. I was seeing a psychiatrist there twice a week, but the person who really helped me wasn't a doctor at all. She was an intern named Marcia Knight.

When I met Marcia in 1975, she was about my age—thirty-two—and she knew all about my days as a Ronette. She was so easy to talk to that some days I'd drop by the hospital in the late afternoon just to say hello. Marcia was usually running around with a clipboard in her hand, but she would always stop to make time for me.

After a while I started visiting her at home. She was working on her doctoral thesis in psychology at the time, and she told me it helped her break the tension to have someone else around. "I'll make a deal with you," she said. "You help me get through my thesis, and I'll help you get through your drinking."

So I started hanging out at her house. I'd watch TV or read, and then, when she needed a break, we'd go out dancing or to a movie. I don't know how much I really helped her, but her friendship worked wonders for me. I didn't kick my alcoholism overnight or anything. As a matter of fact, I wouldn't stop drinking for a long time. But after I made friends with Marcia, I no longer wanted to die. And for me, that was progress.

22

Say Goodbye to Hollywood

y singing career just sat there in 1975. I did do a little record that year, a single called "You'd Be Good for Me" for a tiny label called Tom Cat Records. But like everything else I'd done since the early sixties, the release of that record was practically a secret between me and the label.

Things didn't really turn around for me until the day I bumped into John Lennon outside the Dakota on Central Park West. This was in the spring of 1976, but that wasn't the first time I'd seen him since I got back to New York.

That would've been almost two years earlier, in the fall of 1974. He was still living with May Pang then, and they were staying in a big apartment building on the West Side. One day I ran into May Pang outside the place, and she dragged me up to her apartment to visit John. "C'mon," she said. "John would love to see you."

When we got up there, John was sitting on the bed like an Indian, smoking a joint and listening to records. He hadn't shaved for a few days, and his hair was all tangled. He looked like he was in the middle of a very long hangover, but he sure jumped to his feet when I walked in. "Look who I found walking the streets," May Pang said.

"Ronnie Ronette!" John said, giving me a hug. "I was just thinking about you." Then he swung around and picked up a

45 from a big stack of records next to his portable stereo on the floor. "Have you heard this?" he asked, reaching over to put the record on. "It's the brand-new Phil Spector single, but you're not going to believe it."

He played the record and I heard what sounded a lot like "Baby I Love You," except that it was slowed down to a funeral march. The record sounded so muddy, it could have been recorded underwater. "Wow," I said. "Is that playing at the right speed?"

"Forty-five rpms!" he laughed.

"Who is it?" I asked.

"It's *Cher!*"

"Cher?" I gasped. "Phil produced a record for Cher?"

"Yeah! She's buried in that mix somewhere," John said. "Can you believe *this* is a Phil Spector production?" I couldn't. When the record ended, John picked it up off the turntable and held it at arm's length. "What happened to that guy, Ronnie? I think the poor bastard's completely lost it."

Then John flung the record across the room like a Frisbee. "Oh, well," he said, lighting another joint. "So much for the heroes of our misspent youth. Speaking of which, how are you then?"

And that's how that visit went. I didn't see John again for two years. Then I ran into him outside the Dakota, and he looked a hell of a lot better. He was so thin and fit I almost didn't recognize him until he called out, "Ronnie Ronette!"

I looked up and there he was, walking into the Dakota with another guy, who turned out to be Jimmy Iovine, the record producer. "John," I said, "you look great!"

"I feel great," he said, beaming. "I'm just a happy little housewife now, with not a care in the world. Or is that househusband? Anyway, I've got nothing to do all day but sit at home and play with my new baby. And I've never been more contented."

I was usually a little jealous of anybody who had a baby and a real family life, but I was only happy for John. I knew as well as anyone how long this guy had been searching for peace, and I told him how overjoyed I was to see that he'd finally found the thing he'd been looking for.

"And what about you, Ronnie?" he asked. "What is it you're searching for?"

"Right now I think I'd settle for a good producer," I joked.

"Well, don't look at me," he said. "I'm supposed to be semi-retired, or so I've read in *Rolling Stone.*" Then he pointed to his friend, Jimmy Iovine, who'd been standing there politely this whole time. "Music is Jimmy's department. He knows everyone in New York." Jimmy Iovine is one of the top record producers in the business today, but he was just starting out as an engineer back then.

After that introduction, John put on a funny voice like an old English granny and said his good-byes. "You'll have to excuse me now, luvs, but oi've got a roast in the overn. Ta-ta!" Then he turned and disappeared into the Dakota, where his wife and kid were waiting for him. Jimmy and I laughed and waved him good-bye. I never saw John Lennon again after that. But when I think of him now, I remember that afternoon and I smile.

I walked a little way down the sidewalk with Jimmy before he finally asked me if I wanted to get a cup of coffee. "Sure," I said. He was a sweet guy, and we got to be pretty good friends after that. I think he sensed the rut I'd gotten myself into, so he took it on himself to shake me out of my boredom. A week didn't go by when Jimmy didn't invite me to a club opening or party somewhere. And I soon found out that John was right—Jimmy really did know just about everybody in the music business.

I was sitting at home watching TV when Jimmy called me one night. "Hey, Ronnie," he said. "You want to come down to a session with me tonight?"

"Sure," I said. "Whose session?"

"Southside Johnny and the Asbury Jukes."

"Southside who?" I asked. "Come on, Jimmy. I've never even heard of the guy."

"Then just come down for laughs. The producer's a friend of mine. His name's Stevie Van Zandt. I think you'd like him."

"Oh, I know Stevie," I said.

We got to the Record Plant at around eleven o'clock that night. Stevie was in the middle of recording when we walked in, but he couldn't stop looking over at me. I was wearing a pair of green suspenders over a bright red T-shirt that night, and I had my blue jeans tucked into this pair of knee-high suede boots that I used to wear. I looked pretty good, and Steve wasn't the only guy there checking me out.

After the band finished their take, Steve came over and gave me a squeeze. "Great to see you, Ronnie," he said. "Thanks for coming down."

When Steve went back into the booth, I shot Jimmy a look and whispered, "How did Stevie know I was going to be here?" Jimmy shrugged his shoulders and tried to look innocent. But I knew better. "I smell a setup," I told him.

Sure enough, I hadn't been there five minutes when Stevie walked back over and asked, "So, are you going to sing with us tonight, or are you just here as an observer?"

"You know me, Stevie. Point me to the mike and stand back." He laughed and signaled the engineer to play the backing track for a tune Bruce Springsteen had just written called "You Mean So Much to Me."

"Bruce wrote it for Johnny," Steve told me. "But I want him to rework it as a duet for a guy and a girl. Why don't you two give it a try?"

He didn't have to ask twice. Southside Johnny was this scrawny little blond guy with glasses, and I didn't think he'd be much of a singer. But when he opened his mouth, I flipped. The minute I heard the guy's incredible blues voice, I knew we'd sound great together. "Let's do it!" I hollered.

Steve called Springsteen, and he came down about a half hour later. These guys had all known each other forever, so when Bruce walked in, Stevie just introduced us as casually as he would any two old friends. "Hiya, Bruce," I said. "Nice to meet ya." Then I gave him a kiss on the cheek.

"Hi, Ronnie," he said. "Nice to see ya, too." Then he went off in a corner and rewrote "You Mean So Much to Me" in about fifteen minutes. Stevie grabbed the new lyrics and ran right into the recording studio.

"Okay," he said. "Let's do it."

Three hours later, I'd finished my duet with Southside Johnny and I was in a cab on my way home. "You Mean So Much to Me" was a nice little song, and it was fun to record. But if someone had told me that night that it would be the start of a whole new career for me, I would've laughed in their face.

*   *   *

Dave Zaan called me in March of 1976. He had a gig he thought I might want to do—a small club in Jersey. "The pay's not great, but you'll have an audience," he told me.

I was getting pretty sick of sitting around the house by that time, so I told Dave I'd do the show if he could dig up a couple of new background singers for me, since I hadn't seen Chip or Denise since Vegas.

"Fine," he said. "I'll send a couple of singers by your place tomorrow morning. How's ten o'clock?"

"Better make it noon," I said. Then I hung up.

A few minutes later the phone rang again. It was May Pang. She'd called me a few times since John left her to go back to Yoko, and we got to be friends after a little while. "Hi, May," I said. "What's up?"

"I've got house seats for David Bowie's show tonight at Madison Square Garden. You want to go?"

I didn't know a damn thing about David Bowie, but I figured, why not? And that was the start of my little affair with David Bowie. A sad, funny—and very short—story.

May and I went down to Madison Square Garden and sat in the best seats in the house. We were so close to the stage that Bowie could see us almost as well as we could see him. After the show, May dragged me to this restaurant where they were having a big reception for Bowie. "I hate those kinds of things," I told her. But she insisted we go anyway.

So I went to the restaurant, but meeting David Bowie was the last thing on my mind. Besides, I couldn't have talked to him even if I'd wanted to—he was sitting at a big private table that had been roped off from the rest of the place. He was calling himself the Thin White Duke in those days, and that's just what he looked like behind those gold ropes.

There wasn't anything happening at this reception, and I was all set to go when this guy tapped me on the shoulder and said, "Mr. Bowie requests the pleasure of your company."

I had to laugh. May Pang gave me a wink, and I followed this guy over to Bowie's table. Two other guys lifted the ropes to let me by, and David Bowie greeted me with a big smile. "I'm so glad you came up," he said. "Please, have some dinner."

So I sat down and ate. I thought David was a little strange, and I could tell that he had a pretty high opinion of himself. But for some reason I was attracted to anyone who had that much confidence. Maybe I thought some of it might rub off on me. I could also see that he really liked me. So when he invited me up to a party in his room at the Plaza, I thought, what the hell? I certainly didn't have anything else going on in my life.

We took a limousine over to the Plaza, and when we got to his suite it was filled with these really hip types who spoke with British accents and wore thousand-dollar watches. Most of them were hanging around a long glass coffee table that was literally dusted with a thick white powder.

I only turned my head to look at them for about three seconds, but that was all the time it took for David to disappear. I felt completely out of place around all these snotty people, but I figured I'd try to make conversation until David decided to come back and rescue me.

"Hey," I said, walking up to the glass table. "Can I try some of that?"

There must have been twelve people around that table, but not one of them said a word. They all just looked at me, like, "Who is this piece of shit that David dragged home, and how long do we have to put up with her?"

Then one of the guys finally took pity and handed me a little straw. "Thanks," I said. I leaned down and snorted up what felt like an ounce of this coke into my nose. From all the stories I'd heard about this stuff, I expected some kind of magic. But all it did was make my nose run.

I ran into the bathroom to get some Kleenex, and when I came out there was a guy standing in the hallway with a big snifter of cognac. "David's waiting for you," he said, handing me the cognac. "Follow me."

I was so glad to be rescued from that party, I would've followed this guy anywhere. He led me to a closed door and pointed to the doorknob with two fingers. Then he walked away.

I swung the door open and walked into this huge bedroom that was lit up as bright as Yankee Stadium. I heard music, but I couldn't tell where it was coming from, until I glanced past the gigantic king-sized bed and saw Bowie sitting on the floor, completely naked, popping cassettes into a portable tape player. One look at this guy and I could tell how excited he was to see me. Very.

I wasn't really into sex in those days. I was a drinker, and when you drink a lot, it sometimes takes away your sex drive. But something told me I wasn't going to have any trouble in that department. Sure enough, we made love right there on the floor, and we didn't even bother to kick the cassettes out of the way.

We climbed up on the bed afterward. Everyone else at the party was doing coke, but David and I just lay there drinking cognac from these big crystal snifters. And after a few of those, we were flying as high as anybody there. I tried to go to sleep, but there was so much noise that I finally just reached over and slipped my blue jean skirt back on.

"I've got to get out of here, David."

"Where're you off to?" he asked.

"Back to reality," I said. "I'm going home."

Then he asked if he could come along. He said he could do with a little peace and quiet himself, but I got the feeling that wasn't all he wanted.

"Let's go," I said.

His limousine dropped us off at my place on York Avenue, and we were back on the floor within two minutes. But we'd barely started making love when we heard the sound of running water in the kitchen.

"Shit!" I gasped. "It's my mother!"

I knew she had keys to my house, and it wasn't unusual for her to spend the night over there. But why did she have to pick tonight?

"Your mother?" Bowie asked. He looked at me like I was joking. But when he saw that I wasn't, he started laughing out loud. "Your mother?" he said, still chuckling. "Oh, Ronnie. That's so quaint."

I didn't like being teased, and I had a good idea how to shut him up. I ended up dragging him off to my bedroom, where we fell asleep, eventually.

The doorbell sounded louder than a fire alarm when it woke us up the next morning. "Can't you stop that bloody noise?" David growled from under a pillow.

"No," I said. "Somebody's at the door."

"Who in the world would come by at this hour?"

I glanced at the clock. "It's not all that early, David. It's already a little after noon."

He didn't say anything else, so I figured he'd gone back to sleep. Then the bell rang again. "Well," he said. "Who the hell would come by at twelve noon?"

Noon! Of course. That's when it hit me. Dave Zaan was supposed to be sending those two girls over at noon. That had to be them. I didn't care. Show or no show, I was in no shape to rehearse any new Ronettes today. I pulled my other pillow over my head and tried to go back to sleep. But the doorbell just kept ringing and ringing until I finally gave in.

I carried my tired bones out to the living room and buzzed up these two skinny black girls, one tall and one short. "Hi," the tall one said. "Dave Zaan said you might be just waking up. He told us to keep ringing until you answered."

"Uh-huh," I mumbled. "Thanks, Dave." Then I had them wait in the living room while I ran back to check on David. But he was gone by the time I got to the bedroom. I figured he must have jumped into his clothes and snuck out the back way. And sure enough, I ran to the front window just in time to see him disappear into a cab.

"Your boyfriend?" the short girl asked.

"Not exactly," I said. And then I couldn't resist. "That was David Bowie."

"Oh. Uh-huh," the tall one said. "Sure."

I had a feeling that would be the last I'd see of David for a while. And I turned out to be right.

My night with Bowie wasn't exactly typical, but I did have a pretty strange social life in those days. My career sure wasn't taking up too much of my time in the first few months of 1976, so I pretty much went out with whoever was around. I had a friend named Jeannette who was a lesbian fan from the old days, and one night she took me downtown to see a play called *Women Behind Bars*.

It was a weird show. It starred Divine, and it was full of transvestite jokes and stuff I didn't understand. I finally got so bored I wandered out into the lobby to have a cigarette. When I got there, I noticed this guy standing by the ticket booth who wouldn't take his eyes off me. He was obviously a fan, so I turned and flashed him a great big smile. That was all it took.

"I'm sorry to stare," he said. "But my name is Clifford Terry, and I'm probably your biggest fan in the world. I hate to disturb you, but I know I'd kick myself all night if I didn't walk over here and talk to you."

"You're not disturbing anything, Clifford," I told him. "And if it'll keep me from having to go back into that theater, I'll listen to your whole life story."

He laughed at that, and we spent the rest of the play talking in the lobby. I found out that this guy wasn't kidding—he really was a serious fan. He knew all about records I made but hadn't even thought about in years—"Paradise" and "I Wish I Never Saw the Sunshine" and all the other stuff that Phil never released, at least not in this country.

"A lot of those songs did come out in England," Cliff told me, and I was amazed. When he invited me over to his house to hear some of them, I jumped at the chance. I spent a lot of time with Cliff over the next few months. He told me he was gay the day I met him, but I always said we would have had a great romance if he hadn't been. We'd sit around his place playing my old records and drinking wine for hours on end. It really blew me away to hear some of those old songs. And it finally put me in touch with how good I really was, which was something I hadn't felt in a long time.

"Are you kidding?" Cliff used to say after I'd put myself down. "No one in the world sings like you do. That's a rare gift." Nobody had said anything like that to me in a long time, and I desperately needed to hear it. Cliff helped me boost my self-esteem up at a time when I needed it most. I think that's one of the reasons we hit it off so well.

Cliff also helped me open up and confront the past. He loved to hear my stories. So we'd stay up all night, and I'd tell him all the things I'd never told anyone before about the nightmare of my marriage to Phil, and about all the problems I'd had with my career. Then we'd take a few more swigs from our big gallon jug of wine and we'd laugh—or cry—until morning.

It felt great to finally get some of these stories out of my system. That's when I first realized how much I was still living in the past. I thought I'd given myself a brand-new life when I left Phil, but I never seemed to be able to leave the old one behind. When I talked to Cliff, I finally had to face up to all the things that had happened in my past—and that's when I began to understand what my life could be in the future.

Southside Johnny called me at my mother's house one day in the spring of 1976. I don't think I'll ever forget that call. "Ronnie," he asked me, "what have you got planned for the summer?"

"Not a thing, Johnny," I answered.

"Well, get on your dancing shoes," he said. "You're going on tour."

I nearly freaked. Johnny was going out on the road to promote his first album on Epic Records, and, according to him, our duet on "You Mean So Much to Me" was the hottest thing on the record. *And,* he explained, Epic was willing to pay me to go out on tour and sing it with him every night. "You'll also get to do a few of your own songs, if you'd like."

If I liked? It was like a dream come true. I was out on the road with Johnny and the Asbury Jukes for the next year and a half, and I had the time of my life. The Jukes were all great guys, and they really knew their stuff. It was such a treat to be back on the road with a real rock and roll band.

We opened for Bruce Springsteen and the E Street Band on some of these dates, and those were always great shows. I remember one we did with Bruce at the Cleveland Agora. Even after Springsteen finished his set, the kids just wouldn't stop cheering. I was standing backstage when Bruce came off after about three encores. He was dripping with sweat when he saw me. "Hey, Ronnie!" he said. "You want to go out there and rock and roll?"

"You bet I do!" I answered, and I ran back out onstage with Bruce and did every one of my hits for that wild crowd. Springsteen and all the guys were such Phil Spector freaks, I honestly think they enjoyed that night more than the kids in the audience.

It was no secret how much Bruce and his band loved Phil's sound. That's about all they ever talked to me about. Whenever I sat down to have dinner with Bruce and the guys, he and Stevie would pop up and start asking me all kinds of questions about Phil and his music. "Ronnie," Bruce would ask, "just how many guitars did Phil use on 'River Deep, Mountain High'?"

"I don't know, Bruce," I'd answer. "I was locked up in my room watching an old Cary Grant movie when he did that one." But that wouldn't stop him, and he'd go on grilling me about "Baby I Love You" and the Christmas album for hours on end. Details. He always wanted more details. He drove me nuts asking for details.

But other than that, I got on well with all the guys in Bruce's band. Sometimes too well. I was at a party after one of our first shows when big old Clarence Clemons leaned down and tried to kiss me. "Whoa, Clarence," I said. "You can't be serious. I'm five feet three inches and you're six feet whatever—you *must* know this is never going to work out." He sort of laughed it off. But I think he got the message, because he was a perfect gentleman after that.

Working with Southside Johnny, I made friends with people outside the band, too. Steve Popovich was a big shot at Epic Records, and he was one of my biggest fans at the label. He always told me that he'd love to record me on my own—if he ever found the right song. I knew Steve was a good guy, but I never took him very seriously until he called me from Epic Records one evening in December of 1976.

"Ronnie, Stevie Van Zandt's down here with me," he said. "And we'd like you to drop on by, if you've got the time."

"Sure," I said. "What's up?"

"I think we found a song for you."

I practically flew down to Epic, which kept offices at CBS Records on Fifty-second Street. When I walked in, Steve Popovich already had the mystery song on the turntable. "I was up all night listening to demos when I came across this one," he said. "It's a Billy Joel cut called 'Say Goodbye to Hollywood,' and I think you're going to be surprised."

He dropped the needle on the record and it blew me away. It sounded like it could have been written for me. From the 'Be My Baby' drum beat that opened it up, to the wall of sound production at the fade, it could almost have been a Ronettes record. The singer was a guy, but he used heavy vibrato on the vocals, the same as I would. "That's a Billy Joel song?" I asked. "But that can't be him singing?"

"Yeah," Steve said. "That's Billy doing Ronnie Spector. When I told him I was going to try and get you to do the song, he was floating on air. He wrote the thing three years ago, but he told me he had you in mind the whole time."

Did you ever have one of those days when you just knew that God was smiling on you? Well, He was grinning from ear to ear the day we recorded "Say Goodbye to Hollywood." Everything on that record just fell into place. The E Street Band backed me up, with Stevie Van Zandt producing. And that guy really knew how to bring my voice out. Stevie created a sound that was as close to Phil's as anyone ever got. But the record still sounded extremely modern—and I give credit to Bruce's E Street Band for that.

People have told me that my singing on that record is as strong as it's ever been, and I'm not surprised. "Say Goodbye to Hollywood" is all about a girl who picks herself up and says good-bye to Hollywood and all the people who've let her down. It was the story of my life, and I really got behind the emotion on that one. I wanted "Say Goodbye to Hollywood" to be the best record I'd ever recorded, because I knew that if it hit, I really would be able to say good-bye to Hollywood—and Phil Spector—forever.

When Steve Popovich heard the song he fell back in his chair. "That's a hit," he said, "without a doubt." Steve was so confident in the record that he put it out as the first release on his own label, Cleveland International, which was a subsidiary of Epic Records. Before it even came out, Popovich was already talking about following it up with an entire album.

"I'm sure we can get the E Street guys to do a few more sessions," he told me. "And just this morning I got a call from Brian Wilson—he says he wants to write you a song for the new album."

"That's incredible," I said.

"Ronnie, this is only the beginning," he told me. "I think you're really going to take off this time. I really do."

*   *   *

You'd think I would have learned by now to watch my step anytime someone starts talking that way. But I hadn't. I was still counting the millions in my fantasies when "Say Goodbye to Hollywood" came—and went—in two short months during the summer of 1977.

The record turned out to be what Steve Popovich called a turntable hit, which meant that it was a song the disc jockeys wouldn't stop playing on the radio, even though it wasn't selling in the stores. But that meant nothing to me. As far as I was concerned, if the kids weren't buying it, "turntable hit" was just a fancy name for failure.

I continued to do shows with Southside Johnny for the rest of that summer, and the crowd always seemed to love it when I sang "Say Goodbye to Hollywood" in concert. But after it flopped as a record, I never heard from Brian Wilson or any of these other guys who supposedly wanted to work on my album.

To be perfectly honest, I wasn't in such great shape to do an album then, anyway. I managed to keep myself together through most of the tours with Southside Johnny, but I still drank like crazy whenever I got depressed—and nothing depressed me more than having a flop record.

Still, I've got to hand it to Steve Popovich—the guy really stuck by me. By August, Epic Records had officially dropped their option for an album from me, but Steve still insisted that I meet him down in Nashville. He had suddenly decided we were going to try our luck on a country song.

"Are you sure about this?" I asked him once I got down there. "I mean, I don't even know if I can sing country music."

"Oh, I don't believe in all these divisions between country music and pop, Ronnie," Steve told me. "A good song is a good song, no matter how you do it. And this is a good song." Then he played me a demo of "It's a Heartache," and I had to agree—it was a good song. I had a great time recording it. But it was Bonnie Tyler's version that became the hit—not mine.

I still remember the day we did that song—August 16, 1977— because that was the day Elvis Presley died right down the road in Memphis. In fact, when the news of his death came out, I was in the studio with Chips Moman and a lot of other musicians who'd worked with Elvis. But no one even told us what happened until after the session.

We were just finishing my vocals when this little guy walked into our studio and whispered something to Steve Popovich, who was one of the producers of the session. Steve didn't say a word, but he got right up and ran out of the studio. None of us could figure out what was going on, but when Steve walked back into the studio a few minutes later, his eyes were red, and we thought we smelled liquor on his breath. All he said was, "Let's finish this one up and get out of here."

We did the last few takes, and then Steve gave me a ride back to my hotel. That's when he told me Elvis had been found dead in his bathroom that morning. "Oh, my God," I said. "Why did you wait so long to tell me?"

"I would have told you sooner," he said. "But a lot of those guys in the studio knew Elvis, and I wasn't sure how they'd take the news. I only had this one day in the studio, and I couldn't afford to take a chance that you guys might not be able to make it through the session."

Steve was right. Everyone *was* pretty shaken up—even me. I went over to Chips Moman's house that night and cried myself to sleep. It's not that I was such a big fan of Elvis Presley or anything. It's just that his death got me thinking. Here was a guy who had everything—they called him the *King of Rock and Roll!* But he was so unhappy with his life that he finally destroyed himself. And after he died so suddenly, I couldn't help but wonder if I wasn't headed down that same road.

At least Elvis had kept his singing career going, which was more than I could say. I had just released a great single, and I'd spent the last year and a half on the road, but what did I have to show for it? All that work, and it didn't add up to a damn thing.

That's when I decided I had to have a baby. If I couldn't make my mark on the world as a singer, then maybe I could do it by raising a child. At least then I'd have something I could hold on to, something I could call my own. And it may sound silly, but I was convinced that I would always be a nobody until I proved to my family—and myself—that I could bring a baby into the world.

But as much as I wanted a baby, I had no interest at all in finding a husband. Of course, I still dreamed of living the Ozzie and Harriet life, but I was so down on myself in those days that I couldn't even think about having a real relationship. All I wanted was a man who would get me pregnant and then leave me alone. And I knew just the man for that job.

23

Backstage Pass

I was sitting on Clifford Terry's bed when I asked him to get me pregnant. He thought I was joking. "I don't know if you've noticed," he laughed. "But making babies isn't exactly my forté."

"Because you're gay?" I asked him. "But that's why I picked you."

"Oh?" he said with a little smile. That's when I knew I had him.

"You're not interested in women," I explained. "And I've given up on men. So we're perfect for each other. I want a baby, but I don't need a man attached. You're the only guy who can help me."

Then he started to laugh out loud. "Okay. But if I'm going to do this," he said, reaching for a gallon jug of red wine that he always kept nearby, "I think I'm going to need a little help."

We both got drunk and had sex that night, but no baby came of it. We tried again once or twice later, but I could tell I wasn't going to get pregnant this way. You know what they say, you can bring a horse to water, but you can't make a guy . . .

I got so depressed by the whole thing that I finally gave up on ever having a kid of my own. The truth is, I was lucky Cliff didn't get me pregnant, because I really wasn't ready to be a mother. I still didn't understand what it really meant to have a baby. Looking back at myself in those days, I probably would have been better off just playing with my old dolls.

My romantic life had been one washout after another ever since the divorce, and after a while I just gave up on ever finding a husband. Clifford Terry was my steady date, and I was perfectly happy going out with him. Who needed romance?

That was my resolution in March of 1978. But—wouldn't you know it—by the end of April I had met the man who would be the father of my children. Sometimes I guess the best way to find something is just to stop looking for it.

I met my future husband at a show called *The Neon Woman*. It was another play starring Divine, and it was running upstairs at Hurrah, which was New York's first rock disco. Cliff Terry took me, and he knew everybody in the place, so naturally we got invited to the backstage party after the show.

The first person I saw at the party was Peter Allen, who told me he was one of my biggest fans. I knew Peter had once been married to Liza Minnelli, so we immediately started gossiping about her. I told him how weird she acted when I met her at Alice Cooper's recording session, and then he told me a few stories of his own.

We were still talking about Liza when this young guy walks up and starts listening to us. I thought he was a great-looking guy, and I could tell he was just standing there waiting to say a few words to me. But I got a kick out of how politely he stood there listening, so I left him hanging for a few minutes. He just smiled, patiently waiting his turn. After Peter Allen drifted away, I leaned over and whispered, "Now, don't you dare breathe a word of what you heard here."

"I wouldn't dream of it," he said. I was about to walk away, but I couldn't get over the way this guy kept smiling at me. I finally asked him what he had on his mind.

"I know this is a strange request," he said. But that didn't stop him from asking anyway. "I'd like to hug you."

"Hug me?" I had to laugh. "Sure. Why not?"

Without missing a beat, he leaned over and swept me up in his arms. He was a big guy, so he just kind of rolled me up in his arms and squeezed me until I finally let out a squeal. "Hey," I giggled. "Not so hard."

If I thought he looked happy before, that hug really put him in a daze. "Thank you," he said. Then he started to walk away.

But something made him change his mind, because he swung around and looked me straight in the eye and said, "I saw you sing at Madison Square Garden in 1974. I took one look at you and said, 'Now, there's a real woman.' And I promised myself that if I ever met you, I'd give you a great big hug. So, I just want to say thank you for giving me my hug."

It was such a cute story that I started to laugh out loud. I guess he thought I was laughing at him, because he turned around and was starting to walk away when I stopped him. "Hey," I shouted, loud enough to be heard over all the noise backstage. "What's your name, anyway?"

"Oh," he said, smiling as he walked back over to me. "Didn't I say?" I could tell he was still a little nervous, but he was getting over it fast. "I'm sorry. My name is Jonathan Greenfield."

"Nice to meet you, Jonathan," I said. And then I watched as he started to move away again. He was a big, broad-shouldered guy, and there was something so sweet and open about him that I couldn't take my eyes off him for the rest of the night. He was one of the production stage managers on the show, and I remember how impressed I was by the way all the stage hands and technicians kept walking over to him to get his advice on where to put the sound equipment and stuff like that.

But what amazed me even more was the way he handled one of the high-strung actresses who sang in the show. Ever since the curtain had gone down, this girl had been frantic about some little musical bit that had gone wrong in the show that night. She was pacing around backstage, cursing and just about going crazy, until Jonathan finally walked over and sat down with her. I couldn't hear what he said, but whatever it was, it seemed to calm her down instantly. Two minutes later, he had her laughing and grinning like a cheerleader.

"Wow," I whispered to Cliff Terry. "There's a guy who really knows how to handle a situation." That impressed the hell out of me.

I went back to see *The Neon Woman* every night for a week, which confused Cliff, who knew I didn't even like the show that much. But I finally had to tell him that it wasn't my love of theater that was driving me down to Hurrah every night—I went there hoping to bump into Jonathan.

I'm still not sure what made me go after him that way. I guess I just knew there was something about his personality and style that made me feel at home, and I wanted to know him better. But poor Jon never even guessed I was pursuing him. He thought it was purely coincidence that I dropped by the show night after night. It never occurred to him that his rock and roll idol might actually be interested in him. And that was just one more reason I was falling in love with him a little more every night.

I can't remember the exact moment that Jon and I first started getting serious. By the end of 1978, I had moved into a one-bedroom apartment on the Upper West Side, at Ninety-fourth and West End Avenue. Jon didn't live far away, so I ended up calling him whenever I couldn't handle something. If I broke a closet door, I knew I could get him to fix it. If I couldn't get a guy to leave after a date, I'd have Jon come over and scare him away. Jonathan Greenfield was the one guy who could handle anything I threw at him.

And unlike most of the guys I'd gone out with, Jon never got scared away by my drinking. There were plenty of times when he saw me drunk and depressed. But he stuck by me. He was always there when I needed him, and, except for Cliff, there weren't many guys I could say that about.

The other unusual thing about Jonathan was that, no matter how much time we spent together, he always kept a respectful distance from me physically. And that was something new for me—I was used to going out with guys who couldn't wait to jump on me. Jon never even so much as tried to sneak a kiss. But after a while, his politeness began to drive me nuts.

It was about 2:00 A.M. one morning, and Jon had just dropped me off in front of my apartment building when I decided to ask him about it. "Jon," I said, "is there something wrong with me?"

"No," he said, surprised. "Why would you ask that?"

"I don't know. You don't kiss me, you don't touch me. I thought maybe you didn't like me or something."

"You think I don't like you?" he said. "Ronnie, I idolize you. I'm in awe of you. I always have been."

"Well, you don't show it much."

He got out of the car and started pacing around. I could tell he was getting exasperated, which I thought was really cute. "You don't think I wouldn't love to kiss you and hug you and all that stuff? Well, you're wrong. I would. I'd like to kiss you and hug you, and a lot of other things you haven't even mentioned. But I can't."

"You can't!" I shrieked. "Why the hell not?"

"Because," he said, and then he stopped pacing and looked me right in the eye. "I'm not the right guy for you."

"You're crazy!" I yelled. Then I noticed that my doorman was peeking out of the building to see what all the commotion was about, so I lowered my voice. "You're crazy, Jon."

"No, I'm not," he whispered. "You're a star."

I stood back and looked at him. He was standing in the head-lights of his Chevy, wearing a pair of Converse sneakers and a sweatshirt that was torn under the arm, but he looked like a prince to me. Even so, he was talking like such an idiot that I could've slugged him. I didn't. Instead, I wrapped my arms around his big old bear shoulders and squeezed him until my arms hurt.

It wasn't long before Jon finally came around. They always do. And the more I saw of him, the more I knew he was the perfect guy for me. Jonathan loved my voice, and he wanted to see my career take off almost as much as I did. I had finally found my Mr. Dependable, a man I could count on whenever things got rough. Which was a pretty lucky break for me, because my life was about to get very, very rough.

24

Running Away

It was in the middle of a cold January night in 1980 that I got the call. The phone woke me up at about one in the morning, and I could hear from the static on the wires that it was a long-distance call.

"Veronica Spector?"

"Yeah, I said, shaking the sleep out of my head. "Who's this?"

"My name is Dunham. I'm a social worker with the Los Angeles County Department of Juvenile Correction. Do you have a son named Donté Spector?"

"Yes!" I gasped. "I do. What's happened to him?"

"Nothing. He's fine," the guy said. "It's just that he's run away from home."

That sure woke me up. Donté was only ten years old, but according to this guy, he just climbed onto his bicycle one night and rode away. "Apparently," this Mr. Dunham added, "he wasn't too happy at home."

"Have you talked to Phil?" I asked.

"That's the funny thing," he said. "We've been calling him for three hours, but no one's answering."

I was stunned. All the guilt that had been building up over the past eight years suddenly flooded over me. I had been visiting my son every other month like clockwork, but he never once told me how bad things had gotten at home. In that instant, I suddenly realized how little I really knew about my son.

244

That's when I vowed to get Donté back with me, no matter what it took.

I called my lawyer, Jay Stein, and asked him if he thought I could get custody. "Under the circumstances," he answered, "I'd say the chances are excellent."

That was all I needed to hear. The next morning I withdrew every cent I had in the bank and got on a plane for California. I was going to fight Phil on this one, even if it cost me everything I had in the world.

By the time I got out to California, Jay had already pieced together all the facts, and it was a story that blew my mind. "Apparently," Jay explained, "Donté ran away because Phil wasn't feeding him."

When I heard that, I slumped so far back in Jay's leather chair that I practically slid right down to the floor. The story didn't get any better from there. "According to what Donté told the social workers," Jay said, "Phil would deprive him of supper as a punishment whenever he didn't do his chores."

Jay went on to explain how Donté and the twins would get so hungry that they'd sometimes sneak next door to a neighbor lady's house, where she would take pity and fix them little salads to eat. The twins were three years older than Donté, so they were a little better equipped to deal with Phil's weirdness. But Donté didn't know where to turn, so he finally just hopped on his bicycle and left. The more I heard, the faster my stomach churned. "Oh, God," I sighed. "That poor little kid."

"Oh, that's not the worst," Jay continued, in that bright tone of voice that lawyers use when they're excited about something, even though it's really horrible. "Phil was up to his old tricks. Apparently, he subjected both Donté and the twins to verbal and mental abuse at every opportunity. Whenever they failed to live up to his standards—"

"I know . . . I know," I said. "Phil would curse and yell." I didn't need to hear any more. I knew better than anyone how horrible Phil's yelling could be. And I was a grown woman. I couldn't begin to imagine what it must have been like for a ten-year-old boy.

"Considering what he had to go through to get to this point," Jay added, "I'm surprised he didn't run away sooner."

"When can I see him?" I asked.

"He's at a foster home in Baldwin Hills. I can drive you over there now, if you'd like."

When Jay and I got there, we found Donté playing kickball with some other kids in the yard of this nice, middle-class house. The first thing I noticed was how normal he looked. He waved when he saw me, but he went right on playing the game, just like any other all-American kid.

"Hey, Mom," he shouted. "Watch me kick this one over the fence." I just smiled and thanked God that Phil hadn't completely fucked him up yet. What I didn't see was how much damage had already been done under the surface. I wouldn't even begin to see my son's real scars until long after I got custody and brought him back to New York.

And I did get custody. It cost me every cent I had to beat Phil in court, but I did it. I had to undergo a whole day of psychiatric exams to prove that I was a competent person, and Phil was supposed to go through the same thing. But I think he was scared of what the court psychiatrist might find, so he didn't even show up for his tests. And that was what turned the judge in my favor.

I was thrilled to be a real, full-time mom at last. But it wasn't long before I began to see what a tough job that could be. The sacrifices started the minute we walked in the door to my apartment. The court demanded that a boy Donté's age have a bedroom of his own. Since I lived in a one-bedroom apartment, that meant that I had to sleep on the couch and give Donté my room. I slept in the living room for three months before I could afford to move into a larger apartment in the same building.

Phil was required to pay child support for Donté, but that only came to $850 a month, which barely even covered his private-school tuition. I never knew having a kid could be so expensive! When I used to visit Donté in California, I got into the habit of buying him a present every day. When he came to live with me in New York, I still tried to give him everything he asked for—that's what I thought being a mom was all about. When Donté wanted a bike, I went out and bought him one. If some kid on the playground stole it, I'd go out and buy him another one. I didn't understand that it was okay for a mom to say no sometimes, but I was learning fast. And they were very expensive lessons—I was going broke.

My only hope was to get my career back on track. But that wasn't going to be easy, especially after my big comeback with "Say Goodbye to Hollywood" had flopped so badly in 1977. And with all the stories that were going around about my drinking problems, it's no wonder none of the major labels were interested in me. I knew I was going to need a lot of help to make it back. That's why I was so open when a lady who called herself Genya Ravan called me up out of the blue.

"Is this Ronnie Spector?" she asked when she finally got me on the phone. "Boy, are you hard to track down. My name is Genya Ravan, and I'm going to be your next producer."

"Well, that's nice," I laughed, convinced it was a prank call. "I'm glad you called. Now, who are you?"

But it wasn't a joke. I met Genya a few days later, and she explained her whole story. Back in the sixties—when Genya was still Goldie Zelkowitz—she had been the leader of a Brooklyn girl group called Goldie and the Gingerbreads. She became a producer a few years later, and now she was about to start her own label. And, she added, "I want you to be my first artist."

I told her I'd think about it, but I knew there wasn't really any big decision to be made. No one else wanted to record me, and obviously Genya did. So I finally told her, "Okay. Let's make a record."

Genya was involved in the whole punk scene back then, and she was always trying to drag me into that world, which drove me crazy. "Ronnie," she told me once, "you're great, but you're *so* sixties! We've got to get you into the eighties."

I didn't know exactly what that meant, but I went along with her for a while. Every night she'd take me down to see some new punk band at Max's Kansas City or CBGB. Then she'd always say, *"That's* the sound we want on your record." I tried to like these bands, but frankly, I couldn't stand any of them. It reminded me of heavy metal. The lyrics didn't make any sense to me, and the melodies were lost in all the noise. I tried to tell Genya what I thought, but she just laughed.

"Come on, Ronnie. Loosen up. Grow some hair under your

arms." Then she pointed around the room. "*These* are the kids that buy records. We've got to reach *them*."

I looked around, but all I saw was a bunch of spaced-out kids with blue-and-yellow spiked hair. "I don't know, Genya," I said.

"Don't worry," she insisted. "Wait'll we get into the studio. You'll see."

When we finally went into Electric Lady Studios to make *Siren*, Genya had all these New Wave guys come in to play on the record, and I have to admit they did have a lot of energy. They gave the music a harder edge than I was used to having—which was good, because it inspired me to really cut loose on the vocals. I can actually get sexually aroused when I'm really feeling a song—and I got hot all the time when I recorded *Siren*. I used to love it when Jonathan would come down to the studio because I knew I could drag him off to the nearest dark corner after a take to help me relieve the heat.

Genya was a strong producer who knew what she wanted, just like Phil. Unfortunately, that wasn't the only thing she had in common with him. She was also an obsessive personality and a control freak. There were times when she tried to run my life outside the studio as well as in it. After we started working on the record, Genya even called Marcia Knight to check up on me.

"I *know* Ronnie," Genya would tell Marcia. "And you've got to keep an eye on her at all times. You've got to watch every move she makes."

The strange thing is, I never missed a single recording session with Genya. And I showed up straight to every one. Marcia and I might've smoked a joint here and there, but we were like schoolgirls around all those punk musicians. We'd be sitting there with our legs crossed while Genya and these spiky-haired guys did long lines of cocaine right there in front of us.

I got so tired of Genya's weird demands on me that I was happy to be rid of her after we finally finished the album. *Siren* wasn't very successful, but looking back on the experience, I'm not surprised. Genya tried to turn me into a punk singer, which is something I'm not. And if there's one thing I've learned over the years, it's that you're doomed the minute someone tries to make you into something you aren't. At least that's been the case with my music.

Making *Siren* didn't do much for me professionally, and it sure didn't make my home life any picnic, either. When I'd come home from the studio at four in the morning, all I wanted to do was sleep till noon. But I couldn't. I was a mom now. So I'd be up three hours later making sandwiches for my son. I felt like I was running myself ragged. I was finally beginning to see just how difficult raising an eleven-year-old boy could be. Especially one whose only role model had been Phil Spector.

I couldn't believe how much Donté took after his father. He even tried to bribe the kids at school into being his friends. I discovered *that* after his teacher called to complain that I was giving my son too much allowance. Then she described how Donté would buy a big sack of penny candy and pass it out to all the kids at school in exchange for their friendship. "Donté starts to feel like a real popular kid," she said. "And then the candy runs out."

When I'd try to talk to Donté about things like that, he'd just cross his arms and stare off into the distance. He could be just as moody and stubborn as Phil ever was. And he'd stay like that for days. Marcia and I would take him to the movies, or out to Coney Island with Jonathan, hoping to raise his spirits. But once Donté got in a mood, nothing made him smile. That's when I really began to see how destructive Phil's influence on my son had been.

He really got out of hand the night I took him to see my act. After I started *Siren,* Jonathan helped me put together a band and arrange a few club dates around town. I was doing a show at the Ritz the night Donté came to see me.

I couldn't wait to finally show my kid what his mommy did for a living, so I sat him at a table right in front with Marcia. Halfway through the first number, I glanced down to see how Donté was enjoying the show. But he wasn't even watching me. Instead, he was sitting back in his chair and staring off into the distance. The crowd was whooping and hollering, but all I could see was my son pouting at me in the front row.

After the show, my dressing room was packed with people, but I couldn't find Donté anywhere. I was frantic by the time I caught up with Marcia. "Where's Donté?" I said, grabbing her arm.

She started to answer, but I could barely hear what she was

saying over all the noise in the dressing room. Finally she just pointed toward the far side of the room. I looked over and saw Donté standing off in the corner with his arms folded over his chest, staring at me with a look of total disgust.

I pushed my way through the crowd and asked him what was wrong. "Didn't you like the show?"

"I hated it," he said.

"What?" I was stunned.

"It was horrible, the way all those men were looking at you. And you just stood up there and acted like you liked it."

"But I *do* like it," I tried to explain. "Donté, I'm a performer. People pay money to see me sing and dance. It's what I do for a living."

"Well, do you have to make those noises?"

"What noises?"

"You know, 'ugh, ugh, ugh, ooh, ooh, baby.' *Those* noises."

"Those noises are just a part of the act."

"Well, I hate it," he announced. Then he crossed his arms again, and refused to say another word.

I was flabbergasted. I could understand how a son might want to keep his mother all to himself. But this was ridiculous. I didn't know what to do. My only son couldn't stand to see me do the one thing in the whole world that I really loved. It was too much. Our relationship started to fall apart after that. Donté just got more and more headstrong, until finally he wouldn't listen to a word I said. We had our worst fight on Halloween night 1980.

Donté came home from school all excited that one of his friends had invited him to a costume party that night. I couldn't take him down there because I had a rehearsal, so I told him he had to stay home. He didn't like that one bit, so he stormed off to his room and slammed the door behind him.

My mother was over that night, so I turned to her and shook my head. I thought that was the end of that. But about twenty minutes later, Donté comes walking out of his room wearing a sheet over his head, his hands and feet coated with white talcum powder.

"What are you supposed to be?" I asked him.

"A ghost," he answered. "It's my costume for the party."

Now it was *my* turn to get mad. "Well, you can walk around dressed up like a ghost all you want," I told him. "But you are not going out to any party tonight."

He didn't say a word, but he swung around and gave me the most evil look I'd ever seen. Then he tried to slam the door on me again. It was one of those doors with a lot of glass windows in it, and I caught his eye through one of them as I held it open. *"Don't* slam the door on me! I'm your mother!"

But Donté was having a tantrum, and it was too late to stop him. He pulled his foot back about three feet and let loose a kick that shattered a pane of glass into about ten pieces, and one of them sliced right into my ankle. I grabbed my leg and fell to the floor. My mother came running into the hall to see what had happened, and by that time there was blood gushing everywhere. I looked up to see Donté staring at me with his mouth wide open.

"Grandma," he told my mother, "I think she's really hurt." I'll never forget the panic in his voice, like he was actually shocked to find out that I wasn't indestructible. "I'm sorry, Mom," he stuttered. "I'm so sorry."

I bandaged my leg up and went down to rehearsal. Jonathan was there when I arrived, but he took one look at my leg and drove me straight to the hospital. It's a good thing he did, too. The cut was so deep that the doctor had to perform an emergency skin graft to keep it from scarring my leg for life.

Thank God for Jonathan. He was a source of strength for me in so many ways—personal as well as professional. I don't know what I would've done if he hadn't started working as my manager. He's always been so good at it. Whenever we'd do a show, Jon would stand there in the middle of the stage, directing all the musicians and lighting guys around him. I used to love watching him. He was like a rock in the middle of all this chaos.

Jon was one of the reasons I stopped drinking when I worked. The last time I got drunk before a show was also one of his first shows as my manager. I was completely bombed by the time I got onstage, and I was babbling the lyrics to "It's a Heartache" without a clue as to where the song was going. I was lost and I knew it. Then I looked offstage and saw Jonathan. He was standing there with the most forlorn look I'd ever seen on anyone.

That really affected me. I don't remember ever regretting anything as much as I did getting drunk that night. Jon had gone to all the trouble to book the hotels and rehearsal halls for me, and all I did was walk out there and fuck the whole thing up onstage. But Jon didn't yell at me about it. He just shook his head in disappointment and went on with his plans for the next show.

I was so used to having guys walk away from me that I didn't know what to make of a man like Jonathan, who stuck it out. That made a deep impression on me, and I realized I'd have to start getting serious if I was going to hold on to this guy. So that night, when I was lying in my bed, I made a silent vow that I'd never go onstage drunk or stoned again.

But if my relationship with Jonathan was getting better every day, my dealings with Donté were getting worse. I knew he wasn't happy in New York, so when he asked me if he could spend a week in California, I was all for it.

He was supposed to stay with a friend of his in L.A., a kid named Jerry Goodman. I was a little nervous about sending Donté back to Phil's turf on his own, so I gave Jerry's mother very specific orders not to let Phil anywhere near him. Then I took Donté to the airport and gave him a kiss.

"Here's some money," I said, stuffing three one-hundred-dollar bills into his inside jacket pocket. "Don't spend this," I told him. "Give it to Mrs. Goodman. She's going to buy your return ticket with that money when you come back next week. Understand?"

"Yeah," he said, rolling his eyes the way eleven-year-old boys do.

"Now, you take care of yourself out there," I told him. "And call Mommy every day." The tears were starting to pour out of my eyes, so I let him go. He walked right up to the gate attendant and handed her his ticket, just like a little man. I ran to the window in the terminal and watched him go up the stairs and into his jet. He walked right onto the plane without even turning around to wave good-bye. That hurt. But it was just a little stab compared to what was in store for me.

After he'd been gone about five days, I thought it was strange that Donté hadn't called me once. So I finally called Mrs. Goodman to see how he was doing. When she answered the phone, she sounded cold and distant, like she didn't even want to talk to me. "Oh . . . uh, hi," she said. "Um . . . Donté's not here."

"Ohh!" I sighed. "Well, I was just calling to find out if you bought his ticket home yet."

"Uh . . . no," she said. "Not yet." Then there was a long pause.

After a few seconds I started getting frantic. "Hey, is something wrong out there? Where is Donté?"

"Well," she said, choosing her words carefully. "I thought about it a long time, and taking his feelings into account—"

The suspense was killing me, so I cut her off. "What *are* you talking about? Where is my son?"

"He's with his grandmother."

"What?" I said, stunned. "But my mom lives in New York."

"Not *your* mother. He's with Phil's mother."

"Bertha?" I said. "What the hell is he doing with her?"

"Well," she said, "under the circumstances, I didn't know where else to send him."

"What circumstances?" I demanded to know. "And when is he planning to come back?"

"He doesn't want to go back, ever," she said. "And frankly, after what he's told me, I don't blame him."

After I heard that, I went into shock. My head got light and I started to hear ringing in my ears. I put the phone down for a few seconds to gather my thoughts, but I couldn't make any sense out of it.

Mrs. Goodman kept talking, but the more she said, the worse it got. She told me Donté had called Phil's mother on his first day in California. He told her that I was an alcoholic, that he never knew what I was going to do from minute to minute, and that he was scared to go back to me. So Bertha had come to pick him up, and he was going to live with her now.

"I'm sorry it had to happen this way," Mrs. Goodman was saying. "But I think it's all for the best—" I don't know what she said after that, because I dropped the phone on the floor and walked into my bedroom.

I sat on my bed and tried to cry, but the tears wouldn't come.

I was still too shocked. "Wow!" I said to myself. "So that's all there is to it. I had my fling at motherhood, and I fucked that up, too."

The pain didn't kick in until about two hours later, at around ten o'clock that night. And then it was bad. I started crying and couldn't stop. I felt nauseous and threw up for about a half hour. After that, I walked back to my bed like a zombie and pulled the covers over my head. I thought I'd been through some pretty bad shit in my life, but I guess there isn't much in this life that can prepare you for having your eleven-year-old kid walk out on you.

25

The Bottom Line

I'd already thrown up everything that was in my stomach, so I figured it wouldn't hurt to get drunk. The only liquor I had in the house was a big bottle of Courvoisier cognac that Marcia had brought over to make crepes. We never got around to the crepes, so it was still a full bottle. But it wouldn't stay that way for long.

I lay there in bed drinking that cognac for most of the night. "Why stop now?" I thought. "I might as well keep drinking until I'm passed out. Or dead." At that moment I had no preference either way.

Actually, I take that back. Given the choice, I think I would have chosen death. So much of my self-esteem was tied into being a mom that when Donté walked out on me, I figured that meant I must be the worst person in the world. I was convinced that God wanted me to die, but I wasn't sure why. About halfway through that bottle, I found it easy enough to ask Him directly.

"Hey, God," I shouted at a crack in the bedroom ceiling. "What did I do wrong? Huh? Am I really the worst person in the whole world?"

I stopped and looked around the room, seriously waiting for an answer. I didn't hear anything, but that doesn't mean I didn't get my answer. Because if someone—or something—hadn't been watching over me that night, I wouldn't be alive to write this today.

A little while after my conversation with God, I got so drowsy that I set the bottle down next to my pillow and tried to doze off for a minute. I woke up a few seconds later when I felt something wet seeping over the back of my head, like I was lying in water or something. The smell of alcohol was everywhere, so I sat right up in bed. That's when I noticed that the bottle of cognac had tipped over right next to my pillow. I reached down to grab the bottle before all the cognac spilled out, but I was already too late. I threw the empty bottle on the floor and started cursing my own stupidity.

Damn! I would've killed for just one more drink. But there wasn't a single drop of cognac left, even though my head was completely soaked in the stuff. Once it sunk in that I wasn't going to have another drink, I reached for a Marlboro instead.

Now, anyone who knows the first thing about alcohol will tell you that lighting a cigarette was the dumbest thing I could've done. But I didn't know that cognac burns as quickly as gasoline. And as much alcohol as I'd spilled on that bed, I might as well have been sitting in a molotov cocktail. Considering what could have happened, I really did get off lucky.

I held my lighter steady with both hands in order to light the end of my Marlboro. I was so drunk that I had to flick the thing about five times before I got the spark to catch. But even after all that, the cognac didn't catch on fire. Not yet.

Once I finally got the cigarette lit, I leaned back and took a nice long drag. The last thing I remember was seeing the tip of my Marlboro glowing bright orange. That's when I must've flicked one of the ashes onto the bed and ignited the cognac. Because the next thing I knew, the back of my head was burning, and I was hit by the sickening smell of burned-up hair.

I started screaming. All I could think of was a picture I saw in *Life* magazine of this Buddhist guy in Vietnam who set himself on fire to protest the war. I was sure I was about to burn up just like that Vietnamese guy. But then an incredible thing happened.

The fire burned itself out.

It was all over as suddenly as it started. The whole thing couldn't have lasted more than five seconds. But when I dragged myself over to the bathroom mirror, I was amazed to see how much damage a fire can do in just a few seconds.

My hair—which had been at least nineteen inches long ever since I was a teenager—was gone. It was singed right down to the scalp in some places, and even where it was still hanging on in little patches, it was no more than six inches long. It was horrible—my whole head was just one big, nappy mess. I looked the way a doll does after you've tried to give it a shampoo in the bathtub.

I was devastated. Losing my hair was a very symbolic thing for me. That long, sexy hair was the last thing of pride I had left in my life. Even after I lost my husband, my son, and my singing career, I still had my beautiful, thick Ronettes hair. But now, even that was gone. All burned up.

I walked into the bathroom and threw up about a quart of cognac before I stumbled down to Donté's room and climbed into his empty bed. Then I pulled his scratchy wool blanket over my fucked-up head and went to sleep.

When my mother let herself into my apartment the next morning, she found me still hiding under the covers in Donté's room. "Ronnie! What are you doing in that bed?" she asked. "And what did you do to your room? It's a mess."

"Go away, Mother," I croaked from under my covers. "I just want to die."

"Why you hiding under there?" she demanded to know. Then she reached down and whipped the blanket off my head with one strong tug. "Oh, my God, Ronnie!" she gasped. "You really done it now."

I tried to cover my head with both hands, but there was no point even trying to hide it. I suddenly felt completely naked, and I started crying hysterically. "Oh, Mom! I burned my hair right off my head! What am I going to do?"

My mother didn't have an answer to that one, but she knew what *she* was going to do. She moved right into my house and started waiting on me hand and foot—which was the worst thing she could have done. All I really wanted or needed was independence, but with her cooking me black-eyed peas and fried fish, she made me feel like I was four years old again.

I decided I was just going to stay under those blankets until my hair grew back. Or until I died. And I didn't care which one came first. So I stayed in that bed for a week. I didn't see any point in getting up. What was the use? I'd already burned the hair right off my head, and I was in no mood to find out what worse things were waiting for me outside my bedroom door.

The truth is, there was nothing worse waiting to happen. What was left? There I was, lying in my son's bed with no husband, no career, no baby, and no hair, while my mother dished me out fried fish and black-eyed peas. I didn't see it then, but I really had sunk as low as I possibly could. There really was nowhere left for me to go but up.

It was Jonathan who helped me understand that. I was thrilled when my mother came in and told me that he'd called, and I was already sitting up in bed waiting for him when he came over. I'd pulled one of Donté's old winter caps on to cover my head, but I kept the room so dim that Jon couldn't even have seen me if he'd wanted to. Even so, my eyes were so used to the darkness that I could see him perfectly.

I jumped out of bed the minute Jon walked in and pulled him down on top of me. "Thank God, thank God, thank God," I cried. "I'm so glad to see you. Donté's gone and I don't know what I'm going to do." Jonathan always had the answers, and I figured he would tell me what to do now, the same as always. But he surprised me this time.

"I love you, Ronnie. But I can't hold your hand through this one," he said. I was dumbfounded.

"What? Why not? What's going on?"

"I'm going away for a few days," he said. "To Vermont."

"Vermont! But you can't leave me. You can't." I was so frantic that I tried to grab his shoulders and physically hold him there. But he pulled away and perched himself on the foot of the bed.

"I want to be here for you," he said, very calmly. "But you're just going to have to untangle yourself from this one."

"I can't do it alone, Jon," I said. "I need help."

"No!" he snapped. "You don't need help." He paused for a second, and then continued in a soft voice. "People have been helping you all your life. First your father and mother helped you. Then your grandmother helped you. And your aunts and uncles. And then Phil Spector. All of these people did nothing but help you, Ronnie. And look at where it's got you. You're thirty-seven years old and you're lying paralyzed in your son's bed, *completely helpless!* And now you want *me* to help you. Well, I can't. You've got to get through this one on your own."

I couldn't believe someone who loved me could talk to me that way. And if anyone else had said those things, I probably would have pulled the covers over my head and thrown them out. But I looked at Jon, and I could see how hard it was for him to say things that might hurt me. That's when I realized it was *because* he loved me that he was telling me these things.

"But this is different," I said. "None of this would have happened if Donté hadn't left me."

"But it did happen," he said. "And now nobody can come to your rescue. Not Donté. Not Phil. Not even me. *You've* got to do it, honey, all by yourself."

"But why does this shit always happen to me? Why does God hate me?"

"God doesn't hate you, Ronnie," Jon said. "He loves you. That's why He made this happen. It's fate. This is all part of His direction."

"Oh, like burning up my hair was fate?"

"Maybe so," he said. "I'll tell you this. The same day you burned your hair off I made a call to Alan Pepper at the Bottom Line. He asked me if you could headline at the club on April seventeenth and eighteenth. And I said yes. Do you know what that means?"

Of course I knew what that meant. The Bottom Line was one of the most prestigious nightclub showcases in New York. "It means I'm being given a second chance."

"That's right. Tell me *that's* not fate." Then he got up to leave. "I'm gonna go now, Ronnie. I'll be back in a few days." He went to the door, but before he left, he turned around one last time. "Hey, Ronnie . . . tell me you're gonna survive."

"What?"

"I already know you're going to pull through this thing. But I just want to hear you say it. Come on, tell me you're going to survive."

I honestly didn't know if I could make it through the next few days without him, but something made me want to say the

words he wanted to hear, anyway. "Okay, Jon," I said. "I'm
going to survive."

"That's my Ronnie," Jon said. "I'll see you in a couple days."

Jonathan walked out of the room, but for some reason I
didn't feel alone. Something happened during our little talk—it
was like my whole life was suddenly lit up by a bright, white
light. At that moment I understood everything.

God hadn't turned His back on me at all. The accident was
just His way of showing me that I wasn't helpless. I thought I
had lost everything, but I was really being given a chance to
start over with a clean slate. God let me burn my hair off,
because it was the only way he could make me understand that
everything grows back.

I climbed out of bed and sat down at my dressing room
mirror. Then I pulled my son's winter cap off and started combing out the tangled mess that sat on top of my head. I was
scheduled to do a comeback show in less than six weeks, and I
knew it was going to take a lot of work to pull myself back
together. But I was determined to climb back up on that stage.
I had to. After all, this was the Bottom Line. In more ways than
one.

The show I did at the Bottom Line on April 17, 1981, was a
turning point for me. I'll never forget that night. I had just
finished doing four or five songs from *Siren*, high-energy numbers that got the audience on their feet. Then the band moved
into "(The Best Part of) Breaking Up." I must've sung that one
a thousand times, but for some reason, that song made me
think of Donté that night, and I started crying about halfway
through. I was such a wreck by the time I finished that I finally
turned to the audience and tried to explain my tears.

"I'm sorry," I sniffed. "This is usually such a happy song.
But, uh, about two months ago something happened that
made me understand that it's not just boyfriends and hus-
bands who can break your heart. So I'd like to dedicate that
song to my son, Donté. Wherever you are, Donté, I want you
to know that the best part of breaking up really is when
you're making up again."

The room was so quiet you could hear the traffic rolling by

outside. "Boy," I sighed. "Did you ever feel like you could really use a drink?"

That got a little laugh, and a guy at one of the front tables even reached up and handed me a martini glass filled with vodka. I took the glass in my hand and held it up to the spotlight. "A few weeks ago I might've thought the answer was in this glass. But it's not. At least not today, it's not." Then I handed the drink back down to the guy, and the place broke out in applause.

Hearing the crowd support me like that made all the difference in the world. "Oh, you *are* the greatest," I told them. "I want to give every single one of you a great big kiss, but I can't. So I'm going to pick one of you and that kiss will have to go for the whole group. Who wants to volunteer?" Nobody made a move at first, so I went on. "Woman or man, I don't give a damn. Somebody's gonna get a kiss."

Then I heard a voice call out from the back of the room. "I'll take that kiss," he said. I couldn't see who it was, but I could hear the audience clapping for him. "Well, get on up here, then," I said.

"I don't know if I can make it up there," he said. I couldn't figure out why he wasn't running up to the stage, until I leaned over the footlights and took a look for myself. He was a handsome young man, and I'm sure he would've jumped up on that stage in two seconds if he hadn't been stuck on the other side of a long table in his wheelchair.

"Well," I laughed. "You just wait right there. I'll come to you!"

Then, wearing my spike heels and teeny minidress, I stepped down from the stage, right onto this long table. I walked right across the table until I was standing right in front of this guy. And by the time I made it down there, he was ready for me.

"Hiya, big boy," I joked. Then I climbed down and leaned right into him. I gave him a big kiss. The audience applauded like crazy, and I climbed back up on the table and worked my way back to the stage. When I got there, I looked over and saw how the guy was beaming. I felt great. A few minutes earlier he was just a handicapped guy in the crowd. But not anymore. For the rest of that night anyway, that guy was king of the Bottom Line.

I finished the show without missing a note. And I had to do every encore I knew before the crowd finally let me go back to my dressing room. When I got there, Jonathan was sitting in my chair with tears in his eyes. He stood up and wrapped me in a tender hug, and I just stayed there nestled in his arms for about a minute and a half.

When I sat down at my dressing table, I couldn't stop smiling. There's no feeling in the world like having a crowd applaud for you after a good show. "And," as I told Jon that night, "it sounds even sweeter when you're completely sober."

I couldn't get over the change in my attitude after that night at the Bottom Line. I felt so free, like I was climbing out of a deep hole and looking at daylight for the first time in years. I was still smiling when I turned to my mirror and started brushing my hair, which actually seemed to be growing longer and thicker every single day.

26

Two Pounds, Six Ounces

*A*fter I met Jonathan, my dream of having a baby came back stronger than ever. Of course, I was already thirty-eight by the beginning of 1982, so you'd think I would've hung it up by then. But something told me not to give up that dream of having a kid. Not just yet.

I tried everything I could to get pregnant, at every opportunity. One time Jonathan and I made love on the night train back from a show we did in Chicago. For some reason this train seemed like the most romantic place in the world that night, and I remember how the tracks even seemed to be keeping time to Jon's lovemaking.

Clack-clack! Clack-clack! Clack-clack!

When I felt him starting to come, I reached down and grabbed his balls in my hand. "Baby girl!" I whispered. Then I gave them a quick squeeze. I didn't know if that kind of voodoo would work, but hey, I was thirty-eight years old. I'd try anything once.

We went back out on the road that spring, and suddenly we were too busy to even think about having babies. In fact, the subject of pregnancy didn't even come up again until May, when I practically had to cancel a show because I couldn't get my zipper up. The band was already onstage waiting as I stood in the wings, tugging at the zipper that ran up the side of my very tight minidress. Jonathan finally came running over in a panic. "What's going on, Ronnie? You're on!"

I was so embarrassed. "I'm sorry, Jon. But I can't seem to get this damn zipper closed."

"Let me try," he said. Then I sucked in every bone in my body until Jonathan finally squeezed the thing shut. "I guess you'd better lay off the cheeseburgers," he cracked.

But I hadn't been eating cheeseburgers, and that's what scared me. I'd been eating salads, which is all I ever eat when I'm on the road. But when I looked at myself in the full-length mirror after the show, I could see that I had what looked like a little ball in my stomach.

"Oh, my God!" I gasped. "I'm growing a tumor."

After so many years of trying to have a baby, it never even occurred to me that I might actually be pregnant. Even when I went to the doctor, I continued to expect the worst. "Don't try to spare me, Doc," I told him. "My life has been one disaster after another. I guess I can take one more. I know it's a tumor. Just tell me how long I've got left."

The doctor couldn't resist teasing me just a little bit. "Probably no more than seven or eight months now," he said, smiling. "But after the baby's born, everything should be back to normal and good as new."

I sat down on his couch. "You mean I'm pregnant?"

"The test results won't be back until morning," he said. "But I'd put money on it."

I didn't sleep at all that whole night. I was living with Jonathan by then, and he was lying next to me, snoring, when the phone rang the next morning. It was the doctor.

"It's true," he said. "You're pregnant."

"And this is definite?" I said, taking no chances.

"Absolutely. Of course, I can't guarantee whether it's a boy or a girl, but chances are good it'll be one or the other."

"Oh, either one is fine with me." I laughed. "Thank you, Doctor. Thank you!"

"Don't thank me," he said. "Thank Jonathan. He had a lot more to do with it than I did."

I hung up the phone and kissed Jonathan on the cheek. "Wake up, Daddy!" I whispered. "You're going to have a baby!" Then I flopped myself back on my pillow and watched Jon's eyes pop open.

*   *   *

My whole life changed the day I found out I was pregnant. It
was a miracle—a gift from God. I knew that much, and I sure
didn't want to screw it up. The first thing I did was stop drinking. Totally. It wasn't that hard, either. I only really felt like
drinking when I was depressed anyway, and I'd never been
happier in my life.

Jonathan wanted me to take it easy during the pregnancy,
but I was so excited by the whole experience that I couldn't wait
to burn some of that energy off onstage. We finally com-
promised—I did only those shows that had already been scheduled before I got pregnant, and then I took it easy until the
baby came.

Jonathan was so sweet while I sat around waiting for the baby
to come. He brought me every book ever written about childbirth. And I read them all cover to cover, along with every magazine article on babies and childbirth I could get my hands on.

I was reading one medical magazine when an article on premature births caught my eye. The story said that babies born up
to two months premature had an excellent chance of survival.
I found the story especially interesting, since I was then exactly
seven months pregnant.

"Look at this, Jon," I said, pointing to the article.

"Wow," he said, skimming the article. Then he put the paper
down and started joking. "Hey, if that's true, you might as well
have the baby now and get it over with."

"Oh, I don't know about that," I said. "I think I'd just as soon
use the whole nine months if it's all right with you."

"Knock on wood," Jon said. And then we both tapped the
tabletop twice for good luck.

But maybe we didn't knock hard enough, because that night
I got the worst cramps I've ever felt. I curled up on the couch
and held my stomach with both hands, but even that didn't
help. It felt like something wanted to come out of my body
pretty bad, and I was sure it was the baby.

"Oh my God, Jonathan," I screamed in panic. "I think it's
coming!"

"I'll call the doctor," Jon said. "But I'm sure you just got this
in your mind because of that article."

Jon dialed the doctor and talked to him for about three minutes while I sat there rocking back and forth on the couch in my
flannel nightgown. Every few seconds the doctor would have
Jon ask me something.

"He wants to know what you ate today, honey," Jon said.

It took me a second to answer. "Nothing, Jon. Just that carton
of soup you brought up from the Chinese place on Broadway."

"Okay," he said. He talked to the doctor for another minute,
then he hung up the phone and grabbed his coat. "Are we
going to the hospital now?" I asked. I tried to get up off the
couch to follow him, but Jon turned and gently pushed me back
down.

"No, honey," Jon said. "You stay here. The doctor says you're
probably just constipated. I'm supposed to get you some sup-
positories from the drugstore." Then he leaned forward and
gave me a kiss on the head. "Whatever you do, don't get up
from the couch. I'll be back in about two minutes."

But he wasn't gone two seconds before I had to get up. My
stomach was about to explode and I couldn't stand it another
second. I figured that Chinese soup was finally ready to come
out, so I got up and staggered a few steps into the bathroom.

I barely made it to the toilet before something very big started
sliding out from between my legs. I had no idea what it was—it
felt like a raw chicken. I sat back on the toilet seat, screaming in
pain, and held my legs as far apart as they would go so this
thing—whatever it was—could get out. Then it got stuck halfway, and I started crying out loud. I didn't know what it was,
but I knew I had to get it out of me. I bit my lip and pushed,
until it finally started to move slowly past my thighs.

Then I felt the strangest sensation. All of a sudden, this thing
seemed to be moving all on its own. As it slid through my legs,
I actually felt it reach out and scratch the inside of my thighs.

I tried to jump up from the toilet, but I couldn't even do that.
I was halfway off the seat when I felt this weird tugging, like
there was a rope stretched from me to the toilet bowl. I reached
down between my legs and touched it with my fingers. It was
warm and soft, and I knew in a second that it was my umbilical
cord.

That's when it hit me like a shock. That thing that just came out of me was my baby! I leaped up from the toilet and felt the umbilical cord snap in two. I watched it sink down into the toilet bowl, and that's when I caught my only glimpse of the tiny little creature that was floating in that awful bloody water. I saw it for only a second, but that was long enough.

"Oh my God, no!" I cried. "I just killed my baby!"

Then I really panicked. I wanted to get away from there as fast as I could, so I stumbled into the bedroom in shock. I couldn't get up—I couldn't even move. I just sat there on the bed, screaming at the top of my lungs. "I killed it! My God, I killed my baby!"

Jonathan heard my first screams from out in the hallway, and he came running in a few seconds later. He burst into the bedroom, where he saw me sitting on the bed, crying, with blood streaming down the inside of my legs. "Ronnie!" he called out. "What the hell happened?"

"I knew it was too good to be true," I sobbed.

"What?" he snapped. "What?"

"The baby," I cried. "I lost the baby."

"Where is it?"

"In the toilet."

Jon froze for just an instant while he went over the options in his head. Then he jumped to his feet and ran into the bathroom. He scooped the baby out of the water and wrapped him in a towel. He weighed less than three pounds. The tiny thing wasn't even breathing, and his skin had turned a deep shade of blue. But he'd been in the water for such a short time—less than a minute—that Jon didn't want to give up hope.

"Don't worry, honey," Jon shouted. "I think we can save him."

I just sank back down on the bed crying. "What's the use?" I asked myself. "God didn't really mean for me to have a baby after all. This is just His way of making me drop that stupid dream forever."

Jon refused to give up, but I couldn't even bear to see the baby again, so I stayed in the bedroom. Then Jon carried him into the kitchen and called the paramedics.

"Hello?" I heard him shout. "Yeah, my wife just had a baby and he's not breathing. What do I do?"

"Is there anything blocking the baby's nose?" the guy asked.

Jon looked down and noticed that there was a lot of mucus and stuff clogged up around the baby's nostrils. He grabbed a corner of the towel and wiped it clean. "Okay," Jon said. "Now what?"

"Try praying," the guy said.

Then Jon stared down at this tiny little human being and waited for a miracle to happen. A few seconds later, it did.

He felt the baby make a slight movement under the towel. Then he watched as the baby opened his tiny mouth and struggled to gulp in a mouthful of air. "He's breathing!" Jon shouted to the voice on the phone. "I think he's breathing."

"Good," the paramedic sighed. "Now, keep him warm and don't stop praying. The ambulance should be there any minute."

Then Jon came running back into the bedroom. "Look at him, Ronnie. He's breathing!"

When I saw that he had the baby in his hands, I pushed my face back into the pillow. "I don't want to see him," I told Jon. "Take him away!"

"But, Ronnie," he insisted. "This baby's going to pull through."

"No, he's too little. He's going to die. And I don't want to see him again if he's only going to die."

"Okay, honey," he said, backing out of the room. "But get ready to go. The ambulance is going to be here any second."

"All right," I told him. I was so afraid the baby wasn't going to survive that I didn't want to get any more attached to him than I had to. Even so, something inside made me stop Jon to ask, "Is he a boy or a girl?"

Jon glanced down and announced, "Right the first time, Ronnie. We've got a little boy."

Then Jon heard a knock. "That's them," he said. "Let's go." He ran to get the door, but when he swung it open, there were two cops standing there—a man and a woman—and they looked pretty startled. Poor Jon was a mess. He had blood all over his shirt, which had come unbuttoned in all the excitement. And on top of that, he was sweating like a madman.

"Are *you* the one that's having trouble breathing?" the guy cop said.

"No, it's not me," Jon gasped, holding up the baby in his little towel. "It's him. Our baby."

The woman cop took the baby and led the way down to their car. "C'mon," she said, "we haven't got time to wait for an ambulance. We'll take the squad car."

The lady cop held the baby in the backseat with Jonathan, while I sat in the front, sobbing. I was still in a state of shock, and I had so much guilty anxiety that no one could convince me that I hadn't already killed the baby. "My baby's dead," I just kept repeating. "My little baby's dead."

"No, he's not," the lady cop told me. "Listen!"

The driver flipped a switch and the siren went dead. "There," she said, "hear that? He's crying."

And I did hear it. A tiny noise. A weak, raspy little sound, like a newborn kitten makes when it's crying for milk. It was so soft you almost couldn't hear it. But I did.

"Thank you, God," I whispered. I still wasn't sure if my baby was going to pull through all this, but at least now I had some sign that he really was alive.

"Listen to him, Ronnie," Jon said. "Sounds like he wants to be a singer, just like Mommy."

When the driver heard Jon call me by name, he glanced over at me with a quizzical look. Then he slapped his hand on the steering wheel and got real excited. "Ronnie? Not Ronnie from the Ronettes?"

"Huh?" I looked up, confused. It took me a few seconds to put together an answer, because the Ronettes might as well have been a girl group from Mars at that moment. "Yeah," I mumbled. "That was me."

"I knew it. I knew. I knew it!" he exclaimed. "When I was ten years old, my sister used to take me to the Brooklyn Fox all the time. I saw you sing 'Be My Baby'!"

"Great," I said, wondering if he was going to ask me for an autograph right there in the squad car.

He didn't do that. Instead, he grabbed his walkie-talkie and told me, "I'm gonna have somebody call ahead to Saint Luke's to let them know who's coming in."

He said a few words into the mike, and got connected to headquarters. "Hey, guess who I got in my car?" he told the

dispatcher. "Ronnie Ronette. The girl who sang 'Be My Baby'!
And she's got her baby!" The guy at the other end said something I couldn't understand, and then my cop said, "Yeah,
right! The 'Be My Baby' girl had a baby!"

When he got off the radio, he leaned over and tried again to
put me at ease. "Don't worry about that little guy. The hospital's
gonna have a nice, toasty incubator all ready for him by the
time we get there."

"Thank you," I told him, fighting my tears.

"Are you kidding?" he said. "No way are we gonna lose the
'Be My Baby' girl's baby." I was so touched that I just broke
down crying, right there in the front seat of this speeding police
car. I never dreamed that playing the Brooklyn Fox would ever
have a payoff like this. But I was sure glad it did.

There was an incubator waiting at the emergency door
when we got to the hospital. I got out of the police car, and
before I knew what hit me, one nurse had the baby in the
incubator, and another one had me in a wheelchair and was
rolling me off to the maternity ward. I turned around to wave
good-bye to the cops, but they were gone, just like the Lone
Ranger.

After the nurses brought me up to the maternity ward, it
didn't take me long to get back to my old self. Within a half
hour I was already wandering the ward—dragging my IV behind me—meeting all the other moms and asking if any of
them had a light. It had been nothing to give up drinking when
I got pregnant, but cigarettes were something else again.

I stayed in a semiprivate room with this lady who couldn't
stop moaning from the soreness of giving birth. When she saw
me walking around, she couldn't believe I'd just had a baby
myself. "You're not sore?" she wanted to know.

"No," I told her. "The doctor didn't even have to do any
stitches."

"That's a miracle," she told me. "Your first child! And you
look like you're at least thirty-five."

"Something like that," I said. After what I'd been through, I
figured I could be allowed a little fib.

When Jonathan walked into the maternity ward, we were like
two old soldiers who'd just come back from battle. I hugged

him so hard I almost snapped the IV out of my arm. "Hello, lover," I whispered.

"Hello, Momma," he whispered back. "What do you think about 'Austin'?"

"Austin?"

"For the baby's name. What if we call him Austin?"

Here we go again, I thought. "Jon, I don't know if we should get too attached to him. What if he doesn't make it?"

"C'mon," Jon said, taking my hand.

"Where are we going?" I asked.

"You'll see," he said. And then he walked me down the hall to the ward where they kept the premature babies. He placed me in front of a big window that faced three incubators, and then he pointed to the one on the left and said, "That's Austin. See how well he's doing?"

I looked into the incubator and nearly cried. I could have killed Jonathan for taking me there. It was awful. My baby was a tiny little thing—two pounds, six ounces, and less than nine inches long—and there were wires and probes stuck in every part of his body. His toothpick arms were pinned down at his sides so he wouldn't tear all the wires out. And he was breathing in short heavy bursts, like he was barely alive. His face was perfectly formed, like a tiny doll's, but his features were frozen in a terrible frown, like he was trying to cry, but couldn't.

I shut my eyes and turned away. "Get him out of there," I demanded. "They're torturing that little baby. Make them take him out of there, Jonathan."

"He'll die if they do that."

"But he's so weak," I cried, unable to hold in my tears. "A baby that small can't take that much pain."

I turned and ran back to the maternity ward, dragging my IV stand behind me. I didn't eat or sleep for the rest of the night. Every couple of hours a nurse would come in and tell me how well my baby was doing and ask if I wanted to go see him.

But I refused to go back there. I'd seen him. I knew how slim that baby's chances were. It would've taken a miracle, and I'd been through too many disappointments in my life to start believing in miracles now.

I thought about all the things that had gone wrong in my

life—my rotten marriage, my failed singing career, how my son had left me. It seemed like everything I'd ever really wanted had turned to shit. And that's why I figured my baby would die, too. That was how life worked. "Watch out, Ronnie," I warned myself. "Get ready for the biggest whopper of all."

But the baby didn't die that night. And he was still doing fine when I left the hospital three days later. When I got home, Jonathan was already telling everyone in the world that we'd had a baby. And I nearly had a fit.

"At least wait until he's out of the incubator before you start telling people about him," I said. But Jonathan ignored me. He was in a great mood, but I was still moping around the house waiting to hear the worst.

At times the difference in our moods could be comical. When Jon called his lawyer to brag about the baby, I was bawling my eyes out in the next roon. Finally the lawyer asked, "Is that the baby?" And Jon had to answer, "Oh, no, he's still in the hospital. That's Ronnie crying."

By the baby's fourth day, he was getting stronger, and everyone knew he was going to be fine. Except me. And I probably would've stayed in my stubborn depression forever if Marcia Knight hadn't called me from the hospital.

It was around ten-thirty at night when she told me, "You've *got* to come see your kid. They let Jon take him out of the incubator, and he's *so* cute. But Jon's going crazy because he doesn't understand why you won't come down."

"The baby's okay?"

"The doctor says the worst is over," she said. "Now it's Jonathan who's hurting. He's standing there holding that tiny baby in his arms, and he's crying, Ronnie. Jon's actually crying."

The thought of Jonathan standing there with a two-and-a-half-pound baby in his arms finally melted my heart. I jumped into my clothes and was in a cab about three minutes later.

I arrived at the hospital at about eleven o'clock that night. Everything was quiet at that hour, especially in the premature baby ward. When I got up there I found Jon standing over the incubator, talking to the baby. I tiptoed over to his side and slipped my arm around his waist. "Hello, Poppa," I whispered.

He was so surprised to see me that he had to look twice before he whispered back, "Hello, Momma."

Then I looked into the incubator and saw the baby. The nurses had put a tiny blue knitted cap on his head so he wouldn't catch cold, and they'd dressed him in little yellow pajamas. Now that they'd removed all the wires and probes, I could finally see what a perfect little creature he was. I smiled down at this completely formed miniature human being, and suddenly I believed in miracles after all.

"Hello, Austin," I whispered at last. Then I wiped a tear off the top of the incubator with my sleeve. It was Jonathan's.

A few minutes later the doctor came in. She was an older woman who was so full of love that I knew she belonged in there with all those babies who needed every ounce of love that they could get. She walked over to Austin's incubator just in time to see him kick the little door open with his foot.

I was so startled I gasped. But the doctor just reached over and pushed Austin's foot back in and shut the door. "This one's quite a little tiger," she said.

"Then you think he's strong enough to live?" I asked.

"Oh, honey," she said. "You saw how he pushed that door open, didn't you? This guy wants to go home. He couldn't wait to get out of you, and now he can't wait to get out of there. That baby's in one big hurry to start living his life."

When I heard those words, it was like all the clouds had lifted and the sun was breaking through. All of a sudden I loved that lady doctor more than I've ever loved anyone in my life. I tried to keep from crying long enough to say, "Thank you for making my baby live."

Then I fell into Jonathan's arms and we both had a good, long cry.

Austin had to stay in the hospital for two months, but I was there every day. I insisted on feeding him my own milk, even though the doctors said it wasn't necessary. I went in every night at six o'clock and had my breast pumped. Then I would put on a robe and feed him from a little bottle that was about the size of a large eyedropper. He was so small for the first two weeks that I was afraid he'd break every time I picked him up.

After he ate, the nurses would put him back in the incubator. Then I'd sing him a lullaby. He was born during the Christmas season, and they were always playing my songs from Phil's Christmas album on the radio. So those were the lullabies I'd sing. I'd stand by Austin's incubator every night and sing "Frosty the Snowman" until he smiled and closed his eyes to sleep. I sang to make him happy, but it made me happy, too.

27

Unfinished Business

We finally brought Austin home in February, and that was the most exciting time of my life. I'd never really had a newborn infant in the house. With Donté I always had a nanny, so this was all new to me. The first time Jon and I had to change him, it was like a Jackie Gleason sketch. Jon handled the baby, while I worked the pins, diapers, and talcum. "Quick, Jonathan, pick him up!" I ordered. Then it was, "Okay, now. Put him down. Now, powder. Powder!"

Jon and I finally got married on January 16, 1982. We had planned to have a big wedding just before Austin's original due date, which was in February. But after he came early, we changed our plans and had an informal ceremony in Yonkers, New York. Very informal. The justice of the peace was watching the NFL playoffs that day, and he refused to begin the ceremony until half-time. Then we raced through the vows during three commercials. He said, "Do you?", we said, "We do," and then it was back to the hotel to have sex.

We didn't bother using birth control. It was such a miracle for me to have had my first child, I never even thought about getting pregnant again. But a few weeks later, in February 1983—the same month that Austin was supposed to have been born—I woke up with morning sickness.

"That doesn't mean anything," my obstetrician told me. "New

mothers always get morning sickness. It doesn't mean you're pregnant."

"Well," I told her, "I sure *feel* pregnant."

"Every new mother feels that way," she said. "But I'll tell you what. I'll administer a pregnancy test. If it turns out you are pregnant, *I'll* pay for the exam."

I was feeding Austin when the doctor called me back the next morning. "I'd never have believed it," she told me, "but I'm tearing up your bill right now."

I was flying so high when I hung up the phone that I started dancing around the room with Austin still in my arms. "You're going to have a little sister," I told him, and he stared up at me with one of those smiles that only babies understand. "Of course, he might fool us and come out as a little brother." It didn't matter to me. Either way, I knew I was the luckiest girl in the whole wide world.

My second baby had a little more patience than Austin, but just barely. At least this one waited *eight* months before he started trying to push his way out. But sure enough, one night in October 1983, I was sitting around the apartment with Jon and my mom when those terrible cramps came back.

"Call the ambulance," I told Jon. "The baby's coming."

The paramedics were there in no time, and they whisked us off to Saint Luke's Women's Center. The obstetrician on call examined me for about five minutes before she announced, "False alarm."

"Are you kidding?" I said.

"Relax," she told me. "You're not even dilated. You won't go into labor for another two weeks."

"But this is exactly what it felt like when I had Austin," I argued.

"It may feel the same," she told me, "but it's probably only stress." She stopped talking long enough to make a note on her clipboard, and in the silence we both heard the loud scream of a woman in labor coming from the next room. "When you feel *that* kind of pain," she told me, "that's when you'll know you're in labor."

I wanted to argue more, but then I noticed that my pain had gone down, after all. "Maybe it was just gas," Jon said. "Let's go home." He took me downstairs, where we stood in the rain waiting for a cab to take us back home.

We finally got back to the apartment, but I wasn't home three minutes before the pain started up again, and worse than ever. I laid down on the bed and insisted that Jon call the ambulance again. "I don't care what that doctor says, I'm about to have a baby."

My mother sat by the bedside while Jon called the paramedics. I was in pure torture. The pressure in my stomach got so bad I had to bite the corner of my pillow to keep from screaming. Finally, ambulance or no ambulance, I did what I had to do and pushed until that baby came out.

"Jonathan! You better get in here," my mother was shouting. "He's coming out! He's coming out now!"

Jon ran in with a clean towel and threw it under me. Then he grabbed my hand and said, "That's right, honey. Push! Push!"

The pain got so bad I had to spit the pillow out and start screaming as loud as I could. It was terrible—I stretched and stretched until it felt like there was nothing left to stretch, and it still kept coming. I felt like I was trying to squeeze a refrigerator out from between my legs. And then, just when it felt like I absolutely couldn't take anymore, it stopped.

Suddenly, I felt calm all over. I lifted my head to look around, but my hair was plastered over my face with sweat. Then I brushed it aside and saw something that made me forget all of the pain in less than a second. There was my Jonathan, standing with this tiny creature in his hands. "Looks like we did it again," he beamed. "It's a boy." I reached my arms out and Jon handed me Jason Greenfield—all three pounds, thirteen ounces of him.

Thank God the paramedics got there a minute later. They flew us back to Saint Luke's, where the nurses put the baby in an incubator. Then the routine was the same as when I had Austin—except that Jason was born big enough that he only had to stay in the intensive care center for one month, not two. And one other thing was different—this time around, those nurses couldn't keep me away from my baby.

I was always in there feeding Jason with an eyedropper, or singing him to sleep, the same as I'd done with Austin less than a year before. When I wasn't actually in the premature room with Jason, I was standing outside with my nose pressed up against the glass.

I still remember the day they let us bring him home. We got out of the cab in front of our apartment on Ninety-fourth and West End Avenue. Jon was carrying Austin, and I had Jason, and both of them were fast asleep. I couldn't get over how these babies could sleep right through all that West Side traffic.

Our doorman saw us coming and swung the door open wide. "Looks like you got a whole family now," he said.

And that was when it finally hit me. The doorman was right— after all those years of longing, I finally did have my own little family. I'd been singing "Be My Baby" for twenty years, and now, at last, I had not one, but two little boys who would be my babies. Forever and ever. Or at least until they went to college. All of a sudden I felt so happy I broke out crying right there in the elevator. Jon didn't notice the tears until we got off on our floor.

"What's wrong, Ronnie?" he asked as we walked the few steps from the elevator to our door.

"Nothing!" I said, breaking into a smile. "That's just it. For the first time in my life, there's not a single thing wrong in the whole world. These are happy tears."

"You're really something," Jon said, leaning over to give me a quick kiss on the cheek. "You really are." Then, still holding Austin in his arms, Jon swung the door open and walked into our little home. Jason was still asleep in my arms as I turned to shut the door behind me. I looked down at his sleepy little eyes and thought they looked almost Chinese. Then I gave him a kiss, real soft, so as not to wake him.

I was scraping mashed potatoes off a big china platter when Eddie Money called. That was in the spring of 1986, and I was doing dishes in the kitchen of our apartment on West End Avenue. When I grabbed the phone, my hands were so soapy that I nearly dropped the receiver.

"Ronnie?" I heard a guy's voice say.

"Yeah?"

"This *is* Ronnie Spector?" he asked.

"Yeah," I repeated. "Who is this?"

"My name's Eddie Money," he answered. "I've got this song I want you to sing with me, but everybody tells me you're kind of hard to get."

"That's news to me," I said.

"Well," he continued. "What *are* you doing these days?"

"The dishes," I told him. "When can we get started?"

The kids were only two and three years old then, so I was still spending most of my time raising them. But no matter how much I threw myself into being a mom, I never once considered the idea of retiring. I couldn't—singing is the only way I know how to earn a living. When Eddie called, I hadn't been in a studio for so long, so I jumped at the chance to be on a record. Any record.

The song I did with Eddie was called "Take Me Home Tonight," and it had a cute little part where I sang a short bit from "Be My Baby" in counterpoint to the lead vocal. I liked it as soon as I heard it, and I figured that if anyone was going to do "Be My Baby" on a record, it had better be me. But the main reason I did it was for fun. I never dreamed that when it came out six weeks later, I'd have my first top-ten record in twenty years.

"The single's going through the roof," Eddie told me. And it was. That song just took off out of nowhere, and it kept me jumping for the next six months. Eddie and I did a video that played on MTV, and we sang the song on every TV show from David Letterman to "American Bandstand." Suddenly, I was part of a hit record all over again. After that, everything started going by real fast—just like it did when I had a hit as a kid. One minute I'm doing dishes for my family, and the next minute I'm one of the presenters on the American Music Awards and co-hosting an MTV show with Eddie Money. I love my life.

But it gets even better. A few weeks later, Eddie's label, Columbia, offered me a contract to do a solo album of my own. I freaked out. Columbia Records! It was like the dream of a lifetime come true.

The name of the album was *Unfinished Business*, and I knew how symbolic that title was. In my mind this was the record that was going to tie up all the loose ends. "When this hits number

one," I told myself, "everything's going to fall together. I'll be
back on top, and then I can finally put all the failures of my life
behind me."

But guess what?

Unfinished Business came out in May 1987, and I could tell
within two weeks that it was a flop. I know the excitement that
happens when you've got a hit—the telephone rings off the
hook, and everybody wants a piece of you. But none of that was
happening.

I didn't get a single call from anybody for the entire first
month that record was out. Jack Nitzsche sent a card, which
made me so happy. But that was about it. I just sat at home
playing the record for the kids after that. Jason and Austin
knew every song on *Unfinished Business* by heart, even if nobody
else did.

Let me tell you, I was depressed. Who wouldn't be? This was
about my fourth comeback, and it had fizzled even worse than
the first three. My career was back to square one again, and I
was totally devastated. I got so low that one morning I just
refused to get out of bed. I threw the covers back over my head
and decided I'd stay under there for at least two years. And I
probably would have, except that my kids came running in
about two minutes later.

"Mommy! Mommy!" Austin called. He was only four years
old, and he thought nothing about climbing up on the bed, no
matter how depressed Mommy was. And of course, three-year-
old Jason followed his older brother wherever he went.

"Go away, kids," I told them, pulling the pillow over my head.
"Mommy's depressed. She's going to stay under the covers for
the rest of her life."

"Oh," Austin said. "Why?" Then he pulled Jason up onto the
comforter and settled in.

"Because," I pouted, "nobody wants to buy her record." I felt
so silly. It was so hard to explain such utter devastation to a
couple of kids wearing Spiderman pajamas.

"Oh," Austin answered. He was quiet for only a second before he came back with, "Mommy?"

"What, honey?"

"I want some apple juice."

I could see that these guys weren't about to leave me alone, so I made one last attempt to get rid of them. "Why don't you two run out to the kitchen and have your daddy get you a glass of apple juice?"

"No," Austin said in a matter-of-fact voice. "We want you to do it."

"Why do I have to do it?"

"Because," Jason answered, "Daddy doesn't make it as good as you do."

Then I looked down at my two little boys, standing there with their sorrowful faces, just waiting for me to make them their apple juice. "Oh, well," I laughed, throwing the covers down and climbing out of bed. "Flattery will get you everywhere."

What the hell? I thought. Why am I crying about what the rest of the world thinks of me when I've got a little fan club like this in my corner? Some people idolize me as Ronnie Spector, but these guys idolized me as Mommy, and right then, that seemed a hell of a lot more important. So I walked out to the kitchen to make some apple juice, holding hands with the two greatest fans a girl group singer from Spanish Harlem ever knew.

Epilogue

ou never know how things are going to turn out. If you had shown me a picture twenty years ago of how I'd look today, cooking spaghetti in the kitchen of a Connecticut house for my husband and two boys, I'm sure I would've laughed.

"That *can't* be me," I would've said. "Those people look so normal!"

And even now, I still have to pinch myself sometimes when I see Jonathan and the kids wrestling in the yard or playing Candyland in the living room. I'll ask myself, "Am I in the real world? Or have I been drinking again?"

But my life is not a dream. It may not be Ozzie and Harriet, but it's real. I gave up alcohol eight years ago, before my first baby, and I've only recently started to accept as normal all the stuff most people take for granted—shopping for groceries, reading magazines, going to the PTA. In fact, I've gotten so normal that sometimes I look back on my old life and I wonder if that wasn't really the hallucination.

But the truth is, that life was just as real. The world hasn't changed, I have. And if my story proves anything, it's that you *can* change your life. If I did it, I guarantee you anybody can. Maybe not overnight—but that's okay, too. It's never too late. I didn't have my first kid until I was nearly forty.

Of course, I realize that I wasted a lot of time in my life. And that hurts. When I think about the unspeakable tortures I went through with Phil, the hardest part for me to accept is not that I let him do those things, but that I let him do them *for so long*. I didn't understand that my talent gave me power, and my determination gave me strength. I could have walked away from him at any time. But I was so dazzled by what Phil could do for me that I stood there while he built his wall of sound around me. I didn't realize until it was too late that those walls would one day grow to be ten feet tall and be topped with barbed wire.

There are a lot of Phil Spectors out there, but not all of them keep their wives locked up in twenty-three-room mansions. You can just as easily be a prisoner in a Bronx tenement or a tract house in Jersey. It's not about being locked up in a house at all, really—but about being locked up in your heart. And no one can put a lock on your heart but you.

I put a lock on my heart when I stopped singing. Making music is all I ever wanted to do, but I let someone still my voice when I should have been singing like a bird. I lost a lot of good years, and I'll never get them back. But the only thing I can do now is look ahead.

As I write this, my son Donté just had his twenty-first birthday. He still lives in California, and I haven't seen him since the day he got on that plane almost ten years ago. But if writing my life story did anything, it made me see just how much unfinished business I still have to face. So the day after I wrote the final chapter of this book, I sat down and wrote Donté the letter I should have written a long time ago. We've wasted so many years already—I know that my first son and I will find a way to grow back together. I love him too much to have it any other way.

I still earn my living as a singer, and I still can't imagine ever retiring. How could I? I start to go nuts if I don't get up on a stage at least once every few months. It helps to have a husband who's also your manager. Whenever I get restless, I tell Jonathan to get out there and get me some work. He hasn't let me down yet.

And neither have the fans. I did a show at the Royal Albert Hall in London not long ago, and the fans were still waiting for me outside the stage door three hours after the concert ended. That's the kind of thing that keeps me going.

I'm always running into people who remember me from the old days. Most of them can't believe I'm still alive after what I went through. When I think of Frankie Lymon and all the other rock and rollers who didn't get the chance to play out their stories, I get sad.

And then I think of how lucky I am. You don't often get the chance to start again, and I've had more than my share of second chances. But here I am: free at last, and just beginning my life as a wife and mother. I don't know anyone in the business who's got the life I've got. I just thank God I've made it this far.

So that's the story of my past and present. All that's left now is the future. And God willing, that story's still waiting to be told.

Acknowledgments

*T*here are so many people I want to acknowledge for helping me make it through my life this far, I hardly know where to start. So I guess I'll just go back to the very beginning. To my dad, who was there when I came into the world, and to my mom, who's been by my side ever since, I send my greatest love and thanks. I also want to thank my sister Estelle and my cousin Nedra, who shared good times as well as bad, but always stayed in perfect harmony.

My children are the greatest gift God's given me, so I want to thank Him for sending me Austin and Jason, Gary and Louis, and my first son, Donté. I'd also like to thank my in-laws, Mike and Harriet Greenfield, and their children, Andrew, Ken, and Deborah, for welcoming me into their loving family. I especially want to thank Marcia Knight Greenfield and Clifford Terry, two dear friends who taught me what friendship was all about. I love you all.

After all these years, I'm glad to finally have a chance to say thanks to three of the classiest guys in show business: Dick Clark, David Letterman, and Jack Nitzsche. And I can't even begin to say enough thanks to Paul Shaffer—the Woody Allen of rock and roll, and a man who I'm proud to call my friend. I'd also like to say a special thank you to Cher and Billy Joel for writing those wonderful words for the front of this book. You guys are the greatest!

It only took one person to live my life, but it seems like it's taken a whole army to make a book out of it. I'd like to thank every one of them, beginning with all those who took the time to share their memories with me, including my friends Hal Blaine, David Brigati, La La Brooks, Bobbie Cowan, Danny Davis, Chip Fields, Bobbie and Brielle Golson, Dede Kennibrew, Tony King, Gary Klein, Melanie Mintz, my uncle Ray Mobley, Bruce Morrow, Richard Nader, Jimmy O'Neill, Stu Phillips, Steve Popovich, Ron Resnick, Bobby Sheen, Jay Stein, Nino Tempo, Billy Vera, Cynthia Weil, and Dave Zaan. If you guys hadn't been there to fill in all the blank spots, this book would've had a lot of empty pages.

For opening all the doors that needed opening, I want to thank Jane Arginteanu at Maritime Music, Alan Betrock, Arlene Gallup, Bill Inglot, Jon E. Johnsen at *DISCoveries*, Harvey Kubernick, Marilyn Laverty at CBS Records, Debbie Paull, Dave Schwartz at *Mix* magazine, Jeff Tamarkin at *Goldmine*, Randy Taraborrelli, and Mike Wagner at KRLA in Hollywood. For letting me use their great photographs, I want to thank Ray Avery, Richard Bonenfont, Dave Elkouby, Michael Ochs, Janet Macoska, Maddy Miller, and Mick Patrick. And I don't want to forget Marcia Meldal-Johnsen, whose tired fingers typed the original pages of this book.

I'll always hold a warm place in my heart for that special group of fans who came through for me in a hundred different ways, my rock and roll sweethearts, Jennifer Bartram, Gene Bondy, Ray Coleman, Paul Dunsford, Gordon Flagg, James Fogerty, Bob Hyde, Michael Mitnick, Mike Murdock, Janet Oseroff, Brad Pueschel, Wally Podrazik, David M. Reed, M.D., Randy Russi, Bob Volturno, Danny J. Williams, and David A. Young. And I want to give extra-special thanks to Michael Aldred, Kevin Dilworth, and Jay Lammy, three great guys who really went all out to help me pull this book together. It means a lot to have fans that I can also think of as friends—my deepest thanks to every one of you.

I also want to express my special thanks to Helen MacEachron and Theresa Monks, who read my story over and over again, and made about two hundred great suggestions every time they did. I really don't know how I could've done this book without you. I thank you more than I can say.

And before I forget, I've got to thank Sherry Robb for introducing me to my editor, Michael Pietsch. Finding the right guy to edit your book is as important as finding the perfect producer for a record. Working with Michael reminded me of the first time I sang at a session with Phil Spector—I knew the minute I walked in that I was working with the very best.

Finally, I want to acknowledge my collaborator, Vince Waldron, the storyteller who made my words come alive. For more than a year he saw with my eyes and spoke with my voice. I don't even have to tell him how much I appreciate all that he did, because as this book shows, he can already read my mind.

I've saved my last and biggest thank you for my husband, Jonathan Greenfield, because if it hadn't been for his strength and loving encouragement, I don't think I'd be alive to tell this story today.

Ronnie Spector
Brookfield, Connecticut
April 17, 1990

Ronnie's Hot 101:
A Ronnie Spector Discography

Compiled by Bob Hyde, Jay Lammy, and David A. Young

It's been almost three decades since Ronnie Spector first walked into a recording studio, and since then she's contributed her unique vocal sound to more than one hundred records, including six top-forty hits, another half dozen equally fascinating near misses, and at least a handful of singles that are considered by many to be among the greatest records ever made. This discography is an attempt to list them all—the hits, the misses, and all the records in between that were released by Ronnie, individually or as a member of the Ronettes.

We've also tried to include as many of Ronnie's unreleased tracks as can be verified to exist, as well as most of the contributions she made as a background singer on other artists' records. With few exceptions, we have not listed reissues of her songs on multi-artist compilation albums; nor have we mentioned foreign or promotional records, except in those cases where they differed significantly in format or content from her stock domestic releases.

The songs are listed in the approximate order in which they were recorded, which—as you will see—often had little bearing on when they were released. In those instances where a recording date for a session was unavailable, we based our chronology on aural evidence and—whenever possible—firsthand recollections of the artists and producers involved. We were also greatly assisted by the crack detective work of a small crew of rock and roll scholars whose unstinting energies made this discography possible, including James Fogerty, Randy Russi, Danny J. Williams, Gordon Flagg, Wally Podrazik, Kevin Dilworth, and Bob Volturno. We thank them all for their generous help.

HOW TO READ THIS DISCOGRAPHY

In each entry, title, composer, and highest chart position are given on the left. On the right, all 45's and albums on which the song appeared are listed in order of release.

Sample entry

September 1964[1]

37)[2] **Walking in the Rain**[3] (#23)[4]
(Spector/Mann/Weil)

Philles 123 (Oct 64)[5]; *Presenting the Fabulous Ronettes*—Philles 4006 (Dec 64)[6]; reissued on PSI (UK) 2010 017 (1976) and Collectables 3208 (1983)[7]

[1]date of original recording session
[2]entry number for this discography
[3]song title and composers
[4]highest chart position (Chart number indicates the song's highest position on *Billboard*'s Hot 100, based on Joel Whitburn's *Top Pop Singles 1955–1986*, published by Record Research, Menomonee Falls, Wisconsin.)
[5]label, catalog number, and release date of a 45 rpm single (A label, catalog number, and release date standing alone always refer to a 45 rpm release; albums are designated by title.)
[6]album title, label, catalog number, and release date of an album on which the song appeared (Album titles appear in *italics*. To make this discography more readable, catalog numbers and release dates for albums are noted only after the album's initial appearance in these listings.)
[7]45 rpm reissues of this song (In most cases, this discography lists only those records and reissues that were commercially released in the United States. However, since many of Ronnie's songs made their first—and in some cases, only—appearance in Great Britain, significant releases from the United Kingdom are noted and identified by the initials UK in the catalog number.)

I. RONNIE AND THE RELATIVES

June 1961

Entries 1–12 produced by Stu Phillips.

1) **My Guiding Angel**
   (Tucker/Williams/Evans)

May 111 (Jan 62); *The Ronettes Featuring Veronica*—Colpix 486 (Mar 65)

2) **I Want a Boy**
   (Dinu)

Colpix 601 (Aug 61); *The Ronettes Featuring Veronica*

3) **I'm Gonna Quit While I'm Ahead**
   (Carr Warren)

May 111 (Jan 62); Colpix 646 (Jun 62); *The Ronettes Featuring Veronica*

4) **Sweet Sixteen**
   (Kaye/Springer)

Colpix 601 (Aug 61), retitled "What's So Sweet About Sweet Sixteen" on *The Ronettes Featuring Veronica*

II. THE RONETTES

February 6, 1962

5) **You Bet I Would**
   (Kaplan/King)

May 114 (Apr 62)

6) **You Bet I Would**
   (Kaplan/King)
Alternate take.

The Ronettes Featuring Veronica

7) **I'm on the Wagon**
   (Seneca/Steward)

Colpix 646 (Jun 62); *The Ronettes Featuring Veronica*

8) **Silhouettes**
   (Slay/Crewe)

May 114 (Apr 62); *The Ronettes Featuring Veronica*

1962

9) **Good Girls**   May 138 (Mar 63); *The Ronettes*
   (B. Keyes/Q. Jones)   *Featuring Veronica*

10) **Recipe for Love**   Dimension 1046 (probably un-
    (H. Miller/W. Denson)   released); *The Ronettes Featuring*
                                       Veronica

11) **He Did It**   Dimension 1046 (probably un-
    (J. DeShannon/S. Sheeley)   released); *The Ronettes Featuring*
                                       Veronica

12) **Memory**   May 138 (Mar 63); retitled "The
    (R. Roberts/B. Katz)   Memory" on *The Ronettes Featur-*
                                       ing Veronica

The Ronettes Featuring Veronica was reissued in 1985 as *The Colpix Years (1961–1963)*—Murray Hill 000156.

May 26, 1963

Entries 13–18, 20–23, 26–48, 53 produced by Phil Spector.

13) **So Young**   Label on 45 credits VERONICA;
    (William "Prez" Tyus)   Phil Spector 1 (Apr 64); *Present-*
                                       ing the Fabulous Ronettes—Philles
                                       4006 (Dec 64); reissued on Col-
                                       lectables 3205 (1983)

14) **Why Don't They Let Us Fall**   Label on 45 credits VERONICA;
    in Love?   Phil Spector 2 (Jul 64); *Phil*
    (Spector/Greenwich/Barry)   *Spector Wall of Sound: Rare Mas-*
                                       ters, Vol. 1—PSI (UK) 2307 008
                                       (1976); *The Ronettes Sing Their*
                                       Greatest Hits, Vol. II—PSI (UK)
                                       2335 233 (1981)

Some pressings of PS 2 list title as "Why *Can't* They Let Us Fall in Love?"

The Ronettes Sing Their Greatest Hits, Vol. II was available exclusively as part of the nine-record box set, *The Wall of Sound—Phil Spector*—PSI (UK) WOS 001 (1981).

June 1963

15) **The Twist** (Hank Ballard)	Credited to THE CRYSTALS; *The Crystals Sing the Greatest Hits*—Philles 4003 (Jul 63); reissued on PSI (UK) 2010 020 (1977)
16) **Mashed Potato Time** (Sheldon/Land)	Credited to THE CRYSTALS; *The Crystals Sing the Greatest Hits*; reissued on *The Phil Spector Wall of Sound, Vol. 3—The Crystals Sing Their Greatest Hits!*—PSI (UK) 2307 006
17) **Hot Pastrami** (Roziner)	Credited to THE CRYSTALS; *The Crystals Sing the Greatest Hits*

Why Phil credited these three Ronnie performances to the Crystals is still a mystery. Given the nature of this material—up-tempo dance music of the sort that Ronnie performed regularly in her live shows—it's likely that Phil simply viewed these sessions as extended studio warm-ups for Ronnie's more ambitious efforts with the Ronettes. As such, he may have deemed them unworthy of release as singles, but perfectly suited for filling out a Crystals album.

July 1963

18) **Be My Baby** (#2) (Spector/Greenwich/Barry)	Philles 116 (Aug 63); *Philles Records Presents Today's Greatest Hits*—Philles 4004 (Sep 63); *Presenting the Fabulous Ronettes*; reissued on PSI (UK) 2010 003 (1975) and Collectables 3205 (1983)

August 19, 1963

19) **Getting Nearer**   JOEY DEE; Roulette 4539 (Dec
    (Bell/Watkins)   63)

Background vocals only. Produced by Henry Glover.

The Ronettes' personal and professional ties with Joey Dee and
the Starliters had been well established in the early sixties, but
the extent of their participation in his recordings has been a
matter of debate for some time. Ronnie remembers only that
she sometimes "hung out with Joey and the guys at the studio,"
occasionally contributing a harmony or two. But though she has
no recollection of any of those sessions ever making it to record,
her vocal presence on this entry is unmistakable.

Summer 1963

20) **Frosty the Snowman**   *A Christmas Gift for You*—Philles
    (S. Nelson/J. Rollins)   4005 (Oct 63); reissued on PSI
                                          (UK) 2010 010 (1975)

21) **Sleigh Ride**   *A Christmas Gift for You*; also on
    (L. Anderson/M. Parish)   Philles promotional Christmas
                                          EP—X-EP (Oct 63)

22) **I Saw Mommy Kissing**   *A Christmas Gift for You*; reissued
    Santa Claus   on CBS/Pavillion ZS8 03333
    (Tommie Connors)   (1981)

Portions of entries 20, 21, and 22 were included on the 1981
CBS/Pavillion promotional single "Phil Spector's Christmas
Medley," edited by John Luongo; a segment of entry 21 was
included on the Chrysalis (UK) single CHS 3202, "The Phil
Spector Christmas Mix." *A Christmas Gift for You* was reissued in
1987 as Rhino/PSI RNLP 70235, and most recently on compact
disc as ABKCO/Phil Spector D24005 (1989).

Fall 1963

23) **Baby I Love You** (#24)   Philles 118 (Nov 63); *Presenting*
    (Spector/Greenwich/Barry)   *the Fabulous Ronettes*; reissued on
                                     Collectables 3206 (1983)

September 25, 1963

24) **Be My Baby (Live)**   *Murray the K, Live from the Brook-*
    (Spector/Greenwich/Barry)   *lyn Fox*—KFM 1001 (1964)

Orchestra conductor: Earl Warren.

September 28, 1963

25) **What'd I Say** (Live)   *Memories of the Cow Palace*—
    (Ray Charles)   Autumn 101 (Dec 63)

Orchestra conductor: Phil Spector. *Memories of the Cow Palace*
was reissued in 1983 as Rhino RNLP 105.

1964

26) **Keep on Dancing**   *Phil Spector Wall of Sound: Rare*
    (Spector/Greenwich/Barry)   *Masters, Vol. 2*—Polydor/PSI
                                     (UK) 2307 009 (1976)

27) **Girls Can Tell**   *Rare Masters, Vol. 1* (Erroneous-
    (Spector/Greenwich/Barry)   ly credited to THE CRYSTALS on
                                     LP jacket)

28) **The Best Part of Breakin'**   Philles 120 (Apr 64); *Presenting*
    Up (#39)   *the Fabulous Ronettes*; reissued on
    (Spector/Poncia/Andreoli)   PSI (UK) POSP 377 (1981) and
                                     Collectables 3206 (1983)

29) **What'd I Say**   *Presenting the Fabulous Ronettes*
    (Ray Charles)

A staple of the Ronettes stage show, "What'd I Say" appears here in what sounds like a live performance. But according to Ronnie, this track was recorded at Gold Star Studios, and the audience noises were dubbed in at the mixing console.

April 1964

30) **Chapel of Love**
(Spector/Greenwich/Barry)

Presenting the Fabulous Ronettes; reissued on Collectables 3207 (1983)

31) **You Baby**
(Spector/Mann/Weill)

Presenting the Fabulous Ronettes

32) **How Does It Feel?**
(Spector/Poncia/Andreoli)

Philles 123 (Oct 64); *Presenting the Fabulous Ronettes* (mono pressings only)

33) **How Does It Feel?**
(Spector/Poncia/Andreoli)

Presenting the Fabulous Ronettes (stereo pressings only); reissued on PSI (UK) 2010 014 (1976)

Alternate version, featuring an entirely different background vocal arrangement.

34) **I Wonder**
(Spector/Greenwich/Barry)

Presenting the Fabulous Ronettes; PSI (UK) 2010 017 (1976)

35) **When I Saw You**
(Spector)

Presenting the Fabulous Ronettes; Philles 133 (Oct 66); reissued on Polydor/PSI (UK) 2010 009 (1975); Warner/Spector 0409 (1976)

Spring 1964

36) **Do I Love You** (#34)
(Spector/Poncia/Andreoli)

Philles 121 (Jun 64); *Presenting the Fabulous Ronettes*; reissued on PSI (UK) 2010 003 (1975), PSI (UK) POSP 377 (1981), and Collectables 3208 (1983)

September 1964

37) **Walking in the Rain** (#23)
(Spector/Mann/Weil)

Philles 123 (Oct 64); *Presenting the Fabulous Ronettes*; reissued on PSI (UK) 2010 017 (1976) and Collectables 3208 (1983)

Presenting the Fabulous Ronettes was reissued in 1975 as *The Ronettes Sing Their Greatest Hits*—PSI (UK) 2307 003.

January 1965

38) **Born to Be Together** (#52)
(Spector/Mann/Weil)

Philles 126 (Feb 65); *The Ronettes Sing Their Greatest Hits, Vol. II*; reissued on Collectables 3208 (1983)

39) **Blues for Baby**
(Spector)

Philles 126 (Feb 65)

1965

40) **Is This What I Get for Loving You?** (#75)
(Spector/Goffin/King)

Philles 128 (May 65); *The Ronettes Sing Their Greatest Hits, Vol. II*

41) **Oh I Love You**
(Spector)

Philles 128 (May 65); reissued on A&M 1040 (Mar 69)

42) **Paradise**
(Nilsson/Spector)

Rare Masters, Vol. 1; Warner/ Spector 0409 (1976)

43) **Soldier Baby (of Mine)**   *Rare Masters, Vol. 1*
    (Spector/Poncia/Andreoli)

44) **(I'm a) Woman in Love**   PSI (UK) 2010 009 (1975); *Rare*
    (Spector/Mann/Weil)   *Masters, Vol. 1*

45) **Everything Under the Sun**   *Rare Masters, Vol. 2*
    (Crewe/Knight)

46) **I Wish I Never Saw the**   *Rare Masters, Vol. 2*
    Sunshine (Version 1)
    (Spector/Greenwich/Barry)

47) **Here I Sit**   *Rare Masters, Vol. 2*
    (Nilsson/Spector)

48) **Lovers**   *The Ronettes Sing Their Greatest*
    (Unknown)   *Hits, Vol. II*

November 1965

49) **Be My Baby** (Live)   Appeared in film: *The Big*
    (Spector/Greenwich/Barry)   *T.N.T. Show* (1966)

Orchestra conductor: Phil Spector.

50) **Shout** (Live)   Appeared in film: *The Big*
    (O. Isley/R. Isley/R. Isley)   *T.N.T. Show* (1966)

Orchestra conductor: Phil Spector.

1966

51) **I Can Hear Music** (#100)   Philles 133 (Oct 66); *The Ronettes*
    (Spector/Greenwich/Barry)   *Sing Their Greatest Hits, Volume*
                                       II; reissued as PSI (UK) 2010
                                       014 (1976)

52) **I Wish I Never Saw the**   Unreleased
    Sunshine (Version 2)
    (Spector/Greenwich/Barry)

Probably produced by Jeff Barry.

February 1969

53) **You Came, You Saw, You**   A&M 1040 (Mar 69)
    Conquered
    P.Spector/T.Wine/I.Levine)

Though credited to the Ronettes, Nedra and Estelle do not appear on this record.

January 20, 1970

54) **Earth Blues**   JIMI HENDRIX—*Rainbow Bridge*
    (Jimi Hendrix)   *Original Motion Picture Sound-*
                                   track—Reprise MS 2040 (Oct
                                   71)

Background vocals only. Produced by Jimi Hendrix, Mitch Mitchell, Eddie Kramer, and John Jansen. When asked about this session, Ronnie could only recall that she and Estelle dropped into the studio with Hendrix on a lark one night after running into him at a party. Their efforts earned the Ronettes a credit on the album's jacket, and their vocal contribution is audible on the finished track.

1973

Entries 55–58 produced by Stan Vincent.

55) **Lover Lover**   Buddah 384 (Aug 73)
    (S. Vincent)

56) **Go Out and Get It**   Buddah 384 (Aug 73)
    (S. Vincent)

57) **I Wish I Never Saw the**   Buddah 408 (Feb 74)
    Sunshine (Version 3)
    (Spector/Greenwich/Barry)

58) **I Wonder What He's Doing**   Buddah 408 (Feb 74)
    (S. Vincent)

Entries 55–58 were credited to "Ronnie Spector and the
Ronettes" and featured the revised Ronettes line-up of Ronnie
with Chip Fields and Denise Edwards on background vocals.

III. RONNIE SPECTOR SOLO RECORDINGS

March 1971

Entries 59 and 60 produced by Phil Spector and George Harrison.

59) **Try Some, Buy Some** (#77)   Apple 1832 (Apr 71)
    (G. Harrison)

60) **Tandoori Chicken**   Apple 1832 (Apr 71)
    (G. Harrison/P. Spector)

In his book, *I Me Mine*, George Harrison recalls writing a song
for Ronnie called "You" that was intended for inclusion on her
projected Apple album. "I tried to write a Ronettes sort of
song," he writes, but he got no further than recording an in-
strumental backing track—with Leon Russell on piano—before
the sessions broke down. "We never got to make a whole album," Harrison remembers, "because we only did four or five
tracks before Phil fell over." The backing track for "You" eventually resurfaced on one of George's solo albums, with Harrison
stretching his vocal range to match the higher arrangement
that he'd designed for Ronnie's voice.

1973

61) **Teenage Lament '74** (#48)   ALICE COOPER—*Muscle of Love*—
    (Alice Cooper/Neal Smith)   Warner Bros. 2748 (Nov 73);
                                     Warner Bros. 7762 (Dec 73)

Background vocals only. Produced by Jack Richardson and Jack Douglas.

1975

Entries 62 and 63 produced by Edward Germano.

62) **You'd Be Good for Me**   Tom Cat 10380 (Sep 75)
   (Goffin/Goldberg)

A twelve-inch extended remix of entry 62 was released for promotional use only.

63) **Something Tells Me**   Tom Cat 10380 (Sep 75)
   (R. Cook/R. Greenaway)

1976

Entries 64–67 produced by Miami Steve Van Zandt.

64) **You Mean So Much to Me**   SOUTHSIDE JOHNNY & THE AS-
   (Bruce Springsteen)   BURY JUKES—*I Don't Want to Go Home*—Epic 34180 (Jun 76)

65) **You Mean So Much to Me**   SOUTHSIDE JOHNNY & THE AS-
   (Live)   BURY JUKES—*Live at the Bottom Line*—Epic AS 275 (1976) pro-
   (Bruce Springsteen)   motional release only

December 1976

66) **Say Goodbye to Hollywood**   Epic/Cleveland Int'l 50374 (Apr
   (Billy Joel)   77)

A twelve-inch promotional release of "Say Goodbye to Hollywood" and "Baby Please Don't Go" appeared as ASF-350 (Apr 77).

Winter 1987

67) **Baby Please Don't Go**   Epic/Cleveland Int'l 50374 (Apr
    (Steve Van Zandt)   77)

The label for entries 66 and 67 credited "Ronnie Spector & the
E Street Band." The label also proclaimed that the songs were
"taken from the Epic LP: PE 34683," the catalog number for
Ronnie's projected album with the E Street Band. Though the
LP was never completed, the label's bold promotional claim
does seem to suggest that there may have been more material
recorded at the Van Zandt sessions than these two tracks.

August 1977

68) **It's a Heartache**   Alston 3738 (Mar 78)
    (Scott/Wolfe)

Produced by Kyle Lehning and Steve Popovich.

69) **Cry Like a Baby**   Unreleased
    (Penn/Oldham)

Probably produced by Kyle Lehning and Steve Popovich.

December 1977

70) **I Wanna Come Over (Is**   Alston 3738 (Mar 78)
    That What Time It Is?)
    (Richard and Michael Ben-
    ardi)

Produced by Charles Callelo and Steve Popovich.

71) **You Light Up My Life**   Unreleased
    (Joe Brooks)

Probably produced by Charles Callelo and Steve Popovich.

72) **And the Music Plays On**   Unreleased
    (Shannon/Bourgoise)

Probably produced by Charles Callelo and Steve Popovich.

1979–1980

Entries 73–84 produced by Genya Ravan.

73) **Darlin'**
(Oscar Blandamer)

Polish 202 (Jun 80); *Siren—*
Polish 808 (Aug 80)

74) **Tonight**
(Chris Robinson)

Polish 202 (Jun 80); *Siren*

75) **Here Today, Gone Tomor-row**
(T. Ramone/D. Ramone/
J. Ramone/J. Ramone)

Siren

76) **Boys Will Be Boys**
(Roger Cook/Charles Coch-ran)

Siren

77) **Let Your Feelings Show**
(Roger Cook)

Unreleased demo

Alternate mix.

78) **Let Your Feelings Show**
(Roger Cook)

Siren

79) **Happy Birthday Rock 'n' Roll**
(Peter Gage/Elkie Brooks)

Siren

80) **Any Way That You Want Me**
(Chip Taylor)

Siren

81) **Common Thief**
(William House)

Unreleased demo

April 1980

82) **Dynamite** *Siren*
(Greg Allen/Ralph Fuentes)

83) **Hell of a Nerve** *Siren*
(Glen Robert Allen/Ralph
Fuentes)

84) **Settin' the Woods on Fire** *Siren*
(Greg Allen/Ralph Fuentes)

1984

85) **Tonight You're Mine Baby** *Just One of the Guys—Original*
(Narada Michael Walden/ *Motion Picture Soundtrack—*
Preston Glass) Elektra 60426-IE (May 85)

Produced by Paul Shaffer.

1985

86) **You and Me Go Way Back** Appeared in video: *Deja View—*
(John Sebastian) *The Ultimate 60's Party Video—*
Karl-Lorimar (1986)

Vocal with John Sebastian, Roger McGuinn, Felix Cavaliere.

1986

87) **Take Me Home Tonight** EDDIE MONEY—Columbia 06231
(#4) (Aug 86); *Can't Hold Back—*
(M. Leeson/P. Vale) Columbia 40096 (Aug 86)

Duet with Eddie Money. Produced by Richie Zito and Eddie
Money.

1987

Entries 88–91 produced by Michael Young; entries 93–97 produced by Gary Klein.

88) **Who Can Sleep**
   (Alan Gordon/Jerry Fried-
   man)

Columbia 07082 (May 87); *Unfinished Business*—Columbia 40620 (May 87)

Guest Vocalist: Eddie Money. A twelve-inch promotional release of "Who Can Sleep" appeared as CAS 2701.

89) **Dangerous**
   (Billy Steinberg/Tom Kelly)

Unfinished Business

Guest Vocalist: Susanna Hoffs.

90) **Burnin' Love**
   (Dennis Linde)

Unfinished Business

91) **Unfinished Business**
   (Gregory Abbott)

Unfinished Business

92) **Love on a Rooftop**
   (Desmond Child/Diane
   Warren)

Unfinished Business; Columbia 07300 (Jul 87)

Produced by Desmond Child.

93) **(If I Could) Walk Away**
   (Don Dixon)

Unfinished Business

94) **Heart Song**
   (Douglas Berlent)

Unfinished Business

95) **True to You**
   (Gerard McMann)

Unfinished Business

96) **When We Danced**
   (David Palmer/Phillip Jost)

Columbia 07082 (May 87); *Unfinished Business*

97) **Good Love Is Hard to Find**   *Unfinished Business*; Columbia
   (Alan Gordon)   07300 (Jul 87)

1989

Entries 98–101 produced by Alan Betrock.

 98) **Communication**   Unreleased
    (Marshall Crenshaw)

 99) **For His Love**   Unreleased
    (Marshall Crenshaw)

100) **Something's Gonna Hap-**   Unreleased
    pen
    (Marshall Crenshaw)

101) **Whenever You're on My**   Unreleased
    Mind
    (Marshall   Crenshaw/Bill
    Teeley)

Index